CHARITY
FOR THE
SUFFERING SOULS

CHARITY
FOR THE
SUFFERING SOULS

AN EXPLANATION OF THE CATHOLIC
DOCTRINE OF PURGATORY

By

Rev. John A. Nageleisen

Missionary Priest of the Congregation of the Most Precious Blood

TAN BOOKS AND PUBLISHERS

Imprimatur: ✠ Joseph Rademacher,
Bishop of Fort Wayne
February 2, 1895

Reprinted by TAN Books and Publishers, Inc. in 1982 from the edition published in 1977 by Mater Dei Publications, Inc. Retypeset and republished by TAN in 2008.

Library of Congress Catalog Card No.: 82-83797

ISBN: 978-0-89555-200-6

Printed and bound in the United States of America.

TAN BOOKS AND PUBLISHERS
2009

CANON XXX SESSION VI OF THE COUNCIL OF TRENT

"If any one saith that after the grace of Justification has been received, to every penitent sinner the guilt is remitted, and the debt of eternal punishment is blotted out in such wise that there remains not any debt of temporal punishment to be discharged, either in this world, or in the next in Purgatory, before the entrance to the Kingdom of Heaven can be opened to him—let him be anathema."

DECREE CONCERNING PURGATORY: COUNCIL OF TRENT: SESSION XXV

"Whereas the Catholic Church, instructed by the Holy Ghost, has, from the sacred writings, and the ancient tradition of the Fathers, taught in sacred councils and very recently in this Œcumenical Synod, that there is a Purgatory and that the souls there detained are helped by the suffrages of the Faithful, but particularly by the acceptable Sacrifice of the Altar—the Holy Synod enjoins on bishops that they diligently endeavour that the sound doctrine concerning Purgatory, transmitted by the holy Fathers and sacred councils, be believed, maintained, taught, and everywhere proclaimed by the Faithful of Christ.

APPROBATIONS

Cleveland, 0., February 22, 1893.

Rev. John A. Nageleisen., C.PP.S., Collegeville, Ind.:

Rev. Dear Sir:—Whatever serves to promote the devotion of the faithful towards the Poor Suffering Souls in Purgatory must meet with my cordial approbation. Your book on Purgatory has that for its only object.

May God bless the work and obtain for it a wide circulation. Full of thought, full of piety and eminently practical, it ought to secure many helpers for the Poor Souls in Purgatory. Sincerely yours in Xsto,

† IGN. F. HORSTMANN,

Bishop of Cleveland

Belleville, Ill., March 4, 1893.

"Charity for the Suffering Souls", by Rev. John A. Nageleisen C.PP.S.—a book of instructions for those who are members of confraternities for the Relief of the Poor Souls in Purgatory—is herewith warmly recommended to the faithful. † J. JANSSEN,

Bishop of Belleville

St. Cloud, March 29, 1894.

Rev. John A. Nageleisen., C.PP.S., Collegeville, Ind.:

Reverend Father:—Most cordially and with great pleasure do I herewith comply with your request, namely to recommend to the faithful your book "Charity for the Suffering Souls". The book contains the strongest, most touching appeals in behalf of those Suffering Souls who are still united with us in the love of God. We are exhorted to assist these souls by offering for them, in prayer and sacrifice, the merits of the Precious Blood of Christ. Even now the faithful departed hear the voice of this Blood as the voice of reconciliation; and they will hear it as such, to their complete justification, on the day of the general resurrection. It was, therefore, not more than proper that the book should be written by a member of the Congregation of the Most Precious Blood. Wishing you the best of success and God's blessing for the work you have undertaken, I am, Reverend Father,

Yours most truly in Christ,

† OTTO ZARDETTI,

Bishop of St. Cloud.

Denver, Colo., 255 S. Evans St., September 7, 1894.

Rev. John A. Nageleisen:

Your confrere, the Rev. Andrew Gietl, lately presented to me a copy of your book "Charity for the Suffering Souls". As a zealous friend of the Poor Souls I am greatly delighted to see this splendid work making its appearance among our people.

May God in His infinite goodness bless the author, as I am sure that the Poor Souls bless you for the sake of your charitable mediation! It is in their behalf that you have undertaken this noble work.

† N. C. MATZ,

Bishop of Denver.

ECCLESIASTICUS 7

37 A gift hath grace in the sight of all the living: and restrain not grace from the dead.

ECCLESIASTICUS 24

45 I will penetrate to all the lower parts of the earth, and will behold all that sleep, and will enlighten all that hope in the Lord.

ZACHARIAS 9

11 Thou also, by the blood of thy testament, hast sent forth thy prisoners out of the pit wherein is no water.

PSALMS 141

8 Bring my soul out of prison, that I may praise thy name: the just wait for me, until thou reward me.

DANIEL 12

10 Many shall be chosen and made white and shall be tried as fire: and the wicked shall deal wickedly. And none of the wicked shall understand: but the learned shall understand.

ST. MATTHEW 5

26 Amen I say to thee, thou shalt not go out from thence till thou repay the last farthing.

ST. MATTHEW 12

32 And whosoever shall speak a word against the Son of man, it shall be forgiven him: but he that shall speak against the Holy Ghost, it shall not be forgiven him, neither in this world, nor in the world to come.

Ver. 32. *Nor in the world to come.* From these words St. Augustine (*De Civ. Dei*, lib. 21, c. 13) and St. Gregory (*Dialog.*, 4, c. 39) gather that some sins may be remitted in the world to come; and, consequently, that there is a purgatory or a middle place.

1 CORINTHIANS 3

12 Now, if any man build upon this foundation, gold, silver, precious stones, wood, hay, stubble:

13 Every man's work shall be manifest. For the day of the Lord shall declare *it,* because it shall be revealed in fire. And the fire shall try every man's work, of what sort it is.

14 If any man's work abide, which he hath built thereupon, he shall receive a reward.

15 If any man's work burn, he shall suffer loss: but he himself shall be saved, yet so as by fire.

Chap. 3. Ver. 12. *Upon this foundation.* The foundation is Christ and His doctrine: or the true faith in Him, working through charity. The building upon this foundation, *gold, silver, and precious stones,* signifies the more perfect preaching and practice of the Gospel; the *wood, hay, and stubble,* such preaching as that of the Corinthian teachers (who affected the pomp of words and human eloquence) and such practice as is mixed with much imperfection and many lesser sins. Now the *day of the Lord* and his *fiery* trial (in the particular judgment immediately after death) shall make *manifest* of what sort *every man's work* has been: of which, during this life, it is hard to make a judgment. For them, *the fire* of God's judgment *shall try every man's work.* And they, whose *works,* like *wood, hay and stubble,* cannot abide the fire, shall *suffer loss,* these works being found to be of no value; yet they themselves, having built upon the right *foundation* (by living and dying in the true Faith and in the state of grace, though with some imperfection), *shall be saved, yet so as by fire;* being liable to this punishment, by reason of the *wood, hay and stubble,* which was mixed with their building.

CONTENTS

CHAPTER 4

ON THE MOTIVES FOR HELPING THE SUFFERING SOULS

CHAPTER 5
GRATITUDE OF THE SUFFERING SOULS

CHAPTER 6

APPENDIX
PRAYERS FOR THE SUFFERING SOULS

PRAYER

O MOST HOLY TRINITY, Father, Son and Holy Ghost, I adore Thee profoundly. I offer Thee the most precious Body, Blood, Soul and Divinity of Jesus Christ present in all the tabernacles of the world, in reparation for the outrages, sacrileges and indifference by which He is offended. By the infinite merits of the Sacred Heart of Jesus, and the Immaculate Heart of Mary, I beg the conversion of poor sinners.

I also beg the alleviation and the deliverance of the souls in Purgatory. Amen.

(The first paragraph of this prayer is "The Angel's Prayer," Fatima, 1916.)

PREFACE

THE Omnipotent Word of God, which in the beginning called forth from nothing this magnificent universe, which even penetrated the tomb and compelled death to deliver up its victims; this divine Word which on the Day of Judgment will echo from the rising of the sun to the going-down thereof and summon the dead of all nations to receive retribution: this Divine and Omnipotent Word is even now heard by the dead proclaiming to them pardon and deliverance from the pains of Purgatory. "Amen, amen, I say unto you, that the hour cometh, and now is, when the dead shall hear the voice of the Son of God: and they that hear shall live." (*John* 5:25).

To move this Omnipotent Word to grant pardon and deliverance to the Suffering Souls in consideration of the suffrages of the faithful on earth—such is the object of the following treatises. They are to induce the reader to hasten by his prayer the blessed hour when his brethren and sisters in Purgatory shall hear the summons of the Son of God, "Go forth from your torments; go forth, your punishment is remitted. Enter into the joy of your Lord."

It is, alas, undeniably true that the great majority of men are but little interested in the Suffering Souls who so ardently desire help. Some neglect this duty because they are infidels. They deny the existence of Purgatory, and consequently they do not believe that the faithful can aid the souls confined in it. Besides the infidels, who judge all things religious according to their own limited views, those also deny the middle state, who are separated from the communion of the Catholic Church. Others neglect to assist the

Suffering Souls because they have no true conception of this duty, nor of the great advantages to be gained by performing this work of charity. Those separated from the Church do not help the Poor Souls because they do not believe in Purgatory; and many negligent Catholics, despite their belief in this doctrine, do not aid the Suffering Souls because they consider it too inconvenient to do so.

The disbelief in the existence of Purgatory and the neglect of prayer for the captive souls detained in it are both very harmful. Disbelief is in conflict with the doctrine of the Catholic Church, which from the earliest ages has taught the existence of a middle state and the efficacy of prayer for the dead; neglect of this prayer is contrary to the general duty of charity, which obliges us to come to the aid of our fellowman when and wherever we can. How ungrateful of us and how detrimental to the Suffering Souls, if we Catholics refuse them this Christian charity either because we are ignorant of it or do not sufficiently esteem it! In order to remedy as far as possible this hurtful disregard of duty, we have collected in this volume the most important and instructive points concerning the doctrine of Purgatory. The sources from which these points have been gathered are Holy Scripture, tradition, the decrees of the Church, the writings of the Holy Fathers, the unanimous assent of all nations, and even the writings of non-Catholics. The means by which we can aid the Suffering Souls are extensively treated, especially the expiatory value of Holy Mass; various popular questions are explained at length; the motives for practicing the devotion to the Suffering Souls and the gratitude of these souls towards their benefactors are comprehensively discussed—all this with a view to enkindle our zeal for this charitable work.

As deeds always impress more deeply than words, the instructions are frequently illustrated by examples; but only such examples have been admitted as are of undoubted authenticity. In our times a spurious belief in spiritualism is rampant throughout the world. Thousands and thousands belong to so-called spiritualistic circles and are so being led astray by evil spirits. *Our* spiritualistic belief is essentially true and Catholic, because it is based on the authority of divine faith: namely, we believe in God, in the immortality of the soul, in guardian angels, in the Saints, and in a Purgatory in the next world. May the belief in *this* spiritualistic doctrine gain more and more adherents! And would that every Catholic were filled with fervent, heroic zeal for this work of charity—how many Poor Souls would then be released from their painful captivity! Thereby the number of saints in Heaven would be increased to the greater glory of God, while at the same time the salvation of souls here on earth would be greatly promoted.

Concerning the extraordinary events related in this book the author declares, in conformity with a decree of Pope Urban VIII, that he claims for them only human credence, excepting such as are favored with the authoritative decision of the Church. Credence derived from human testimony may however furnish us with the same certitude concerning the truth of a question as does human science, provided the credibility of the person stating a fact is beyond doubt. When once it is established that the conditions required to make a certain fact credible have all been fulfilled, then it is clear that a doubt concerning the truth of that fact is no longer reasonable. When the trustworthiness of the witnesses cannot be called in question—that is, when it is proved that they knew the fact to be true and were willing to testify to its truth; when we are sure that we have received an authentic account of the event—then deception is impossible; and in such cases human testimony is perfectly reliable. Among the great number of occurrences relating to the Suffering Souls we have selected only the most pertinent, and of these again the best authenticated.

Finally, in order to induce the reader to make practical use of the instructions contained in this volume and because the Holy Sacrifice of the Mass is the principal and most effective means of helping the Suffering Souls, we concluded to add to this work an explanation of the aim and object of the Archconfraternity of the Most Precious Blood for the Relief of the Suffering Souls, and of the Spiritual Benevolent Fraternity instituted for the same purpose. These instructions are followed by a selection of prayers calculated to assist pious souls in their devotions for the relief and ransom of their suffering brethren.

Who can describe the ecstasy, the heavenly joy with which our souls will be enraptured, when we shall meet in the realms of bliss a parent, a brother or sister, a friend or acquaintance, whose release from Purgatory we obtained by our suffrages, whose entrance into everlasting glory we hastened by our prayers! Most sweet indeed is the consolation contained in the doctrine of our holy religion which teaches us that true love, founded in God, is not extinguished by death, but gains its realization in and through God; and that by this love, which is the bond of perfection, the Church suffering, the Church triumphant and the Church militant are made one family, one body, united for a diversity of ministrations under one Head, Christ our Lord.

May these treatises move fervent and charitable hearts to hasten to the Fountain of the Most Precious Blood, to draw down its cooling dew on the Suffering Souls.

The author formally declares that he submits everything contained in this volume to the infallible judgment of the Holy Catholic Church, whose office it is to scrutinize and approve whatever is taught as Catholic doctrine. In her saving communion he hopes to live and die.

THE AUTHOR

St. Joseph's College, Collegeville, Indiana.

PREPARATORY PRAYER

COME, Holy Spirit, fill the hearts of Thy faithful and enkindle in them the fire of Thy love.
V. Send forth Thy spirit and they shall be created.
R. And Thou shalt renew the face of the earth.

Let Us Pray

O God, Who didst instruct the hearts of the faithful by the light of the Holy Spirit, grant us by the same Spirit to have a right judgment in all things and ever to rejoice in His consolation. Through Christ our Lord. Amen.

THE ANGELIC SALUTATION

Hail Mary, full of grace, the Lord is with thee, blessed art thou among women and blessed is the fruit of thy womb, JESUS. Holy Mary, Mother of God, pray for us sinners, now and at the hour of our death.
AMEN

CHARITY
FOR THE
SUFFERING SOULS

Chapter 1

The Existence of Purgatory

Eternity

THERE is no doubt but that the question of our existence after death is the most important and consequential of all questions. It is the fundamental question of life, decisive of our eternal destiny. Therefore it ever was, and must be, the ultimate and essential purpose of Religion to answer this question.

Eternal thanks to Our Divine Redeemer! We Catholics have the reasons of the faith that is in us implanted deeply in our hearts. Christ, "the Way, the Truth and the Life," who dispels all darkness, lifted the veil that covers the next world and expressed Himself in the most emphatic manner that annihilation is not our destiny, but that we are created for an everlasting life, either of bliss or of torment. "And these shall go into everlasting punishment: but the just, into life everlasting." (*Matt.* 25:46).

The body, taken from the earth, returns to dust; but the soul, the spirit breathed into man by his Creator, appears, after death, before God's tribunal to be judged. The soul is immaterial, invisible, a spirit, created in the likeness of God, and immortal. As a child that resembles its parents is the image of its father or mother, because it has similar features, etc., thus man is the image of God, because he possesses similar (not the same) attributes as God. "And God created man to His own image." (*Gen.* 1:27). Like God, man was to be pure, immaculate, an heir of the Kingdom of Heaven; he was to be gifted with great knowledge and to be

1

free from concupiscence, misery, pain, and even from death. Thus was the being, which is by nature an immortal spirit, endowed with reason and free will, gifted by the Creator with supernatural qualities. But sin destroyed the work of God. It dishonored Heaven and thinned out the ranks of the Angels; it destroyed Paradise and man's eternal happiness, until the former was regained and the latter restored by the Son of God at the price of His Most Precious Blood.

Joseph was the saviour of Egypt from famine: Jesus Christ became the Saviour of mankind from eternal damnation. Joseph was persecuted by his brethren, ill-treated by them and sold for twenty pieces of silver: Jesus was betrayed by Judas, denied by Peter, and sold for thirty pieces of silver. After many trials and tribulations Joseph was placed over all Egypt, for Pharao said to him: "Seeing God hath shewn thee all that thou hast said, can I find one wiser and one like unto thee? Thou shalt be over my house, and at the commandment of thy mouth all the people shall obey: only in the kingly throne will I be above thee. And again Pharao said to Joseph: Behold I have appointed thee over the whole land of Egypt. And he took his ring from his own hand, and gave it into his hand: and he put upon him a robe of silk, and put a chain of gold about his neck. And he made him go up into his second chariot, the crier proclaiming that all should bow their knee before him, and that they should know he was made governor over the whole land of Egypt. And the king said to Joseph: I am Pharao; without thy commandment no man shall move hand or foot in all the land of Egypt. And he turned his name, and called him in the Egyptian tongue, the saviour of the world." (*Gen.* 41:39-45). Now Joseph had power over life and death in the land of Egypt. To him all had to go that desired to escape the pangs of hunger; even his father and his brethren had to bow before him and accept of him the necessaries of life. Pharao's order was, "Go to Joseph!" Although Joseph opened the full granaries and provided Egypt with bread, yet those only were saved that made personal application to him and received the gift out of his own hand. Therefore all the people flocked to him; old and young, relatives and strangers, friends and foes, flocked to him from all countries to purchase provisions.

Our Lord Jesus Christ also had to suffer, and His sufferings were greater than those of Joseph in Egypt, because He was to be the Saviour of all mankind from eternal death. But He showed Himself as the "Wonderful," as the valiant Hero of whom Isaias foretells, "The people that walked in darkness have seen a great light: to them that dwelt in the region of the shadow of death, light is risen." (*Is.* 9:2). "For a CHILD IS BORN to us, and a son is given us, and the government is on his shoulder, and his name shall be called Wonderful, Counsellor, God the Mighty, the Father of the world to come, the Prince of peace. His empire shall be multiplied, and there shall be no end of peace: he shall sit upon the throne of David, and upon his kingdom, to establish it and strengthen it with judgment and with justice, from henceforth and forever." (*Is.* 9:6, 7)—Jesus "received from God the Father, honour and glory: this voice coming down to Him from the excellent glory: This is my beloved Son, in whom I am well pleased; hear ye Him." (*2 Peter* 1:17). Jesus says of Himself: "All power is given to me in heaven and on earth." (*Matt.* 28:18)—"For which cause God also hath exalted Him, and hath given Him a name which is above all names: that in the name of Jesus every knee should bow, of those that are in heaven, on earth and under the earth." (*Phil.* 2:9, 10). His victory was accomplished in sacrificial death. Redemption was achieved when Jesus, in view of Heaven and earth, exclaimed dying on the Cross, "It is consummated." (*John* 19:30).

Then death, man's eternal ruin caused by sin, was overcome through the victory of Christ, and life was restored by Him "Who was delivered up for our sins, and rose again for our justification." (*Rom.* 4:25). The power of darkness was destroyed; mankind was delivered from disgraceful captivity; the abyss of Hell was closed and the gates of paradise were reopened. Christ's treasury of atonement is superabundant and forever inexhaustible; it is not diminished or depleted even if millions upon millions draw from it grace upon grace, health and strength, light and life. As all the country flocked to Joseph, thus do men "of all nations, and tribes, and peoples" (*Apoc.* 7:9) come to Jesus Christ, the Saviour of the world, to obtain the eternal heritage of Heaven. Without the command of chaste Joseph "no man shall move hand or foot in all the land of Egypt"; without the will of Jesus Christ no man shall enter paradise recovered for us by Him. To attain salvation all must obey Him; we must personally use the means of grace instituted and ordained by Him; we must, moreover, cooperate with the graces He grants us. On this depends our eternal destiny.

Eternity! Eternity!—Heaven or Hell, one of the two we must choose by our lives. Because "the unjust"—such either by transgression or through unsatisfied justice—"shall not possess the kingdom of God" (*1 Cor.* 6:9), the ineffable mercy of God, in consideration of the merits of Jesus Christ, created, in the next world, a place of purification for those who, at the time of their death, are not entirely pure: this place is called *Purgatory*.

Purgatory

Between Heaven, "the place of refreshment, light and peace," and Hell, the abode of eternal torment, there is, till the day of general judgment, a middle state, called Purgatory, for those souls that depart this life justified, but still in need of final purification. In this place of punishment and purification, of justice and mercy, dwell the souls that have venial sins to expiate, or temporal punishment to undergo, or both. The doctrine of the Catholic Church concerning Purgatory is expressed in the following two sentences:

1) There is, in the next world, a temporary place for the atonement of such venial sins, and temporal punishments of sin, as man is found guilty of on his departure from this world.

2) The faithful can, by prayer and good works, especially by the Holy Sacrifice of the Mass, assist the souls suffering in Purgatory.

Concerning the location of Purgatory, the nature of its torments, the extent of its suffering, etc., the Church has made no official declarations, hence only the two above sentences are dogmas which we must believe under pain of excommunication. Nevertheless we should be guilty of culpable temerity if we were to reject the generally accepted doctrine of the holy Fathers and of notable spiritual writers relative to some other points concerning Purgatory.

In connection with the Catholic doctrine concerning Purgatory it is necessary to bear in mind the doctrine of remission of sins. With the remission of mortal sin there is necessarily connected the remission of its eternal punishment. But the case stands quite differently with regard to the *temporal* punishment of sin which God permits to remain even after the remission of its guilt. The sinner who committed a mortal sin and thereby became an enemy of God becomes, through the Sacrament of Penance, a friend, a child of God; his eternal punishment is condoned, but a temporal punishment remains. It is, however, the general doctrine of theologians that at least a part of the temporal punishment is remitted, every time, in the tribunal of penance, and that this part is in proportion to the contrition and penitent disposition of the repentant sinner. The remaining part must be atoned for in this world by penance, or in the next by the torments of Purgatory.

Both the temporal punishment yet due to sin remitted, and the stain of venial sin yet unremitted are, in the sight of God, a defilement of the soul. Venial sin, to which man is so prone, is not remitted by merely external works of penance without true contrition; its remission depends on the interior disposition of the penitent soul, on perfect charity, patience and resignation to the Will of God. "Whether remission is obtained gradually by means of repeated acts," says Deharbe (*Explanation of the Catechism*, vol. II. p. 409) "or at the parting of the soul from the body through one act of perfect charity, is a question on which theologians do not agree. Suarez defends the latter opinion, because such an act is followed by an increase of charity or sanctifying grace, and may be made so perfectly as to cleanse the soul from every inclination to sin."

We must not, however, conclude from this that all souls shall be excluded from the beatific vision of God until they shall have passed through the fiery furnace of Purgatory. Such a view is untenable. Unquestionably true as it is that many souls are banished forever from the presence of God immediately after the particular judgment, it cannot, on the other hand, be denied that they that were cleansed from all their faults in this life, soar up, after the particular judgment, into the heavenly Jerusalem, the city of peace, whose inhabitants are blissful in love.

Moreover, from the fact that a soul is sentenced to chastisement in Purgatory the conclusion is not to be drawn that it will be inferior in heavenly glory to souls admitted to Heaven without undergoing purification by fire. The most precious stones and metals sometimes need longer and more thorough purification than less valuable ones. The degree of their value depends on their interior worth and not on the dross and corrosion that surrounds them. Thus also the degree of heavenly glory depends on the merit of each saint. Thus it may happen that souls eminent for works of penance and full of merit, may nevertheless have to remain in Purgatory longer, and yet, after their purification, they may attain to a higher degree of glory than such as were not in need of purification. Each one shall receive his reward according to his merit, after having paid the last farthing of his debt, being "purified as if by fire."

The religious innovators of the last centuries, by denying the existence of Purgatory, made an attempt indefensible both before the tribunal of religion and of reason. They desire to replace this consoling doctrine by one more pleasing to the "father of lies," only for the sake of innovation, and instigated by pride, avarice, envy, sensuality, etc. The rebels dare to weigh God's mercy and judgment in the scales of their darkened reason. By rejecting prayer for the dead and the doctrine of temporal punishment of sin, they disrupt one of the most sacred bonds with which faith has encircled mankind, viz. the communion of saints. The Church Militant, Suffering and Triumphant in its entirety composes the Mystical Body of Christ, who is the Head, while the faithful are the members. The departed, then, who died in the Lord, are an integral part of this great Mystical Body, either as saints in Heaven, or as suffering souls in Purgatory. But the misguided innovators have only the darkness of the grave to place between the human heart and its departed loved ones. Their presumption is condemned by Divine Revelation and the constant Tradition of the Church, by the unaminous belief of all nations, and by non-Catholics themselves, by reason and by sentiment. Leaving these gloomy and rebellious men to deny the Suffering Souls a prayer, we shall seek to prove in the following pages how all nations and all ages concur in the sentiment: "There is a Purgatory; and 'it is therefore a holy and wholesome thought to pray for the dead, that they may be loosed from sins.'" (*2 Mach.* 12:46).

Sentiment

Like unto a mourning dove, the beloved Spouse of Christ, the Church, never interrupts her sighs and prayers for the faithful departed until they have arrived in the port of eternal bliss. She renews in Holy Mass our Divine Redeemer's sacrificial death, offering it up to His Heavenly Father; she invites the Church Triumphant and the Church Militant to join in persevering prayer for the Church Suffering. What a consolation for the dying, what a reassurance for the living to profess a religion so comforting: consoling to the dying who, though cleansed from all mortal sin by the holy Sacraments, yet are uncertain whether they shall be found sufficiently pure, and worthy of Heaven, but rest assured that the Church Triumphant and Militant will come to their aid after death; comforting for their surviving friends, because they continue to show them their affection in case they should stand in need of their assistance in the purifying flames. Hence we can never be sufficiently thankful to God for having called us to a religion whose maternal care, charity and zeal goes beyond the confines of our earthly pilgrimage and follows us even after our eyes have been closed in death.

How sorely we feel the parting from our dear ones! When the dying husband bids farewell to his loving wife, recommending himself to her prayers; when affectionate children stand around the deathbed of a dear mother, listening to her parting words; when the death of a dear friend is announced to us, we are overwhelmed with sorrow; the smart of parting well-nigh breaks our heart. At such moments religion, with its heavenly consolation, comes to our aid, exhorting us to lift up our hands in supplication to our brethren of the Church Triumphant, to distribute with liberal charity among our suffering dear ones our prayers, alms and suffrages. How beautiful is this faith, how consoling this doctrine of the communion of saints!

Therefore, Christian soul, do not abandon yourself to sorrow; follow the advice of St. Paul, "Do not mourn as those who have no hope." Remember the parting words of St. Monica to her son, St. Augustine, "Remember me at the altar of God!" Glancing at the battlefield of the Machabees, make an act of faith in the existence of Purgatory, saying with the inspired writer, "It is a holy and wholesome thought to pray for the dead that they may be loosed from sins."

Reason

Reason, when assisted by the higher light of revelation, gives us satisfactory evidence of the existence of a middle state, and, to our consolation, compels us to profess our belief in it. Our dissenting brethren ask: Why is it that souls who departed this life in the state of grace must nevertheless suffer so severely? Why must they, after having devoted their earthly career to true love of God, to the renunciation of all wickedness and worldly aspirations, after living in self-denial, justice and piety, why must they nevertheless suffer, why are they denied entrance into eternal bliss?—Let the inquirer rest assured that if it were not necessary, God would not permit it; for He finds no pleasure in the misfortune and pain of man, but in his salvation and eternal happiness. As a father will not hurt his child except in case of necessity, thus also our Heavenly Father will not hurt us except it be necessary for our true welfare.

God-fearing persons conscientiously avoid mortal sin; yet, either from a want of due vigilance or from human frailty, they commit venial faults which, trifling as they may appear, are punished by God; for Jesus says: "But I say unto you, that every idle word that men shall speak, they shall render an account for it in the day of judgment." (*Matt.* 12:36). True, we know that these venial faults are blotted out by an act of contrition, and that they are remitted by voluntary acts of penance, as well as in Confession: but nevertheless, may a person not be overtaken by death before having thus blotted them out, even before thinking of doing so? Then, when appearing before the tribunal of God, the soul is immediately confronted with its unatoned faults, and remembers with sorrow and terror its delinquencies. It acknowledges as supremely just the sentence of God condemning it to the purifying flames of Purgatory. And how will they fare whose faults approach in dangerous proximity to mortal sin? It is related of a poor woman that she sometimes covertly permitted her cow to graze in a neighbor's field. It was rarely done, for she was very conscientious. The damage caused amounted to, perhaps, twenty cents a year. But as she continued the practice for nearly twenty years, the amount finally reached the sum of four dollars. Simple-minded as she was, she never thought of this. She died and appearing before her Judge, was reminded of her indebtness. She is confused, can scarcely believe that she owes such a sum, but nevertheless it is so. In sorrow and contrition she acknowledges her fault, and goes to Purgatory for it.

We so often have little regard for small matters, and are thereby led to contract bad habits. Many a person is accustomed to complain of his hard lot and to regard himself as less fortunate than his neighbors: this is a fault which must be atoned for. Another is over-sensitive, and hangs his head when contradicted; or he is talkative and mixes in every conversation; or he is morose and vindictive, prone to making sharp remarks; another has contracted the habit of making only half genuflections before the Blessed Sacrament, etc., etc.; all these faults must be atoned for. Thus there is a number of faults, bad habits, weaknesses and negligences, of which even good Christians are guilty: they must be atoned for. For of Heaven Holy Scripture says; "There shall not enter into it anything defiled." (*Apoc.* 21:27). Pure as gold chastened by fire must the soul be before it can be admitted to the beatific vision of God.

There are others who have been guilty of mortal sins, but returned to God before their death by a true conversion, obtaining forgiveness of their sins and remission of eternal punishment in the Sacrament of Penance. Divine justice nevertheless demands satisfaction for these remitted sins; some temporal punishment is due to them. This we see in Moses, Aaron and David, in St. Peter and in St. Mary Magdalen: God had forgiven them their sins together with the eternal punishment due to them; He Himself, or His prophets had assured them of pardon: yet He punished David by the death of the son born to him (*2 Kgs.* 12:14); He punished Moses and Aaron by denying them entrance into the promised land (*Num.* 20:12). All these servants of God, though freed from the guilt and eternal punishment of their sins, continued nevertheless to deplore them all their lives, and to atone for the temporal punishment due to them by penance. Yet, who can say whether they ever attained to a point when they could say truly: Now we have destroyed all the evil effects of our sins in ourselves and in others? According to the words of Christ, "Thou shall not go out from thence till thou repay the last farthing." (*Matt.* 5:26).

Many die when they have scarcely begun their penance, others in the midst of it, others again at its end. Many a one who continued all through life in his wickedness, returns to God on his deathbed; he makes an act of contrition, confesses his sins and receives absolution, and feels happy at the thought that the burden of guilt is lifted from his soul. He dies, and is not condemned; but on his deathbed he neglected voluntary satisfaction and hence he is sentenced to undergo punishment in Purgatory. Entire satisfaction may be rendered in a short time: the Good Thief on the cross rendered sufficient satisfaction in his last moments to be admitted immediately into paradise. But many render but little satisfaction during a long time; numbers of people die without having even atoned for the sins of their youth: they must atone in Purgatory.

There is no doubt that in all these cases each one receives a gracious sentence; that all are saved because they died in the grace of God: but can they enter Heaven immediately? No; "there shall not enter into it anything defiled." (*Apoc.* 21:27). Hence they are debarred from the beatific vision of God until they shall have been purified, and have rendered satisfaction to Divine Justice. Having glorified His mercy, God now illustrates His justice in them. This being so, we are compelled to admit the existence of a middle state, where the just undergo temporal punishment and render satisfaction. This is impossible either in Heaven or in Hell. In Heaven there is no pain or punishment; in Hell torment and punishment is everlasting: there sin is avenged, but not atoned for. Therefore the just, who as yet are not worthy of Heaven, but saved from Hell, must undergo their purification in a middle state, where God cleanses them by punishment and thus renders them capable of His beatific vision.

Hence reason, praising God's mercy and justice, unites with the Catholic Church in the joyful declaration: "There is a Purgatory, and 'therefore it is a holy and wholesome thought to pray for the dead, that they may be loosed from sins.'" (*2 Mach.* 12:46).

The Unanimous Concurrence of all Nations in the Belief of Purgatory

The doctrine of Purgatory being thus consonant with reason, even the heathens professed it; for what is easy of belief is accepted, at least in its fundamental theory, by all nations. Hence they all believed in the existence of a Supreme Being; so that Plutarch could refer to cities without walls and without laws, but was forced to declare that there were none to be found without belief in a deity to whom they zealously rendered homage and sacrifice. We find the doctrine of the creation of man, of the prevarication of our first parents, of the flood, etc., among the most savage and rude nations. In the same manner, they all had some idea of a state of purification in the next world, however crude and perverted it might be. Thus we find this belief a part of the doctrine of the roaming savage who took with him on his predatory excursions the mortal remains of his father, and of the refined Greek and Roman, who scrupulously adhered to the customs by which he sought to placate the *manes* of the deceased. Widely as mourning customs differed, we find everywhere expiatory sacrifices for the dead, prayers for them: hence the holocausts, the cremations, the libations, offerings placed on tombs, funeral ceremonies, etc., as related in history. The Africans, the Chinese, the Japanese, the Celts and the Slavs professed their belief in purification in a middle state by the doctrine of the migration of souls, and of other modes of atonement. Similar views are found with the Esquimaux, Greenlanders, North American Indian tribes, etc., all concurring in the belief that the soul, on its way to Heaven, has to undergo many trials, in overcoming which the living can assist them by prayer, sacrifice and funeral celebrations.

Whence this universal sentiment which, though it does not appear everywhere with equal distinctness, yet is common to all? Undoubtedly these distorted views of an everlasting truth are founded in human reason which believes in the immortality of the soul and distinguishes between absolute purity and total depravity, between human frailty and obstinate perversity. Plato states the doctrine of paganism on this subject as follows: "As soon as the departed have arrived at the place to which they are conducted by demons, the separation of the just and holy from the wicked takes place. Those found to have led nearly a good life are conducted to the Great Lake to dwell there and atone for their faults till they are absolved. They whose condition is judged to be beyond remedy because of the wickedness of their transgressions, are plunged into Tartarus, whence they are never released. They whose

faults have been great, but remedied to some degree,
are also plunged into Tartarus; but after remaining a
year, the waves throw them ashore and they are transferred back to the Sea of Acherusia. If they are received
there by them against whom they offended, their punishment is ended. They, however, that shall be found
to have made great progress in holy life, escape all
these prisons in the interior of the earth, and proceed
to the pure abode above the earth."

The Jews also, though accepting only the Old Testament, believe the doctrine of purification in the next
world. They lay great stress on it, and are zealous
defenders of its practice. For instance, with them a
child is bound to say for a whole year a certain prayer
called *Kadis* for his deceased father. When there are
no children, strangers are paid to say this prayer. Jose-
phus remarks that this custom is very ancient.

It is impossible that nations of such diversity of
faith, morals, laws and languages should concur so
unanimously in this one point, except they all drew
from the same source, the fountain of truth. Here we
may well say, *Vox populi vox Dei:* "The voice of the people is God's voice." This voice of all nations and tribes
come to us from ages past, loudly attesting: "There is
a Purgatory; and 'it is therefore a holy and wholesome
thought to pray for the dead, that they may be loosed
from sins.'"

Opponents of Purgatory

While reason compels all nations to proclaim their
unanimous belief in Purgatory, a certain class of gloomy
and proud men, whose dull intelligence admits only of
an intercourse through the medium of the senses, pre-
sumes to deny this consoling doctrine. It is deplorable
to see men calling themselves Christians, and pro-
fessing to have progressed far in general culture, walking in the darkness of unbelief. Like owls, whose eyes
sparkle and shine but do not see in daytime, such men

surround themselves with the semblance of knowledge, deceiving by an appearance of brilliant scientific attainments, yet sitting in the dark. They do not see the day that dawned with Christ and advanced with the propagation of His doctrine till it now shines in meridian splendor. They resemble, says St. Ignatius, the fallen angels; for as these were incited to pride and brought to their fall by their sublime position, thus they are made enemies of Christ, enemies of revealed religion, by their pretended science and sham learning, thus sinking in the estimation of sound reason even below the most uncultured nations. For though it is not clearly demonstrated that the ancient Carthaginians, Egyptians, Celts, Slavs, etc., believed in Hell, yet there is no doubt that they believed in a state of purification after death. Whence this remarkable fact? St. Thomas Aquinas says, that while real science renders its possessor humble and makes all things except ourselves appear great, false science puffs up and shows everything as small and insignificant, except self. Hence we know of no other explanation but the senseless fanaticism of such as revolt in rabid haughtiness against the existing order of things, at the same time considering themselves too good, and others too wicked for Purgatory; which spirit is the result of singularity, prejudice and obstinate adhesion to preconceived ideas, and of a mean, narrow mind, intent on measuring divine things by the rule of dulled human perception. Thousands of souls were led into a labyrinth of error and unbelief by pride and presumptuous inquisitiveness regarding the mysteries of religion, by negligence in fulfilling their religious duties, by wickedness of life, by the reading of bad books and papers, by promiscuous association with scoffers at religion, with infidels, and with others whose company endangers faith.

And as even some so-called Catholics are presumptuous enough to doubt the consoling doctrine of Purgatory because, deluded by false logic, they believe the Church to be wrong on this point, we give a brief, comprehensive statement of the errors concerning Purgatory; in order that they may have a chance to recognize more easily their indefensible position, rise above their prejudices, and put to flight the serpent of pride and error.

The Gnostics of the first centuries of Christianity believed that the human soul is destined to free itself by degrees from the dominion of sensualism by going through a kind of purification here on earth. These heretics retained but little of Christianity, and their system had no place for Purgatory. For according to them the soul, once freed from the body and purified by earthly sufferings alone, returns to God in the realms of light, while everything else is engulfed in the darkness of eternal night.

In the fourth century, Aerius, a follower of the heresiarch Arius, called the doctrine of prayer for the dead immoral, claiming that it caused men to abandon themselves to vice and sin in the presumptuous hope that they were enabled, by gifts of money, to obtain the prayers and good works of others to escape punishment.

In the twelfth century, the Waldenses were at variance among themselves concerning the doctrine of Purgatory. The Albigenses and Catharers, who followed Gnostic views, and denied a future life in general almost universally, were logically bound to reject Purgatory. In southern France, the adherents of the apostate, Peter de Bruis, denied Purgatory, because they regarded themselves too good, and others too wicked for it.

Until then the enemy of God made use only of one or the other of the objections to Purgatory hitherto mentioned, in order to gain adherents opposing Purgatory. In the so-called Reformation of the sixteenth century, however, all these objections were united into one heresy denying the existence of Purgatory. For fifteen centuries the Church had offered up the Sacrifice of Expiation for the Suffering Souls, when Luther, an apostate monk, disturbed her peace and assailed her sacrifice by divulging a new doctrine. Of a morose and bitter disposition, he attacked the Catholic doctrine of indulgences, thus assailing the clemency of his spiritual Mother. Logically, he was soon led to deny the efficacy of her intercession, thus robbing the faithful of the consolation of her prayers after death by declaring that man, once justified, had no need of satisfying Divine Justice either in this world or in the next. Hence he denied the efficacy of prayer for the dead, and consequently the existence of Purgatory. But as he thus proclaimed a doctrine rejected both by Catholic Faith and by reason, a doctrine that aimed at the same time at being consonant with divine truth and conniving at the sinful inclinations of man, hence Luther wavered in his position and in his teaching. Lies are unstable, but truth remains steadfast forever. "The lip of truth shall be steadfast for ever: but he that is a hasty witness, frameth a lying tongue." (*Prov.* 12:19). The Protestant theologian, Fritschel, in his "Review for Lutheran Theology and Church," mentions the conflicting views of Luther concerning the doctrine of Purgatory as follows: In 1518 and 1519 the "Reformer" declares the existence of Purgatory as undeniable, and insists on its acceptance. In the following years, until 1530, his views underwent a change. He wished to retain Purgatory, but was not willing that it should remain an article of faith, "because," he maintained, "its existence can neither be proved, nor ought it to be denied." Then, in 1530, Luther published a "Denial of Purgatory;" a "powerful argument against this error," as Fritschel calls it. In the Schmalkaldian Articles of 1537, the heresiarch calls Purgatory a "Devil's Mask." Nevertheless, he again wavers on other occasions, and in 1543, permits the insertion of prayers for the dead in the official edition of his Church Directory. No wonder that Fritschel repeatedly calls Luther's position "remarkable." It must appear "remarkable" to every person capable of reasoning, no less so than the following prayer taken from his Directory: "O God, if the soul is in a condition to be assisted, I beseech Thee to be gracious towards it." Still more remarkable it is, that so many persons adhere to his wavering doctrine.

Calvin calls Purgatory "a dastardly invention of Satan, a blasphemy against Christ which annihilates His cross." Yet he concedes that prayer for the dead is an ancient and pious custom, and says that the souls of the just are detained until the last day in the bosom of Abraham. (*Lib. Inst.* 3. 5).

Luther's illogical error was the result of wounded pride, nourished by intemperance like fire is fed by fuel. Smothering reason through exciting the passions, he aroused in his followers the seven-headed hydra of vice, causing them to show less logic than the Esquimaux and Greenlanders, by rejecting the consoling doctrine of a middle state in the next world.

The views and speculations concerning Purgatory, which originated in the diverging doctrines of Protestantism, are too manifold to be noted here. It is sufficient to mention that some of its adherents admit Heaven and Hell alone, others a place of purification and Heaven, others again no Hell and no Purgatory, but Heaven alone.

Nevertheless there are, and always have been, a great many dissenters from the Catholic Church who, intent on living justly and uprightly, cultivate a profound logical religious sentiment, and hence agree with the learned Protestant Leibnitz who says: "It always was the teaching of the Church that they that have departed this life, though acceptable to God through Christ and therefore elected to eternal life, must sometimes suffer natural punishment or purification for their sins, especially if they have not cleansed themselves sufficiently from their faults while on earth. True, the holy Fathers do not agree as to the mode of purification; but nearly all agree in the opinion that after this life a paternal punishment or purification, whatever its nature may be, will take place, by which the souls, after their departure from the body, are enlightened, and then, convinced of the imperfection of their past life and of the turpitude of sin, are filled with sorrow, and themselves desire it, unwilling to be admitted to the height of beatitude without having undergone it." And he concludes: "It always was a doctrine of the Church that we should pray for the dead, because they receive assistance by our prayer."

Collier, also a Protestant, remarks: "Prayer for the dead is one of the most ancient and best authenticated practices of religion. It quickens the belief in the immortality of the soul, draws the veil of darkness from the grave, and joins this world with the next. Had it been retained, most likely we should not have experienced so much skepticism and unbelief among us. I cannot find a reason why a dissenting Church, which cannot claim supernatural gifts, and is quite foreign to the early ages of Christianity, has rejected, or permitted the neglect of, a custom which is not condemned." True, the so-called Reformers, if they would be logical, could not admit Purgatory; but it was a rather hazardous proceeding to draw, by mere deduction, a negation of truths so firmly rooted in faith and so consonant with reason and sentiment. Hence the untenable position of Protestantism, which loudly proclaims to the world that despite its doctrinal negation, many of its adherents unite with the Catholic Church in declaring: "There is a Purgatory; 'it is therefore a holy and wholesome thought to pray for the dead that they may be loosed from sins.'" (*2 Mach.* 12:46).

Uninterrupted Tradition of the Church and Purgatory

Protestants admit that the belief in purification after death, and the custom of praying for the dead, were both universal in the Church for fifteen centuries. And indeed, if we would but go to the trouble of examining the pages of history, we should find the view correct, as a few proofs from the writings of the holy Fathers, the inscriptions in the catacombs and the decrees of the councils of the Church will show.

St. Chrysostom, in his third homily, says: "The Apostles did not ordain without good reason a commemoration of the departed to be made during the celebration of the sacred mysteries; for from it the deceased draw great gain and help. Why should our prayers for them not placate God, when, besides the priest, the whole people stand with uplifted hands whilst the august Victim is present on the altar? True, it is offered only for such as departed hence in the Faith." St. Gregory of Nyssa writes: "The Apostles and disciples of Christ have handed down to us what since has obtained the force of law everywhere in the Church of God, namely that the memory of those that died in the true Faith be recalled in the celebration of the sacred and illustrious mystery." In the fourth century, St. Jerome presents to our view the pious Pammachius mourning over the mortal remains of his consort, less with tears than with prayer and by alms. St. Augustine relates with touching emotion the parting words of his mother, St. Monica: "Lay this body anywhere; be not concerned about that. Only this I beg of you, that wheresoever you be, you make remembrance of me at the Lord's altar." Even as early as the second century, Tertullian wrote: "On the anniversaries of the dead we offer the Holy Sacrifice for the departed. Even though Scripture did not warrant this, the custom originates in Tradition; it was confirmed by universal adoption and sanctioned by faith."

A touching proof of the belief that the living are able to help the dead is found in the history of St. Perpetua. She beheld her own brother Dinocrates, seven years of age, in the torments of Purgatory. The Saint continued assiduously in prayer for him, and in a new vision saw his pain gradually lessened, until he finally appeared to her with a luminous countenance leaving the place of his suffering to engage in childish sport. "I then awoke," she remarks, "and knew that my brother's punishment was over."

The catacombs, the subterranean tombs of the martyrs, give eloquent testimony of the belief in Purgatory, which is all the more impressive because it leads us back to the very cradle of the Church, to the bloody persecutions overcome by the faith and virtue of thousands and thousands of victims. A number of renowned cemeteries, for instance that of SS. Peter and Paul, of St. Priscilla, St. Domitilla, etc., date back to the first century, to the very time of the Apostles, and the others are as old as the second and third century. In the numerous incriptions found there, abundant proof of the belief in Purgatory is expressed in prayers for the departed. For instance: "Here, dearest son, thy life has come to an end. But Thee, O Heavenly Father, we implore to have mercy, to take pity on the sufferings of our dear one, through Christ, Our Lord." "To Lucifera! Whosoever of the brethren chances to read this, let him pray to God to take unto Himself her holy and pure spirit." "Eternal light shine upon thee, Timothea, in Christ!" Verily, the reading of these few specimens among the hundreds of inscriptions dating from the first centuries, present to us in a true mirror the reflection of the faith of the Church of our own times.

But how strange! Dissenters ask us to regard Purgatory as a mere conjecture, which received its form and shape by SS. Gregory and Augustine, and by later Councils. In return, the Church points to her constant Tradition, as embodied in her ordinances and customs, and triumphantly vindicates the doctrine of Purgatory by her councils.

Long ago, the Council of Carthage recommended prayers for the dead; the same was done by the Roman Synod, in 502; by the Synod of Orleans, in 533; by the Council of Braga, in 563; by the Council of Toledo, in 675; by the Synod of Chalons, in 813; by the Synod of Worms, in 868. The second Council of Lyons, in 1274, says: "The Holy Roman Church declares and teaches, that when truly penitent souls die in charity before they have atoned for their faults of commission and

omission by worthy fruits of penance, they are purified after death in the torments of Purgatory." The
Council of Florence, in 1439, states the same doctrine
in the very words of the Lyonese Council. Finally, the
Council of Trent (Session VI. 22, 25), declares formally,
first, that the faithful are able to assist the souls
detained in Purgatory by their prayer and by the Holy
Sacrifice of the Mass. Moreover, it threatens with excommunication those who affirm that after receiving the
grace of justification the penitent sinner's debt and
eternal punishment are remitted in such a manner,
that no temporal punishment remains to be undergone
in Purgatory.

Thus the belief in Purgatory is clearly and unmistakably expressed in the writings of the holy Fathers,
by the testimony of the Catacombs, and the decrees of
the Councils. Besides eternal Heaven for undefiled
souls; besides everlasting Hell for souls departing with
the guilt of mortal sin on them, there is a middle
state—Purgatory. Hence: "It is a holy and wholesome
thought to pray for the dead, that they may be loosed
from sins." (*2 Mach.* 12:46).

Divine Revelation and Purgatory

The Council of Trent, assembled for the defense and
vindication of the ancient Faith, branded the auda-
cious innovators of the 16th century with the note of
excommunication, condemning their nefarious doctrine,
and reaffirming Catholic belief in Purgatory. By the
declaration of this dogma the Church did not invent
a new doctrine, but simply sustained and made an
authentic declaration of the faith founded on ancient
Tradition and on Holy Scripture. She set the seal of
her divine authority on it, sustained it by her authoritative declaration, and thus consummated our consolation by her authentic evidence for the existence of
Purgatory.

In Holy Scripture we find this evidence even in the

Book of Genesis. It informs us that Joseph, on his father's death, ordered the Egyptians to hold a mourning celebration of seventy days, and a funeral celebration of seven days. In the First Book of Kings we read that the inhabitants of Jabez Galaad fasted seven days at the death of Saul, Jonathan and Abner. The learned divines Suarez and Bellarmine declare in conformity with the holy Fathers, that these practices are not to be understood simply as expressions of mourning alone, but must be regarded also as suffrages for the dead. If fasting was nothing but an expression of sorrow, it is difficult to explain why David fasted during the illness of his child, but ceased to fast immediately after its death. It is evident that he was of the opinion that a continuance of his fast was no longer to any purpose, because the child, having died in innocence, was no longer in need of prayer, and good works. The royal prophet describes in a touching manner the doctrine of Purgatory when he refers to the ineffable bliss of those souls that, having passed through the flood and fire of affliction, at length have found the long desired deliverance. The prophet Micheas takes comfort in advance in the consolations of Purgatory, saying: "I will bear the wrath of the Lord, because I have sinned against Him, until He judge my cause and execute judgment for me: He will bring me forth into the light." (*Mich.* 7:9). Hence the declaration of Ecclesiasticus (7:37): "A gift hath grace in the sight of all the living, and restrain not grace from the dead." One hundred and fifty years before the light of the Gospel shed its saving rays on the world, belief in Purgatory finds unmistakable expression in the history of the victorious Machabee, Judas. This renowned hero, having lost a great number of warriors in battle, is not content with honoring them by a pompous burial: he orders a collection to be made, and sends the proceeds—twelve hundred drachms of silver—to Jerusalem, to have sacrifice offered for the deceased. "For," adds the inspired writer, "if he had not hoped that they that were slain should rise again, it would have seemed superfluous and vain to pray for the dead. And because he considered that they who had fallen asleep with godliness, had great grace laid up for them. It is therefore a holy and wholesome thought to pray for the dead, that they may be loosed from sins." (*2 Mach.* 12:44-46). Holy Scripture itself, then, draws from the action of this chieftain the conclusion that Purgatory exists, and that our prayers and sacrifices are accepted in suffrage for the release of the departed.

Our Lord Himself, though He was most zealous in correcting abuses, and well knew that the Jews prayed for the dead, not only did not interfere with this practice, but confirmed it. For He said, "And whosoever shall speak a word against the Son of man, it shall be forgiven him: but he that shall speak against the Holy Ghost, it shall not be forgiven him, neither in this world, nor in the world to come." (*Matt.* 12:32). From these words SS. Augustine, Gregory the Great, Bernard, the Venerable Bede and others conclude as follows: Whatsoever may be the nature of this speaking against the Holy Ghost mentioned here as an unpardonable sin, whether it be understood as referring to the obstinacy of the Jews or of the unbelievers in resisting the acknowledged truth: one certain, clear and indisputable fact follows from this passage of the Gospel by the very exception made in it: it proves convincingly that certain sins *are* forgiven in the next world. Now this forgiveness is not obtainable in Heaven, because sin does not gain admittance there, nor in Hell, where there is no redemption. There is only one possibility: these sins are forgiven in Purgatory—hence there *is* a Purgatory.

Moreover, Our Lord exhorts us: "Be at agreement with thy adversary betimes, whilst thou art in the way with him: lest perhaps the adversary deliver thee to the judge, and the judge deliver thee to the officer, and thou be cast into prison. Amen I say to thee, thou shalt not go out from thence till thou repay the last farthing." (*Matt.* 5:25, 26). Many holy Fathers, among them Origen, St. Jerome, St. Ambrose and others, declare that this passage is to be understood not only as referring to a place of eternal punishment, but also to one of temporal atonement in the next world, because deliverance is promised to those that "repay the last farthing."

The doctrine of the Apostles agrees with that of their divine Master. Like Him, they never reproved the Jews for believing in a middle state, nor did they ever prohibit prayers for the dead. St. Paul mentioning the Jewish custom of pious practices for the dead, refers to these as to a baptism, or religious rite, and draws therefrom the conclusion of a future resurrection. He writes, "What shall they do that are baptized for the dead, if the dead rise not again at all? why are they then baptized for them?" (*1 Cor.* 15:29). Thus he teaches us that the custom of praying for the dead is one beneficial to them, and hence to be retained by the Christians. But if there were only Heaven and Hell in the next world, such prayers would be unprofitable.

St. Paul affirms this doctrine still more explicitly when he teaches that there are faithful who attain Heaven by fire, or, to use his own words, they "shall be saved, yet so as by fire." (*1 Cor.* 3:15). According to the Apostle there are such as make Christ the foundation of their salvation, but build on this foundation an edifice of wood, hay or stubble, that is, they believe in Christ, but mix many imperfections with their good works. "If any man's work abide, which he hath built thereupon, he shall receive a reward. If any man's work burn, he shall suffer loss; but he himself shall be saved; yet so as by fire." (*1 Cor.* 3:14-15). "The fire shall try every man's work, of what sort it is," whether "gold, silver, precious stones, wood, hay, stubble." (*1 Cor.* 3:12, 13). The holy Fathers remark that by gold, silver and precious stones are meant good works, by wood, hay and stubble venial sins and imperfections. Hence St. Augustine says, "Punish me in Thy wrath, that I may be cleansed in this world, and so transformed that I shall not stand in need of the purifying flames like those that are 'saved as if by fire.' Whence this? Because they built on the foundation with wood, hay and stubble here below. Had they built with gold, silver and precious stones, they would be safe from both fires, not only from the everlasting one that shall torment the wicked forever, but also from the one that purifies those that are saved by fire." The learned commentator Allioli, explaining the above words of St. Paul, says: "Remark well, the fire of which the Apostle speaks cannot be understood to mean the tribulations of this world; for he speaks of a fire burning on the day of judgment, consequently after the time of this life. It cannot be understood to mean the great examination by the Judge, for you are not only examined, but made to burn, so that you suffer by fire. It cannot mean the fire of Hell; because he that suffers by the fire mentioned is saved after suffering loss. It can be understood only as meaning the cleansing fire after death called Purgatory, which burns the soul departed in imperfections, during the time of cleansing, and shall be extinguished at the general judgment in the destruction of the world." Our works, then, shall be subject to examination; they shall be cleansed from every base alloy in the flames enkindled by divine wrath, the same as gold and silver are purified in the crucible of the refiner. Hence the learned Bellarmine remarks, "It is a doctrine held in common by all divines, that in this passage the words, 'by fire' are to be understood as referring to a temporal fire of purification, to which they are sentenced after death, who, according to the verdict of their particular judgment, have built with wood, hay and stubble. This explanation is not only warranted by the text, but agrees with the general opinion of the Fathers." The renowned theologian then adduces the testimony of SS. Cyprian, Ambrose, Jerome, Augustine, Gregory, Anselm, Thomas, Bonaventure, etc.

St. Paul himself gave us the example of praying for

the dead. Having received hospitality at Rome in the house of Onesiphorus, he reminds his disciple Timothy of it, saying: "The Lord give mercy to the house of Onesiphorus: because he hath often refreshed me, and hath not been ashamed of my chain . . . The Lord grant unto him to find mercy of the Lord in that day." (*2 Tim.* 1:16, 18). Allioli remarks: "The Apostle does not send greeting to Onesiphorus when speaking of his past merits, but to his family. For the deserving man himself he prays that the Lord grant mercy unto him on the day of judgment. Hence it is apparent that at that time the good man was dead, and that the Apostle teaches us by his example to offer up suffrages and prayers for the souls of those that died in the Lord: this, however, can be done only if we believe in a middle state—Purgatory."

Hence the existence of Purgatory, demonstrated and proved as it is by reason, revelation and theological evidence, is an accepted Catholic dogma. It is a doctrine contained so unmistakably clear in the sources of revelation, in Scripture and Tradition, and is presented so concisely as the outcome of faith in eternal reward and punishment, that it would be a Catholic dogma even if it had not been declared as such by the authority of the Church. It is a dogma because there is indisputable evidence that the whole Church, in all ages and in all countries, accepted it as such, and because it was declared as such by the solemn declaration of the Church's supreme teaching authority.

The doctrine of Purgatory does away with the foolhardy doctrine of the soul's mortality; it convinces us that death is but a transient occurrence. "In the sight of the unwise they seemed to die: and their departure was taken for misery . . . Afflicted in few things, in many they shall be well rewarded: because God hath tried them, and found them worthy of Himself" (*Wis.* 3:2, 5), so that He will not destroy their souls. "My soul shall live." (*Ps.* 118:175). For God solves the mortal bonds of the just only to lead them to the place of purification. "As gold in the furnace He hath proved them, and as a victim of a holocaust He hath received them" (*Wis.* 3:6) to open for them the portals of the abode of refreshment, light and peace. "For grace and peace is to His elect." (*Wis.* 3:9).

We love to hear this doctrine. It brings us consolation in affliction; it renders easy the sacrifices we have to make for virtue; it moves us to joyous praise of the Lord's justice and mercy; it makes us love our Faith; it elevates us above ourselves and transports us into the land of the living, that is, into the regions of immortality, into the Church Suffering and Triumphant. On the other hand, denial of this doctrine brings death. Bellarmine observes: "The doctrine of the existence of Purgatory is so Catholic a dogma, that they who nevertheless deny it assuredly have to fear not Purgatory, but rather the flames of Hell."

And thus we hear faith and nature, all nations and all ages proclaim for the welfare of mankind: "It is therefore a holy and wholesome thought to pray for the dead, that they may be loosed from sins." (*2 Mach.* 12:46).

Chapter 2

The Condition of the Suffering Souls in Purgatory

The Spiritual Condition of the Suffering Souls

THERE is a middle state—a state of purification—after this life: this is a natural claim of the human heart's affection, acknowledged unanimously by all nations, but of which we receive certainty and a complete and correct conception only by revealed religion. The souls of those who died in the state of grace, but were not found sufficiently pure to enter the heavenly Jerusalem, are sentenced to this state. The most dreaded time for man, dreaded even by saintly servants of God, is the hour of death, that decisive hour on which depends Heaven or Hell. At this dangerous hour our Guardian Angels are a most potent help for us. These spirits, endowed with supernatural intelligence and privileges, servants of God and protectors of man, assist and encourage us. They put to flight the evil spirits, and are the first to receive the parting soul and conduct it to God. Therefore the Church in her recommendation of a departing soul says, "Go forth, Christian soul, from this world, in the name of the Angels and Archangels." The holy Angels are invited to receive the departing soul and to conduct it before the throne of God. This is also expressed in the prayer of the Church: "Let St. Michael, the Archangel, prince of heavenly hosts, receive him. Let the holy Angels of God come forth to meet him and conduct him to the city of the heavenly Jerusalem."

After the soul has appeared before the tribunal of God, sentence is passed, and then it goes to the abode decreed by divine justice. St. Thomas Aquinas and St. Bonaventure say that it is probable that the souls sentenced to temporal punishment are conducted to the place of punishment by good Angels, and there begin a new and abstergent life. We add, in a few general sentences, a description of this spiritual life of the souls in Purgatory, as well as it can be given.

The prerogatives and dignity of man in this world are founded in his spiritual being, in his immortal soul. By this his ennobled, rational and free nature man is endowed with the faculty of thought, of judgment, of liberty and will. Is it, then, not apparent at first view, that among all beings of visible creation man predominates and is the most prominent, that everything else is created for his service? All things must bow before man's power, because reason elevates him above the whole material world, if he knows how to bring it under his dominion. The soul's power of cognition at the time of its departure from the body remains its property also in Purgatory, but a new degree of cognition is, generally speaking, not added, for the aspect of visible creation with its manifold wonders is shut off from it. The soul is in prison, under punishment. The learned Bautz writes: "With St. Augustine theological writers are of the opinion, that the Suffering Souls have cognizance of many things that specially interest them. As the holy doctor remarks, the souls of the deceased are beyond the reach of earthly influences, and as a rule remain so, although their affection for us is not diminished. Whatever of mundane affairs interests them can be brought to their notice in various ways. They are informed of it partly by other souls who depart this life at a later period, partly through the intervention of Angels, partly by special divine revelation, partly also by being permitted to re-appear among us." The natural perceptive powers of a soul are, therefore, as a rule restricted to its place of captivity. It has a direct cognition of itself, and of the other spirits into whose company it was transferred. According to Bautz the soul, at its separation from the body, is endowed with all the faculties corresponding to its new phase of existence, and is thus enabled to communicate with the other souls and with the heavenly spirits that appear in the abode of torment.

Even during mortal life the soul of man is capable of elevating itself into the realm of the supernatural; it is impressed with ideas imperceptible to the bodily senses so as even to entertain a conception of the infinite. Instructed by revelation, it becomes enthusiastic in the service of the true, the beautiful, the good, and the divine; it finds a pleasure in Christian virtue in comparison with which all other enjoyments become insipid. The souls in Purgatory retain possession of this supernatural cognition. It is not an intuition, but essentially a species of faith that has become part of their existence. Some points of doctrine which are articles of faith in the Church Militant are such no longer for the Church Suffering, because to the latter they have become matters of cognition, intuition or experience. Particular judgment, Purgatory, the Guardian Angels, perhaps also Satan and Hell; are part of their experience. Other mysteries of faith, however, are veiled to the Suffering Souls the same as to us.

The Creator endowed human nature with such glorious prerogatives and revealed His paternal Providence to man so manifestly, that he will be the most blessed creature for all eternity, provided he attains his final destiny. The Suffering Souls in Purgatory have as yet not attained it, hence they yearn for it, full of hope and confidence. They feel the pangs of an insatiable hunger and thirst, and are consumed by a longing for essential life, beauty and truth, for imperishable greatness, for eternal happiness and glory in God. Like faith and hope, the Suffering Souls also possess charity. As Suarez remarks, the Suffering Soul, though not yet enjoying the contemplation of God, is nevertheless possessed of a fixed measure of infused divine love, corresponding to its merit, which latter can no longer be increased.

The course of this life once finished, the time of forbearance, mercy and merit is over. Then God is no longer our Father, but our Judge, our severe Judge, who sentences us to pay the last farthing. Personally, the Suffering Souls cannot do anything to escape their wretchedness and misery. For them the time of labor, when they were able not only to increase their merit, but also to atone for their sins, is over. The darkness of that night has overtaken them, "when no man can work" (*John* 9:4) for his own profit. To them are applicable the words of Scripture: "If the tree fall to the south, or to the north, in what place soever it shall fall, there shall it be." (*Eccles.* 11:3). The soul's eternal destiny is not only decided, but it moreover can no longer use the time during which it is debarred from entering eternal glory to increase its own merits. The Suffering Souls no longer have time to do penance for their sins, or to increase their merit, or to pray to God for their own deliverance, or to hasten their admittance to eternal bliss. Theirs is a time of suffering, of suffering without merit, of suffering without the possibility of relieving themselves.

Just as the time of merit is over for the Suffering Souls, so also is their time of combat past. They are forever exempt from probation, temptation and the possibility of committing sin; all who die united in charity with God have finished their course, fought the good fight and ended their pilgrimage. With St. John Damascene the holy Fathers and ecclesiastical writers say, "Death is for man what the fall was for the Angels."

The doctrine, that the Suffering Souls can do nothing for their own relief, is certain in that sense, that they cannot acquire new merit to be applied in atonement for their sins. They cannot themselves do anything to render satisfaction to God. If these holy Souls, remarks Suarez, could obtain their release by some act of satisfaction, they would liberate themselves in a very short time simply by making an act of perfect contrition. Nevertheless, this same author concedes that they can move God by their prayer to apply to them the intercession of the faithful on earth; that they can invoke their Angels for some refreshment and mitigation of their torments; and lastly that they can entreat these heavenly spirits to incite the faithful to a greater zeal in the performance of good works in their behalf, which office these good spirits fulfill most readily and of their own accord. Bellarmine calls this opinion of Suarez not only probable, but indubitable, and argues that the Suffering Souls pray for themselves in the manner described. Gregory of Valencia, adducing the authority of the renowned Alexander of Hales, is still more positive. "I maintain," he says, "that the souls in Purgatory pray for themselves and implore God to deliver them from their torments by some means ordained by His eternal Providence, perhaps by the intercession of the faithful on earth. This is the doctrine of Alexander of Hales, who relies on the authority of Pope Gregory the Great. For if, as the latter says, the souls in Purgatory invoke the aid of the faithful, they also, presumably, implore God to impel the faithful to come to their assistance."

If the Suffering Souls can pray successfully for themselves; if, as we shall show later, they can intercede and obtain favors for us, as is maintained by Suarez and St. Catherine of Genoa: then it is probable that they also console and succor each other to the full extent of their charity, as far as they are permitted to do so by God. Or does it seem improbable that, impelled by an unselfish and sublime charity, they voluntarily renounce the suffrages of their relatives and friends in favor of others, thus suffering one for the other? True charity is forgetful of self, as St. Paul remarks; and this same apostle is himself an example of this charity. Like Moses he desired to become a reprobate, if he might thereby save his brethren. Tertullian relates the same also of the early Christians. To save their brethren they exposed themselves to every danger, they suffered stripes, fire and death. If charity achieved such triumphs on earth, may we not expect the same, and more, of the charity of these just and holy souls? Their charity is undoubtedly pure and unselfish; they love God in His creatures. The holy Angels watch over us, not for the sake of adding to their merit, but for the love of God. God's own love for us is an unselfish one, proceeding from His pure, superabundant and infinite charity for us. "Indeed," says Binet, "suffering for the welfare of another is an act worthy of those magnanimous and charitable souls who are less sensitive of the purifying flames than of the fire of divine love." And Bautz concludes: "Whether such a mutual devotedness is actually permitted by the order of divine Providence in Purgatory, and to what extent, is beyond our knowledge." Certain it is, that by their own act the Suffering Souls cannot help themselves, nor assist others: we must aid them by our good works.

Confirmed in the grace and love of God, the souls in Purgatory are the adopted children of our heavenly Father, infinitely surer of this adoption than the most pious and saintly souls during earthly life. Though their conscience inform the latter, that they are "if sons, heirs also; heirs indeed of God, and joint heirs with Christ" (*Rom.* 8:17), they are nevertheless not sure to remain such, because they are in danger every moment of losing the grace of God by sin, and of becoming children of damnation. But a soul in Purgatory, being out of this danger, has no longer any cause for fear. It is assured of remaining an elect child of God forever, and certain to possess the heritage of Heaven. Though such an elect spouse of Christ is detained in the most terrible torments, and is not permitted to hasten to the wedding feast, because

admission thereto must be purchased by the satisfaction due to the sanctity and justice of God, she
nevertheless dwells in the realms of peace, resting in
Christ Our Lord, as the Church testifies in the commemoration of the dead in Holy Mass. The soul, though
suffering grievously, suffers with such resignation and
conformity to the Will of God, that it experiences neither confusion nor terror. It is strong in patience; pain
does not deaden its love of God, and therefore does
not disturb its peace, which is firmly established in
the hope of future glory.

Spiritual Torments of the Suffering Souls

Convinced of the existence of Purgatory, and having
reviewed in spirit some features of the condition of
those detained therein, let us now devote our pious
attention to the contemplation of the abode itself in
which these souls are sentenced to dwell, and consider
the extent of their misery.

Although nothing definite can be said concerning the
means applied in Purgatory in order to effect that
purification which renders the souls worthy of the
beatific vision of God, we are nevertheless reminded
by Holy Scripture that "it is a fearful thing to fall into
the hands of the living God." (*Heb.* 10:31). Revelation
affords us no clue to the nature of the punishments of
Purgatory; we know, however, that they are two-fold:
a pain of loss, and a pain of sense. On both let us hear
the common and more probable opinion of theologians.

As the soul, by its noblest inspirations, is drawn irresistibly to God, therefore the exclusion from the beatific
vision of God is the supreme, the most excruciating
pain that it can endure. To understand this, at least
in part, we must consider the anguish of a heart that
has lost the object of its affection. In such a heart love
and grief are united, for true love cannot but suffer
by the absence of its object. Lovers yearn for each
other's presence, pining away in sighs and tears. Not

unfrequently they commit suicide because the one will not outlive the other. Asylums for the insane give eloquent testimony of the sad consequences of unrequited love. Now man is not created for this world, but for God. His inmost nature, his noblest and sublimest faculties and powers impel him and draw him on toward God. True, we mortals do not behold God, and, being devoted wholly to the perishable things of this world, we are quite unconcerned thereat. The distracting turmoil of the world, its unhallowed enjoyments, the profane bonds binding us to it, the overwhelming cares with which we overload ourselves—all this combines to compensate us, so to say, for the loss of God's vision. But in the same measure as man frees himself from these fetters his spirit ascends by the wings of insuperable desire to the supreme, all-beautiful Being. With some Saints this spiritual ardor of love was so great, that their heart, their countenance, their whole body glowed with and reflected a physical heat. It had this effect on St. Peter Alcantara, St. Catharine of Genoa, St. Magdalen of Pazzi, St. Stanislas Kostka and others. The more they became convinced of the supremacy of things heavenly and divine over things earthly, the more ardently they became desirous of attaining them, a yearning much greater than that resulting from mere human affection.

As soon as we have deposed the robe of mortality in death, as soon as the boundless circle of eternity has received us, the soul, in its solitude and forsakenness, is seized with an invincible desire to be admitted to the beatific vision of God. Such souls have been ransomed and cleansed by the Blood of Christ; they have the indelible mark of God's grace; the imperishable crown of victory is prepared for them, for they are faithful, holy souls that love God alone. These souls, destined for Heaven and sentenced to the darkness of a disconsolate solitude, are seized with the most ardent desire of seeing their God, and they see Him not! Their torment is so much the greater, the more they are conscious of the supreme beatitude of being admitted to His vision. Whoever once had the experience of the agonies of homesickness may form a faint idea of the extent of their sorrow. Hence St. Augustine exclaims, "Give me a loving soul: it will comprehend what I intend to convey."

Besides the pain arising from unrequited desire, deprivation of the beatific vision of God causes another great torment to the Suffering Souls: this results from the consciousness that it is not God's fault, but their own, that they cannot enter Heaven; it is a consequence of their sins. Thus their sins are brought back in all their hideousness to their spiritual view, and indescribable sorrow fills them. When Absalom was called back from his flight and permitted to enter Jerusalem, his father David would not let him come into his presence, but said, "Let him return into his house, and let him not see my face." . . . "And Absalom dwelt two years in Jerusalem, and saw not the king's face. He sent therefore to Joab to send him to the king . . . I beseech thee therefore that I may see the face of the king: and if he be mindful of my iniquity, let him kill me. And Absalom was called for and he went in to the king: and prostrated himself on the ground before him." (*2 Kgs.* 14:24-33). So great was his sorrow at having offended his father. It is related of St. Aloysius that he swooned away with sorrow for his few and insignificant faults. St. Stanislas fainted when he heard immodest words; St. Oringa was attacked with nausea when obliged to listen to them.

The Suffering Souls are called to the nuptials of the Lamb; a splendid throne is prepared for them; they have escaped all dangers threatening their salvation; their loving desire of seeing God is most vehement. With St. Paul, they often repeat, "Unhappy man that I am, who shall deliver me from the body of this death?" (*Rom.* 7:24). "Having a desire to be dissolved and to be with Christ." (*Phil.* 1:23). The veil of flesh which separated them from their Beloved has fallen: now they shall see Him and share His bliss! But, alas, the Lord remembers their misdeeds; the Most Holy One delivers them to the tormentors; because they are in need of purification, they are sentenced to the dark prison, where they must languish until they shall have paid "the last farthing." At the end of their earthly pilgrimage, at the very threshold of Heaven, they are debarred from its entrance through their own fault: oh, how bitter a sorrow, how sad a condition!

Yet the punishment is not alike for all souls. God can join with it a species of consolation; He can mitigate it by the hope of a speedy deliverance. Severe as the pain of loss is, its infliction concerns a loving soul, a soul willing to suffer and to atone in order to be made worthy of being united with the object of its eternal love. To such a loving soul God grants the necessary strength to bear its great trial with patience. Sure of the complacency of their Beloved, the Suffering Souls joyfully bear every pain of Purgatory with resignation to the Will of God. With St. Ignatius the Martyr they say: "Let the demons exhaust all their power in me, if I but possess Christ!" Thus, undoubtedly, they are not without consolation; but their consolation is mixed with sorrow. Purgatory is not a place of reward, but of punishment.

We read in *St. Benedict's Stimmen*, 1880: "A soul appearing to St. Mechtildis declared to her: 'I feel no pain, except that I am debarred from the vision of God, whom I long to see so ardently that if all the longings of all men on earth were united, they would seem nothing in comparison to the desire that consumes me.'" Thus the Souls in Purgatory suffer the whole burden of the pain resulting from their separation from God, and from their unrequited desire of beholding Him, and this in so high a degree, that a pious religious, after an apparition he had, declared that he would suffer a thousand deaths for his bitterest enemy in order to save him from Purgatory, because its torments so greatly exceed the pains of this earth. The Suffering

Souls' thirst for God is more intense than the panting hart's longing for water; yet it shall not be quenched until they shall have paid "the last farthing."

The Suffering Souls' Pain of Sense

Another kind of punishment to which the souls in Purgatory are subjected consists in the *pain of sense.* We cannot doubt its reality, knowing as we do that God even in this world makes use of various kinds of sufferings in order to purify a soul pleasing to Him. Temporary deprivation of God's vision is the soul's punishment in Purgatory for having, on earth, turned away from God, its supreme good; but the soul also sinned by turning to created things and enjoying in their possession a spurious delight and satisfaction. The punishment for this illicit sensual enjoyment is a sensible pain, by which the unlawful delectation is atoned for. According to the general opinion of theologians, the pain of sense consists in fire. In his work *De Civitate Dei*, Book XXI, St. Augustine says of the pain of sense in the next world: "If the fire be not immaterial like the pain of the soul, but material, causing us to smart only when we touch it, then the question may be asked: how can it constitute a punishment for spirits?" And he answers: "It is not necessary to engage in a long disputation or argument on this question. For what prohibits us to believe that spirits can be made sensitive albeit in a miraculous manner, of a material fire, when the spirit of man, which is truly immaterial, can be enclosed in the human body during natural life and after the day of judgment? The spirits, then, though having no body, will be bound to a material fire, experiencing pain from it, but giving it no nourishment. For also that other manner by which spirits are now joined to bodies, is truly wonderful and above the conception of man, and yet it is what constitutes man. I might say the spirits burn without having a body, the same as Dives burned in Hell when he exclaimed, 'I

am tormented in this flame' . . . But that Hell, which
is called by Scripture a lake of fire and brimstone,
shall be a material fire as was declared by eternal
truth." Theologians, with St. Thomas, teach that by
divine co-operation fire exerts its influence on the soul
physically and really; it confines the soul to a certain
space, and limits its activity there in a manner most
violent and unnatural. The pain of sense, then, consists principally in a purifying, material fire. Although
the suffering souls are destined for Heaven, they are
nevertheless denied admission there because in the
heavenly Jerusalem only the purest and finest gold is
accepted. The Suffering Souls, through gold, are still
defiled by the dross of the earth from which they were
created. Therefore the Lord detains them in a fiery
furnace, there to purify them, like unrefined gold,
of all dross and spurious material. "And He shall sit
refining and cleansing the silver, and He shall purify
the sons of Levi, and shall refine them as gold, and
as silver." (*Mal.* 3:3). This fire is a most fierce, penetrating and all-consuming flame; a fire whose power
immeasurably exceeds the strength of natural fire; a
fire which causes infinitely greater pain than all pains,
torments and penitential works of this world; for the
souls are no longer limited in their power of endurance
by the body, which can suffer only to a certain degree
without succumbing. The Latin Church, through Pope
Eugene and the Fathers of the Council of Florence,
was about to declare as a dogma that the fire of Purgatory was a material one, because this was and is
the continual belief of the Church; but in order to
facilitate the union between the Latin and Greek
Churches, this declaration was deemed inopportune,
the Greeks declaring their belief in Purgatory, "but
we do not argue whether it consists in fire, darkness
or tempest;" and for the sake of peace the Council was
content with this declaration. At all events the dis-
cussion served to establish clearly the Church's belief
in Purgatory.

The existence of fire in Purgatory is vouched for also by numerous apparitions and private revelations. They demonstrate to our very eyes this fire as a material one, thus indicating that the words "fire" and "fiery torments" used by Scripture are to be taken in a literal sense. St. Bridget, of whom the Church, in her official prayer, says, "O God, who through Thy Divine Son didst reveal to blessed Bridget heavenly mysteries," was permitted in one of her ecstasies to witness how a soul was sentenced to a three-fold punishment: to an external and internal fire, an intense cold, and to furious assaults of the devil. Mechtildis of Magdeburg saw a lake of fire mixed with brimstone, in which the Suffering Souls had to bathe in order to be cleansed. According to St. Frances of Rome, Purgatory consists of three apartments, one above the other, all alive with a clear, sparkling fire, unlike that of Hell, which is dark and somber. Bautz, whom we follow in the above, relates of the Venerable Mary Anna Lindmayer: "Her friend Mary Becher and her mother appeared to her and left marks of fire on one of her feet, which she saw and felt for weeks. At one time she beheld Purgatory in the shape of a torrent of fiery water, at another, as a prison of fire. The souls themselves appeared to her as sparks of fire falling about her. The appearance of some souls caused her to shiver with frost caused by the cold proceeding from them."

With the sole exception of their duration, the torments of Purgatory are the very same as those of Hell; the only difference is that the former are temporary, the latter everlasting. This is the doctrine of St. Thomas, who says: "The same fire punishes the damned in Hell and the just in Purgatory, and the least pain in Purgatory exceeds the greatest we can suffer in this world." It is true, then, that our works have to undergo purification after this life. As gold and silver are refined in the crucible, so are they cleansed of the dross of earthly imperfections in the flames of divine wrath. Oh, what an indescribable sea of fire in which the Suffering Souls are immersed! Flames encircling them, flames penetrating them, flames unceasingly tormenting them!

Other Punishments of Purgatory

Although some theologians maintain that it is uncertain whether other methods of punishment are applied in Purgatory, we yet find proofs of it in Holy Scripture, in the writings of the Fathers, and in private revelations of trustworthy and saintly persons. In the Book of Wisdom we read: "And He will sharpen His severe wrath for a spear, and the whole world shall fight with Him against the unwise." (*Wis.* 5:21). St. Bonaventure remarks on these words: "Therefore the damned are punished not by fire alone, but the other elements also cooperate, in order that every creature might be enkindled for the punishment of the wicked and arm itself for revenge. But if we ask what is the condition of the elements in Hell, we must answer that they are not separated from one another there, nor kept in a certain order, but they are in a state of confusion and disorder." Fire being accepted by some theologians as the only means of punishment, Bautz endeavors to reconcile both opinions in the following manner: "The interior of the earth being pervaded by fire, all the elements are penetrated with it, and thus the whole creation appears armed with fire to avenge the injury done to the Creator. And because a means of punishment suited to all spirits is at hand, God, who creates no superfluities, makes use of this same means for the purification of the Suffering Souls."

The following examples from private revelations and apparitions had by saintly persons will explain this. Though these revelations are not dogmas of faith, it would nevertheless be temerarious to dispute or deny them; for Holy Church herself, in the acts of the Saints, affirms that the latter were endowed with the gift of supernatural vision and prophecy. These miraculous revelations disclose to us not only the punishment of fire, but also other punishments in connection with it; they inform us of souls surrounded at the same time by fire, by darkness, by cold, and by evil spirits tormenting them. St. Thomas Aquinas says: "Their sufferings shall be the same as those of the damned except in their duration." The Venerable Catherine Emmerich assures us: "There are places in Purgatory where evil spirits torment and frighten the souls. These places are the most terrible, and we would be inclined to believe them to be Hell, except for the inexpressibly touching resignation of the Suffering Souls." Dionysius the Carthusian relates the apparition of a religious in England, who affirmed that the Souls in Purgatory are assaulted, beaten and tormented in various ways by the devils.

The Suffering Souls are not only assaulted by their enemies, but they are also afflicted in consequences of the pious and zealous aspirations they had on earth. Let us instance this by the three theological virtues. The soul was imbued with divine faith: why did it not live accordingly, thus rendering its present purification unnecessary? Why did it lose so much time in transitory things, when it hoped to gain Heaven by the grace of Jesus Christ? Why did it profess to love God alone, when it divided its love between Him and the creatures? Thus all the virtues combine to confound the soul most painfully. Saul, having been captured by his enemies, said in desperation: "Draw thy sword and kill me, lest these uncircumcised come and slay me, and mock at me." (*1 Kgs.* 31:4).

In Purgatory, as in Hell, those of our senses will have to undergo particular punishment, that served us more specially in committing sin, according to the adage: "Wherein man sins, therein is he punished." Thus St. Hedwig saw in a vision how the proud were plunged in mire and filth; the disobedient were burdened and bowed down as if by a heavy load; the intoxicated appeared as bereft of consciousness; the gluttons were

tormented by continual hunger and thirst, the impure
by fire. The Venerable Sister Frances saw a notary
handling his writing instruments; a locksmith with a
red hot hammer; a drunkard with a fiery cup; a vain
woman clothed in burning rags and having a loath-
some face; an immodest person inexpressibly ugly, and
surrounded by fire. Blessed Margaret Mary Alacoque
saw a deceased Sister lying on a fiery couch in punishment for her slothfulness, her heart plucked to pieces
for her murmurings, her tongue eaten up for her uncharitable remarks. Of the Venerable Sister Mary Ann Lindmayer we read similar visions. A negligent priest
appeared to her in the shape of a miserable candlestick with the stump of a candle. Those excessively
fond of certain animals were sentenced to bear them
about their necks. (Bautz, page 613.)

Such and similar are the punishments to which the
souls are condemned in their abode of misery, in their
prison of darkness. The Venerable Bede relates an occurrence which in his time created a great sensation in
England and was readily believed. A man by the name
of Drycthelm died after a severe illness. After being
dead for a night, he rose again to the great terror of
the bystanders. Then he related his experiences in the
next world as follows: "A young guide conducted my
soul into an extensive valley full of horrors and darkness, so that I was filled with terror. It was divided
into two apartments, one filled with fire and flames,
the other with snow, ice and frost. There I beheld a
countless number of Suffering Souls, hideously disfigured and fearfully tormented, and pressing forward
like a stream from one apartment into the other. They
precipitated themselves from the icy lake into the
flames, from the cold into the fire, finding no rest. I
imagined I saw the torments of Hell, so great were the
sufferings I witnessed. But my guide corrected me,
telling me it was only Purgatory, and in particular the
abode of such souls as had delayed their repentance
till on their deathbed, for which they were sentenced

to Purgatory till the day of general judgment. But the prayers of the faithful, their suffrages of alms, penance and fasting, and particularly the Holy Masses offered up for them, relieve them in their torments, abbreviate their punishment and hasten the time of their deliverance." This portrayal of the sufferings in Purgatory is far from overdrawn: it rather does not justice to the reality. Convinced of this, St. Bernard exhorts us: "Brethren, put away from you the old leaven as long as there is time. The days of probation pass away, whether we use them for our purification or not; but woe to us if they are fulfilled before our cleansing is accomplished, so that we have to be purified in that fire, than which nothing in this world can be imagined more painful, smarting and acute." The holy Fathers and theological writers in general coincide with this view.

Consolations in Purgatory

Every soul in Purgatory is a beloved child of God, and is conscious of this childhood with a higher degree of certainty than are the most saintly and godly souls in this world. This consciousness fills the Holy Souls with consolation amid the greatest torments of Purgatory. When St. Francis of Assisi had been assured in a vision that he was among the elect, he exclaimed in an ecstasy of heavenly delight: "Paradise, O Paradise! We shall enter Paradise!" So great was his rapture at this assurance, that he henceforth despised all transitory things.

Mindful of the consolation of the Holy Souls at the assurance of their future beatitude, St. Francis of Sales says, "The thought of Purgatory is productive rather of consolation than of terror. Most persons are afraid of Purgatory, because they regard themselves rather than the glory of God." And he ascribes this to those preachers who refer only to the punishments of the middle state, and do not remind their hearers also of

the consolations and joys by which the sufferings of
the Holy Souls are mitigated. "Great as the torments
of Purgatory are," he continues, "so that they cannot
in any way be compared with the utmost suffering in
this world, the interior consolations granted there are
nevertheless so ineffable that no earthly bliss and
enjoyment can equal them."

Even in this life there are occasions when joy and
sorrow dwell together in the human heart. For years
the lover suffers for his beloved, enduring hunger and
thirst, cold and heat amid self-denials and labors, in
order to prepare a home for himself and the object of
his affections. The Saints did the same in a still higher
degree to attain the divine object of their love. How
resignedly, how joyously they suffered on the rack, the
cross, by fire, in torments of every description—all the
while loudly praising God! Remember St. Stephen,
St. Lawrence, St. Ignatius, St. Agnes, St. Felicitas,
St. Apollonia and others. God is admirable in His Saints,
as on earth and in Heaven, so also in Purgatory.
Undoubtedly all the souls in Purgatory join with grateful hearts in the words of St. Chrysostom, "If I had to
pass through a thousand hells, but were assured of
finding paradise in the end—how pleasant these hells
would be to me!" The Holy Souls, in their sufferings,
experience a greater consolation than the Saints on
earth do in theirs. The former are conscious of their
impeccability, they are confirmed in charity, and are
no longer in danger of offending God.

The Holy Souls are not only sure of their eternal
destiny, but know also how long they have to suffer,
and that every moment of delay prolongs the duration
of their exclusion from paradise. Accustomed to sub-
mit to the Will of God in everything, they joyfully
endure their pains; yea, they hasten to betake themselves to the flames in order to accelerate their purification. The Saints on earth did the same. Many of
them retired voluntarily to a desert, to a convent cell,
to a high pillar, to serve God in austere atonement;

others delivered themselves to their executors, willingly suffering the torments of fire, of the rack and the sword to cancel the indebtedness contracted by their own sins, and to make reparation for the sins of others. The Holy Souls in Purgatory are animated by the same zeal for appeasing God's justice. Their zeal is so great, that not only do they not decline to suffer, but they would consent to their very annihilation for the greater glory of God; for God's Will is their will. They praise God's justice, their suffering is voluntary and loving. Unselfish, their sole desire is to please God by love alone. They find sweet satisfaction in the exercise of charity and patience for these virtues' own sake, without reference to any other reward but that of pleasing Him whom they love, and who loves them with a divine love. This is essentially a heavenly consolation for these Holy Souls.

On the consolations of Purgatory, St. Catherine of Genoa remarks: "There is no peace to be compared with that of the souls in Purgatory, save that of the Saints in Paradise, and this peace is ever augmented by the inflowing of God into these souls, which increases in proportion as the impediments to it are removed. The rust of sin is the impediment, and this the fire consumes, so that the soul in this state is continually opening itself to divine communication. On the other hand it is true that the souls in Purgatory suffer torments which no tongue can describe nor intelligence comprehend unless assisted by a special grace of God. True, the love of God by which the soul is suffused fills it, as far as I can see, with an ineffable contentment; but this contentment does not take away from the souls in Purgatory the least particle of their torments. On the contrary, this love, feeling itself impeded, is the source of their pain, which is increased proportionately to the perfection of their love. And it seems to me that I see the punishment of these souls to consist rather in discerning in themselves something displeasing to God and in having voluntarily admitted it despite His great goodness, than in any other torment they have to suffer in Purgatory. They are so contented with the divine dispensations in their regard, and with doing all that is pleasing to God in the way in which He chooses, that they cannot think of themselves. They see nothing but the divine operation which is so manifestly bringing them to God that they can reflect neither on the pain nor on the consolations of their state. It would seem insupportable to a soul to see that due reparation was not made to God; to be freed from this remnant of rust it would suffer a thousand Hells rather than appear before Him without being completely cleansed. Thus knowing that Purgatory is intended for the cleansing of these stains, the soul casts itself into it, and considers the removal of the impediments a great mercy." (*Lechner, Life and Works of St. Catherine of Genoa*).

The Church, in the Office of the Dead, confirms this doctrine, and describes in a touching manner the joyously sorrowful condition of the Suffering Souls. Their past, their present state, and their blissful future is placed vividly before our eyes. We are reminded of their ardent love, of their joyful praise of God; of their undisturbed peace, their sweet, unshaken hope. On the other hand we are shown their ineffable pain, profound sorrow, bitter want, their insatiable yearning and mournful plaint.

In order, however, to fully understand what was hitherto explained, and what appears to us full of mysteries, we must attentively contemplate the most sacred humanity of our Lord Jesus Christ. At the consummation of His Passion, when suffering the agonies of death, He not only seemed forsaken by His Heavenly Father, but so to say by His own Self, because He would not permit His divinity to console His humanity. Blissful in His divinity, Jesus was so encompassed by sorrow in His humanity, that He exclaimed in the Garden, "My soul is sorrowful unto death" (*Matt.* 26:38); and on the Cross, "My God, my God, why hast Thou forsaken me!" (*Matt.* 27:46). This is a true image of the gladsome yet sorrowful condition of the Suffering Souls in Purgatory; on the one hand they are unhappy, on the other replete with hope and heavenly consolation.

The torments of Purgatory ought to imbue us with a holy fear of offending God; they ought to excite us to the performance of penitential works and fill us with a continual dread of the judgments of God. Drycthelm, whose resuscitation was referred to in a preceding paragraph, thenceforth was not content to lead a truly Christian life; but intent on living a model of penitence and dying a saint, he divided his property among his family and the poor, and retired to a monastery, where he lived so austerely, that his rigor astonished all England. He imitated the meekness and fervor of the Holy Souls; and when asked by his religious brethren how he was able, at his advanced age, to persevere in so austere a life, he replied, "My dear brethren, the rigors that I witnessed exceeded mine by far. These practices are nothing in comparison to what I saw in Purgatory."

There are people who cannot bear the thought of Purgatory. They are distressed to think that after serving God all their lives, after passing victoriously through their many trials, they should proceed from the sufferings on their deathbed to remain for years in the cleansing flames of an unparalleled fire. Let them abandon their unreasonable dread. If we die in the love of God we will be reconciled to the ordinations of His Will. We will rejoice at escaping Hell, at being sure of our salvation, at suffering purification according to the Will of God and for love of Him, without expecting increase of our merit or our reward; we will rejoice that every obstacle to the operation of grace and to the practice of virtue is removed from us, and that we are drawing nearer and nearer to God without the least danger of ever losing Him. Justified souls rejoice at undergoing that final purification which enables them to render complete reparation to the

offended majesty of God, and they regard their sufferings as a favor of divine mercy. Therefore, to feel
distressed at the prospect of Purgatory indicates a want
of submission to the Will of God. Faber observes, that
whosoever considers himself as having deserved Hell,
is glad and grateful to go to Purgatory.

Finally, there are others, such as do not wish to
amend their lives, who are wont to declare that they
will be satisfied to go to Purgatory after death, if only
they escape Hell. They speak without reflection and
know not what they say. For if they continue voluntarily in their vices and sins, they will have to suffer
a most intense Purgatory if they are so fortunate as
to escape Hell. Then there may be even pious persons
inclined to make little of the punishments of Purgatory, because of the consolations granted to the Suffering Souls, albeit the pain is thereby not diminished
in the least. Such depreciation of the torments of purification is offensive to God. Faber informs us, that when
Blessed Henry Suso, as a consequence of his familiar
intercourse with God, began to think less of the punishments of Purgatory, Our Lord warned him that this
was displeasing to Him. For Purgatory is a place of
punishment, not of reward. Therefore many theologians
declare that the least pain of Purgatory exceeds by far
not only every temporal suffering, but the sum of all
temporal sufferings.

The Duration of Purgatory

At the Last Judgment the condition of purification
comes to an end for all souls in Purgatory. This is the
belief of the Church, founded on the doctrine of that
final event. "And these" (the wicked) "shall go into everlasting punishment: but the just, into life everlasting."
(*Matt.* 25:46). Hence St. Augustine remarks: "The Christian is therefore to hold that there is no Purgatory,
except before the last and tremendous judgment."
Those that die shortly before the Last Judgment will

have to suffer greatly by the occurrences preceding it, which God will perhaps reckon for their punishment. Moreover the holy Fathers declare that God may so increase the intensity of their punishment that they atone for their faults in a short time. It is certain, then, that the punishment of Purgatory is not ever-lasting, for in this case there would be no difference between it and Hell. It is certain also that the dura-tion of Purgatory will not last beyond the final judg-ment, for after it there will be only Heaven and Hell. Finally, it is beyond doubt that the torments of Pur-gatory will not be of the same duration, nor of the same intensity for all souls; for justice admits not of equality of punishment where there is no equality of guilt.

It is difficult, or rather impossible, to demonstrate how long the punishment of particular souls will last. St. Augustine teaches that the duration of punishment in Purgatory for a soul is fixed according to the mea-sure of sin and penance of each individual. The dura-tion may be measured by days, and yet, on account of the intensity of pain, it may seem much longer. Brother Constantine of the Redeemer appeared after his death and said, "I suffered three days, and they seemed to me to have been three thousand years." For certain souls Purgatory, not abbreviated through the inter-cession of the faithful, may last until the end of time; for our Judge is just, and "it is a fearful thing to fall into the hands of the living God." (*Heb.* 10:31). It is only by the special favor of the goodness and mercy of God that we are permitted to shorten the sufferings of the souls in Purgatory. When, therefore, souls suf-fer a long time in it, it is in great part the fault of surviving Christians, who are either careless and luke-warm in their prayers for them, or have too high an opinion of their virtues. Another reason for the long duration of the suffering of some souls is their inabil-ity to do anything for themselves, the great number of faults and negligences of which they have been guilty, and particularly their neglect and want of charity during life for the souls of the faithful departed; finally, the immaculate purity required of those that enter Heaven. We append a few examples of long suffering in Purgatory, taken from the revelations of saintly persons.

According to Venerable Marina of Escobar some souls are sentenced to a punishment of twenty, thirty, forty, fifty, sixty years and more. One soul told her that it had been sentenced for a period of almost inconceivable duration, but by the aid of suffrages the time had been shortened. The Venerable Sister Frances of the Blessed Sacrament relates: Some pious Carmelite Sisters had to suffer for twenty, forty and fifty years, and still their deliverance was delayed. A pious bishop was in Purgatory ninety-five years for some negligences; a priest forty years for similar reasons; a nobleman sixty-five years on account of his fondness for gambling; another soul had suffered for eighty years when it appeared to Frances. The Venerable Catherine Emmerich, a great friend of the Suffering Souls, mentions souls that were in Purgatory for centuries. She relates: "I was led to the various abodes of the souls, and remember being transported to a mountain whence a soul advanced towards me, wearing a chain and surrounded by a red blaze. It had been there for a long time, abandoned by everybody, remembered by and prayed for by no one. It was the soul of a man whose education had been neglected, and it seemed to me, by the fault of his mother. He had retained a kind of dread and respect for the Blessed Virgin Mary. Once, when passing an image of the Blessed Mother, he was tempted to destroy it, but refrained from doing so by some emotional impulse. After this he was attacked by a malignant fever, and desired to make his Confession, but became unconscious before he could do so. Yet, he had the grace to make an act of perfect contrition before his death, and thereby was saved. He said that Holy Masses would be of particular assistance to him, and that his term of punishment would be shortened greatly by suffrages of every kind." (*Schmoeger, Revelations of Catherine Emmerich*).

Faber, speaking of the duration of the punishment in Purgatory, says: "If Sister Frances beheld the souls of many pious Carmelite Sisters, some of whom had been favored with the gift of miracles during life, still suffering in Purgatory ten, twenty, thirty and sixty years after their death, and even then not near their deliverance, what must become of us and ours?"

Many Holy Souls not found sufficiently pure to enter Heaven at their death, suffer long in Purgatory because we deny them the aid of our suffrages in the belief that they are high in the glory of Heaven, while they are helpless in the torments of the middle state. We deem it an act of Christian charity to regard our deceased beloved ones as beyond the need of purification; hence the misplaced phrase, "The dead are at rest; they are better off than we," etc. This is a delusion, by which Satan but too often succeeds in causing us to neglect our dead. For though the souls in Purgatory are assured of their salvation, and are no longer subject to temptation, they are yet deprived, as long as they are detained in Purgatory, of giving that glory to God which He receives by the adoration and praise of perfectly pure souls. By thus influencing persons to refrain from praying for their deceased friends, the devil evidences his hatred of God and his envy of the Holy Souls, and we, by listening to his suggestions, become instruments of his malice if we neglect, under the semblance of charity, to come to the aid of our suffering friends. In this respect St. Augustine is an example worthy of imitation. It is related of him that for twelve, yea, for thirty years after his mother's death he continued to celebrate Holy Mass himself, and caused it to be celebrated by others, for the repose of her soul, and that he urgently implored the prayers of the faithful for her.

The Venerable Curé d'Ars, J. B. Vianney, reckons

among the forsaken souls those of bishops, priests and other pious persons who died in the fame of sanctity, or at least had better opportunities of sanctifying themselves than common Christians. According to the rule that much shall be required of them to whom much has been given, such souls are subjected to a severer scrutiny than the generality of Christians. Ecclesiastical writers often dwell on the fact that priests and superiors have to undergo a particularly long and painful purification in Purgatory. Moreover, it is a sad experience that no person is forgotten so easily and so soon after death, as the priest; in some instances the faithful have so high an opinion of his sublime dignity and virtue that they resent the thought of his being in Purgatory; in other instances it is a punishment of his neglect in coming to the relief of the Suffering Souls.

The Venerable Sister Frances had apparitions of two Popes, who begged her prayers for the abbreviation of their long Purgatory; of a Cardinal, who suffered thirty years for some negligences; of a Spanish Bishop, who had been in Purgatory seven years for seeking his own advancement in his high office, and for neglecting some of its duties; of several priests of Pampeluna, who had suffered forty and fifty years for faults of idleness, of ambition, and of neglect of duty. One priest that appeared to her had to suffer for distractions during the recitation of the Divine Office, for undue haste in the celebration of Mass, for ambition and for fickleness in his good resolutions. To these examples might be added a number of others from unimpeachable sources; but we deem them sufficient to fill us with intense pity for the Suffering Souls, and to induce us to reject the practice of praising the deceased for their good qualities and actions, meanwhile forgetting that their debts have to be paid "to the last farthing," which we can and ought to do for them by our prayers. It does great harm to them and to us to believe that they do not need our prayers. Such souls become the most

forsaken and forgotten ones, and we expose ourselves
to the danger of experiencing the truth of the words
of Scripture: "With what judgment you judge, you shall
be judged; and with what measure you mete, it shall
be measured to you again." (*Matt.* 7:2).

That Purgatory is of long duration, that it is extended
to centuries, and, for some souls, even to the day of
general judgment, can be gathered also from the works
of theological writers, and from the prayers of the
Church. Some of the holy Fathers explain the difficult
passage in the first epistle of St. Peter, where he mentions those as saved "which had been some time incred-
ulous, when they waited for the patience of God in the
days of Noe." (*1 Pet.* 3:20). Many, they say, seeing the
prediction of Noe fulfilled, were undoubtedly converted,
and repenting, were pardoned by God. They perished
in the waters which covered the earth, and their souls
were detained in the prison of which St. Peter speaks,
until the Redeemer appeared among them after His
death, and announced to them their deliverance. Thus
they had to suffer in Purgatory many centuries.

The heinousness of mortal sin, the multitude of sins,
though pardoned and remitted as to the guilt and eternal punishment, by their very nature demand a long
duration of temporal punishment. In her ancient liturgical prayers the Church intercedes for all the departed
since the creation of the world. Another proof of the
possibility of a long duration of the punishment in Purgatory is found in the fact that there are so called perpetual foundations of Masses, of Masses to be said as
long as the church in which they are founded exists.
In the ages of faith this laudable pious custom was
very general, and it is most commendable. For who
knows but what the souls of our departed ones are
among the number of those unfortunates, who, if they
are not assisted by our suffrages, see the end of their
sufferings only after the lapse of years, so that they,
poor children of the Sacred Heart, pine and sigh for
relief in their torments? Oh, how few Christians know

the true state of their conscience, the actual amount of their indebtedness to divine justice, to be paid after their departure from this world! True, our Judge is merciful, but His mercy does not abate His justice; and this is appeased only by good works in Christ Jesus, our Redeemer: by Holy Mass, prayer, almsdeeds and acts of mortification, or other works for the relief of the Holy Souls.—Christian soul, what have you done, what do you do for this purpose?

The Location of Purgatory

The general opinion of scholastic theologians, adhered to also by Bellarmine, is that Purgatory is located in the interior of the earth, very near to Hell. This, also the common belief of the faithful, is confirmed by the liturgical prayers of the Church, and by the testimony of Holy Scripture.

The Church prays: "Deliver, O Lord, the souls of the faithful departed from the punishment of Hell and from the deep abyss." In this passage she calls Purgatory "hell," that is, a deep subterraneous cavern next to the Hell of the damned. St. Thomas teaches explicitly, "Purgatory is connected with Hell, and this in such a manner that the same fire torments the damned and purifies the just." Hell, however, according to the unanimous acceptation of theologians, is located in the interior of our earth. St. Augustine finds this quite appropriate, and in support of this theory he quotes Ecclesiasticus: "I will penetrate to all the lower parts of the earth, and will behold all that sleep, and will enlighten all that hope in the Lord." (*Ecclus.* 24:45). St. Bridget, speaking of the severity of the punishments of Purgatory, refers to its location as follows: "The severest pains and torments are above hell, in its neighborhood, where the devils also trouble the souls." Venerable Bede also notices, in his history of England, the well-known revelation of Brother Dryc- thelm, by which the general opinion is confirmed, that

Purgatory proper is in the interior of the earth.

Nevertheless we must not view Purgatory as being always one and the same local prison. In the visions of many saintly persons are mentioned various places where the Holy Souls are purified and suffer their Purgatory. Faber observes: "Some revelations relate of souls that are not confined in a local prison, but undergo their punishment in the air, or next to their graves, or near the altars of the Blessed Sacrament, or in the rooms of those praying for them, or amid the scenes of their former frivolity and vanity." According to the *St. Benedict's Stimmen*, the Venerable Sister Frances of the Blessed Sacrament had visions of Sisters who were sentenced to suffer in their former homes, in their convent cells, in choir, or in other places where they had committed faults. The Venerable Bernard Colnago, S.J. saw at Rome a soul that expiated its faults for forty-three years in one of the streets. According to the opinion of most spiritual writers the souls suffering in various places by far outnumber those of the Church Militant. Hence Our Lord said in a vision to St. Marina, "Do not be astonished, but know that in proportion to those that remain in Purgatory the number of souls you are to liberate is like a drop of water in a mighty stream." Declaring that scholastic theologians generally coincide with this view concerning the great number of souls sentenced to suffer in various places, Bautz says: "St. Thomas remarks that the opinion of the saints and numerous revelations render the acceptance of a two-fold place of purification probable. Purgatory proper is located in the depth, adjacent to Hell. But by divine decree there are other places of purification, for we read that Suffering Souls were found here and there on earth. God has so disposed: first, for the conversion of the living, that they might learn from such evidence how sin is punished in afterlife; secondly, for the relief of the departed, in order that the living might be reminded of the needs of these souls and hasten to come to their aid."

What a view is opened to us in this phase of future life! Such a number of souls suffering in so many places of purification! And again, the multitude in Purgatory proper, in that silent, quiet abode of sufferers, presided over by the Mother of Mercy, the Blessed Virgin Mary, where Angels are the ever willing ministers of her clemency! For these souls the suffrage of our prayers is asked, that their deliverance may be hastened by the application of the expiatory merits of Jesus Christ and His saints. Christian soul, what part have you hitherto taken in their deliverance? Were you intent, at least to some degree, on coming to their aid by prayer, almsdeeds and Holy Masses? "Blessed are the merciful: for they shall obtain mercy." (*Matt.* 5:7).

Credibility of Apparitions of Departed Souls

Bellarmine proposes the question whether souls return from Purgatory to this world. This question is by no means irrational, as many are inclined to believe. It is remarkable that in our day there are so many, even pious and learned persons, who are in general disinclined to believe in apparitions of the dead, not even admitting that there may be exceptions; and yet such apparitions are fully corroborated by the testimony of Holy Scripture and attested by most reliable witnesses. In the Old Testament we have apparitions of Samuel, Jeremias and Onias; in the New Testament Moses and Elias appear on Mount Thabor. At Our Lord's death on the Cross, "the graves were opened: and many bodies of the saints that had slept arose, and coming out of the tombs after His resurrection, came into the holy city, and appeared to many." (*Matt.* 27:52, 53). The Venerable Catherine Emmerich, in her book of visions, says in relation to this passage, "The highpriest Zacharias, slain between the temple and the altar, appeared in the *sanctum* and spoke threatening words; he also referred to the death of that other Zacharias, whom Herod had ordered to be killed, and to that of

St. John, and to the murder of the prophets in general. Two sons of the pious highpriest Simon the Just,
an ancestor of Simeon who prophesied at the presen-
tation of Jesus in the temple, appeared in the great
pulpit as spirits of enlarged form. They denounced the
murder of the prophets, declared that the sacrifice was
now at an end, and exhorted all to believe in the doctrine of the Crucified. At the altar Jeremias appeared
issuing threats, and declaring that the sacrifice of the
Old Law now gave way to that of the new dispensation. The apparitions and exhortations in places to
which Caiphas alone had access were kept secret and
denied, and those that dared to mention them were
threatened with severe penalties. Then I saw the portals of the sanctuary open amid a great noise. A voice
exclaimed, 'Let us go hence!' and the Angels left the
temple. The altar of incense trembled and a censer fell,
the case containing the Scriptures was overturned, and
the sacred books were tumbled out. The confusion
increased, and the time of day was forgotten. Here and
there lay dead bodies; other dead walked about among
the people and spoke threats; at the sound of the voice
of the Angels leaving the temple they returned to their
tombs. While this was going on in the temple, similar
consternation was visible throughout all Jerusalem.
Immediately after three o'clock many graves opened,
particularly in the northwestern part of the city. Pilate,
confused and superstitious, was greatly terrified and
incapable of attending to his duties. The earthquake
shook his palace, which rocked to and fro while he fled
from one room into another. The dead appeared in the
adjoining courtyard and upbraided him with his unjust
sentence and contradicting judgment. Herod, in his
palace, was beside himself with fear, and had all his
apartments closed up."

Apparitions of Angels are also frequently mentioned
in Scripture. These pure spirits, though never clothed
with a body, yet appeared in visible form to Abraham
and partook of food with him. Angels appeared to Hagar,

to Lot, to Jacob, to Balaam, to the Israelites, to Gideon, to the mother of Samson, to David, to Elias, to the servant of Eliseus, to Tobias, to Sidrach and his companions, to Judas the Machabee and his warriors; to the Blessed Virgin Mary, to St. Joseph, to the shepherds at Bethlehem, etc., etc. Verily, whosoever denies the possibility of such apparitions, professes little knowledge of the supernatural, and denies his belief in Holy Scripture, which attests that souls and spirits appeared from the other world.

The holy Fathers also regarded the apparitions which the martyrs and other saintly persons had as genuine. Who would have the presumption to fix a boundary in this matter, thus circumscribing the omnipotence of God by a denial of the possibility of apparitions? St. Augustine relates that a deceased father appeared to his son, declaring invalid a debt he was said to have contracted before his death. St. Gregory of Tours mentions that St. Vitalina appeared to St. Martin. St. Peter Damian describes how a priest saw the soul of St. Severin, archbishop of Cologne. Sister Frances of the Blessed Sacrament was continually visited by the Holy Souls; at all hours of the day and night they thronged about her, asking her prayers and help. Often they would appear to her surrounded by fire; at other times, black and emitting sparks; again as shadows, or in hideous forms. If she was in choir, they would wait near the door; and when she left, they followed her to her cell or wherever she went, to inform her of their wants. If they found their benefactress asleep, they would remain standing at her bedside without disturbing her in order not to frighten her. On All Souls' Day especially they appeared in great numbers. Among them were many souls long ago forgotten on earth, particularly those of poor patients who had died in hospitals, and of soldiers fallen in war. Concerning the latter she remarked, "They seemed to be a whole army." She would liken the number of souls about her with the throngs crowding a church on extraordinary occasions. Sometimes these souls brought her messages of other souls that were not permitted to visit her. Thus one of the deceased Sisters of her convent brought her a message of four other Sisters who were not allowed to leave Purgatory.

Similar instances are related of Louis of Blois, Mary of the Angels, Joanna of Jesus-Mary, Gertrude of Dominico, Bernardine of the Cross, Benedicta of Brescia, and a great number of others, particularly of Catherine Emmerich. St. Bernard, St. Thomas Aquinas, St. Alphonsus Liguori, and the holy Fathers generally, accept these apparitions unhesitatingly and refer to them in their writings as to facts. The same is true of other spiritual writers, for instance Dionysius the Carthusian, Louis Blosius, Thomas à Kempis; also of the most renowned historians of the Church, such as Baronius, Surius, the Bollandists, Calmet, Stolberg, Butler, etc.; then of the great theologians, Blessed Peter Canisius, Bellarmine, Suarez and others. Finally, the Church herself, after due investigation during processes of canonization, often declared the authenticity of such apparitions and recognized them as genuine by pontifical Briefs. The possibility, then, of such apparitions is demonstrated by an uninterrupted chain of facts running back through centuries, and supported by a mass of trustworthy and reliable, yea, ecclesiastical and divine evidence.

In view of this mass of facts, which might easily be increased, it is inexplicable how a faithful Catholic can entertain doubts concerning this matter. According to St. Augustine it would be great temerity to deny that the souls of the departed cannot, with God's permission, return to us; for nobody can doubt with any show of reason the testimony of these unimpeachable authorities concerning the return of Suffering Souls to this world. To the objection, that spirits have no body, and are therefore invisible, we reply: If it was and still is possible for Angels to appear, why not also for souls, if God empowers them to act on the corporeal world?

If it was possible to God's omnipotence to permit Angels and souls from Limbo to appear to men on earth, it is certainly not unreasonable to ascribe to the same omnipotence the possibility of permitting souls to appear to men for the purpose of invoking the aid of or thanking their benefactors.

Concerning the manner how these apparitions and manifestations of souls from Purgatory are brought about, St. Thomas and St. Augustine incline to the opinion that in many cases there occurs a supernatural action of Angels on the mind of those to whom they are granted. Moreover, it is likely that the souls, like the Angels, can manifest themselves in such a manner that they produce perceptible images on a person's mind without appearing visibly to him. Of the Venerable Lindmayer we read that she often heard the Suffering Souls calling on her for help, felt them fanning a cold wind to her face or tugging at her dress, though she did not see them. Other souls manifested themselves by groaning or rustling which was heard also by others in the house. The souls can also appear as phantoms, and are able, with the assistance of the Angels, to reproduce all the actions of a real body, such as movement, sound, speech, light and warmth.

Whenever our attention is directed to the departed souls by any one of these kinds of manifestation, it is a sign of the great mercy of God towards the Suffering Souls and towards us. Such apparitions make us aware of the great distress of the Church suffering, of which Church we on earth often have not the least conception, and which yet is entirely dependent on us for help. A Holy Mass, a Rosary, an alms, a mortification, some other good work, even a compassionate ejaculation or pious thought offered up confidently to the Sacred Heart of Jesus for the Suffering Souls, is powerful to create an ineffable joy in that mystic abode. At the same time the apparition of a Suffering Soul, or a visible manifestation of its distress, is a salutary admonition for the living, whereby they are reminded most impressively amid their carelessness, frivolity and tepidity of the severe judgments of God.

Chapter 3

On the Means of Relieving the Suffering Souls

On the Means of Relief in General

ACH member of the human body has its own duty to perform: the feet walk, the hands work, the ears hear, the eyes see. Whatever a member does, it does it not for its own sake alone, but also for the sake of the other members thus contributing to the welfare of the whole body. Our members are united with one another in such a manner that the sensation of pleasure or pain is felt not only by the member immediately affected, but more or less by all. By this sympathy the various members are moved to cooperate with and assist one another as much as possible. The head is the most prominent part of the body; from it proceeds all life; without it the members are dead. The Catholic Church is constituted similar to the human body. The members of the Church of Jesus Christ either triumph together in Heaven, militate on earth, or suffer in Purgatory. And because they are all most intimately united, they sympathize most cordially in their mutual joys and sufferings. We on earth rejoice at the blissful state of our glorified brethren and sisters in Heaven; we feel afflicted at the sufferings of the souls in Purgatory; we are filled with consolation or sorrow according to the intelligence we receive concerning our living brethren. This sympathy impels us to assist one another in all our needs and troubles. The spiritual goods of the Church are the common

property of her children; they all share in them in as
far as they have need and are worthy of them. The
Head of this body of the faithful is Christ Our Lord,
as the Apostle says, "And He is the Head of the body,
the Church." (*Col.* 1:18).

The communion of Saints is a most consoling doctrine, for it assures us of the great prerogative of having friends at the throne of God, the Saints who pray
for us and obtain for us the spiritual blessings and
graces of which we stand in need for time and eternity. It is most consoling for the souls in Purgatory;
because, being in communion with them, we are enabled
to come to their aid in their great affliction by the
means at our command. As the souls in Purgatory can
only suffer and expiate, but not acquire merit, the
Church Militant takes their place in the work of atonement, offers up suffrages to the merciful and just Judge,
and implores Him to accept them in expiation of their
delinquencies. The justice of God demands the payment of the debt incurred by sin, but His mercy is
appeased by vicarious atonement, and is moved by the
intercession of the living to act with great lenity toward
the Suffering Souls. The reason of this is to be found
in the communion of Saints. Charity, particularly
supernatural charity, unites so as to make one of many.
As a consequence what is performed by one is accepted
by God as the work of the other. Had those souls, during their mortal life, been more fervent in prayer, in
self-denial by fasting, laboring and suffering, they would
have entered Heaven immediately after death; now
others do in their place what they neglected, thus giving security for them. But as he that gives security
assumes the debt, the indebtedness of the Suffering
Souls is cancelled by the suffrages of their friends.

The Church Triumphant cannot atone in the proper
sense, for the Saints in Heaven no longer perform the
works of expiation that are necessary for the relief
and release of the Suffering Souls. Atonement, in its
proper sense, is the reparation of an offense by some

work of penance. By atonement the sinner not only repents of his sins, but seeks to reconcile divine justice by penitential works. The Suffering Souls were called to depart from this world before they had propitiated divine justice by atonement; and now their living friends, who alone can perform voluntary meritorious acts, can make the necessary reparation in their place by penitential works. These latter cannot be performed in Heaven, which is the abode of eternal bliss.

The relief and aid rendered to the Suffering Souls by the Church Triumphant is in the form of prayer and intercession. The Saints in Heaven have recourse to the clemency and mercy of God; they ask His pardon and the remission of punishment for the Suffering Souls simply as a gift, offering in return only the merits of Jesus Christ and of the Church Militant. Though many theologians assert that prayer as such, irrespective of its atoning power, has of itself the effect of obtaining of God the remission of temporal punishment, the learned Suarez and the greater number of theologians call the other opinion more probable, which teaches that God glorifies not only His mercy but also His justice, and that He therefore does not remit temporal punishment in answer to prayer alone; for in this case the Saints in Heaven might, by their prayers for the Suffering Souls, release all souls from Purgatory in a short time. And do not the merits of Christ Himself constitute the entire treasure of Heaven? Does He not surpass all Saints of Heaven in love and mercy? But whether He bestows His merits on the Suffering Souls by His own free will, or is moved to do so by the prayers of the Saints—this is a question which appears difficult to decide. For according to the arrangement instituted by Christ, the ministers of His Church on earth are appointed to draw on the treasure of the merits of Christ and His Saints after certain good works have been performed by the living. According to this arrangement it can be assumed that Christ will not transfer anything from this treasury without some reciprocation on the part of the faithful on earth. The Saints in Heaven implore nothing that is contrary to the arrangement made by Christ. The prayers of the Saints in Heaven are directed to the end that God may enlighten and impel the faithful on earth to make reparation for the souls in Purgatory, and that He may accept these acts of atonement performed by the living. Prayer by itself, and atonement by expiatory works, or both happily united, constitute the suffrages for the souls in Purgatory.

The Church Militant has this advantage over the Church Triumphant, that by her prayer, atonement and suffragatory expiation she can assist the Suffering Souls in cancelling so much of their debt as is yet due. The living who desire to help the Suffering Souls can assume debt for debt, cancelling by fasting their neglect of it, by tears their want of sorrow, etc.—so much for so much—thus giving them relief in their torments. The means, then, of helping them are as numerous as the means of obtaining grace for ourselves; for we can apply our merits by way of suffrage to the Suffering Souls.

The holy Fathers divide the means of helping the Suffering Souls into three kinds, viz., the Holy Sacrifice of the Mass, prayer and works of expiation, for instance almsdeeds, fasting, pilgrimages and the like. It is an incontrovertible dogma of faith always believed in the Catholic Church, and founded on indisputable evidence, that the faithful are able to aid the souls in Purgatory. Hence St. Augustine, observes: "While others weep and mourn at the death of their relatives, be thou intent on coming to the relief of the departed soul by sacrifice, prayer and alms." Prayer for the dead was regarded at all times as founded in Divine Revelation, as a tradition of faith. The holy Fathers sometimes represent to us how the Angels gather the Most Precious Blood of Our Lord, into golden vessels, and pour its refreshing dew on the souls in Purgatory, who

are cleansed by its purifying application, and enter
the abode of eternal bliss. They describe the consolation which we are able to impart to these souls during their captivity by having recourse to the treasury
of the Most Precious Blood for their release, which we
do by making a diligent use of the means placed at
our disposal.

Catholic Burial

Generally speaking, the first effect of a beloved person's death is weeping and lamenting by the relatives.
Then follow the preparations for burial, the ordering
of mourning apparel, a pompous funeral, and visits of
condolence, which latter are in most cases a mere cour-
tesy made for the sake of appearances. The corpse is
clothed in expensive robes, placed in a rich casket, covered with costly flowers and buried under a splendid
monument. In truth, the whole performance is very
often nothing but a pagan spectacle arranged with a
view of resulting in honor and praise for the surviving relatives, while not the least is done to hasten the
release of the soul from the torments of Purgatory. The
Suffering Souls do not receive the least benefit or consolation from a showy funeral. On the contrary, they
are grieved at witnessing how Satan is served and
ambition flattered thereby. At Baptism, to the question: "Dost thou renounce Satan?" answer was made
in the name of the soul, "I do renounce him." "And all
his pomps?" "I do renounce them." And we imagine to
do honor to a soul that departed this world fortified
by the holy Sacraments, that was intent during life on
laying aside everything ungodly and un-Christian, by
bestowing more attention on the mortal remains than
on the immortal soul, by following instead of renounc-
ing Satan's works and pomps, rather than seeking God
and His divine pleasure! The soul protests: "I renounce
all satanic pomps," and nevertheless its lifeless body
is surrounded with the impious splendor of the adver-

sary of God; silken shrouds, costly caskets, expensive floral decorations seem indispensable; the funeral cortege must be of the grandest order to render tribute not so much to the memory of the deceased as to the vanity of the surviving family. Even the house of God is trespassed on by these vain demonstrations, the minister of God even is expected to make himself subservient to them by lauding the virtues of the deceased in an affecting funeral address—and all this while the poor departed soul is languishing for assistance. Could the deceased speak, he would proclaim loudly from out of his coffin: "I renounced all this; how can you thus dishonor me?" Not satisfied with paying tribute to Satan by the funeral cortege and appurtenances, and by a show of excessive grief and lamenting, the world also must have its share of folly; a costly monument must announce to every passer-by what a rich harvest Satan reaped in the vanity displayed over the remains of the deceased. "To what purpose is this display at funerals?" asks St. Jerome; "must vanity take the first place even amid tears and mournings?" There can be no greater dishonor shown to the memory of a great man, than to arrange mourning celebrations that are in contrast with all his life and principles. Thus it would be a effront to Washington, the Father of our Country, were anarchists to celebrate his memory. What greater ignominy could be heaped on the blessed memory of the saintly Pius IX, than to raise for him an anti-Christian monument? But this is the spirit animating the actions of those that give the first place to worldly pomp at the funerals of their relatives. The deceased renounced Satan, all his works and all his pomps, and they exhibit in a most unwarrantable manner all his tokens at the funeral! Worldly pomp is in its right place at the funeral of an enemy of God, but not at the burial of a follower of Christ, "whose kingdom is not of this world."

As severely as the holy Fathers condemn the practice of pompous funerals, as earnestly do they exhort us to aid in having burials performed according to the rites of the Church, in a manner befitting the character of the deceased; for to bury the dead is a spiritual work of mercy. The departed soul is the chief gainer at an ecclesiastical burial. The ceremonies of the Church, the bearing of the Cross, the ministers in their sacred vestments, the blessings, incense, holy water, blessed candles, ringing of the bells, the consecrated burial ground—all is replete with sweet and abundant consolation for the departed soul; for all is done to its former abode, the body, now loved by it more truly than in life as the masterpiece of the Creator's hand, the sacred temple of the Holy Ghost, the future companion of its glory in eternal bliss.

After death there is question not only of consolation for the soul, but also of abbreviation of its punishment. The Church prays, and every prayer of faith, even that of individuals, has expiatory power. Practiced in the spirit of the Church, prayer hastens the expiation and atonement of the deceased. Moreover, some of the Church's means of suffrage have the character of a sacramental, for instance holy water, consecrated ground, etc. We have seen that a pompous worldly funeral is painful to the soul of the deceased. On the other hand, its joy is great at being treated by the Church as a child of God, and at obtaining mitigation of its sufferings in Purgatory by her mediation. Over the grave the cross, the plain cross, is to be raised, victoriously proclaiming to the world that here rest the mortal remains of a soldier of Christ. We never witnessed a more consoling, a more affecting sight than that of a Catholic cemetery on Long Island, New York, where a plain cross over every grave proclaims to the world that there a truly Christian spirit has triumphed over the enemy of God, over his pomps and works. There external splendor does not distract the visitor when he breathes the short but fervent prayer, "Eternal rest grant to them, O Lord!" We know of congregations that have honored their deceased pastors by the erection of costly monuments—but is the Holy Sacrifice of the Mass celebrated for the repose of their souls? At present, perhaps, the members of the congregation pray for their deceased pastor; but in the course of years the present generation will pass away, and he is forgotten. Had monthly or annual Masses been founded for the benefit of his soul, his memory would have lived in the congregation; it would remain united with him in a charity not bounded by the limits of mortal life.

Do you then wish, Christian soul, to confer a real benefit on the souls of the departed? Do you desire to demonstrate your love and kindness for them? Pray for them! St. Chrysostom observes: "Do you wish to honor the dead? Give alms for them! For what will weeping alone avail? What good can a pompous funeral and vain display achieve? Rather be intent with all your might to assist the departed soul by almsdeeds, prayer and Holy Masses. Let mourners weep and show their grief; let them find consolation in tears; but let them not forget to come, with still greater zeal, to the aid of the departed by the Holy Sacrifice, by prayer and almsdeeds." St. Augustine, though exhorting earnestly not to neglect the decent burial of and appropriate monuments for the dead, nevertheless declares, "Pompous funerals and costly tombs may console the living, but do not assist the dead." He reproves too great display on such occasions and reminds Christians to act according to their profession, and not to imitate the heathens, but rather to pray for the relief of the souls in Purgatory. Touchingly describing the last moments of his sainted mother Monica, he writes: "When the day of her dissolution was at hand, she had no thought for the sumptuous covering of her body, or the embalming of it, nor had she any desire for a fine monument, nor was she solicitous about her sepulture in her own country. None of these things did she recommend to us, but only desired that we should make a remembrance of her at the altar of God, at which she had attended the Sacrifice without one day's inter-mission, whence she knew was dispensed that Holy Victim by which was cancelled the handwriting that was against us. (*Col.* 2). Let her therefore rest in peace, together with her husband whom she dutifully served in much patience, that she might gain him for the Lord. And do Thou, O Lord God, inspire Thy servants, my brethren; do Thou, O my Master, whom I serve with my voice, my heart and my writings, incite Thy children; that those who will read this may remember at Thy altar Thy handmaid Monica, and Patricius, for-merly her husband. These were my parents in this transitory life. May they be remembered with pious affection, so that, what my mother asked of me as her last request, may be more plentifully performed for her through these my confessions and prayers." (*Con-fess. Book 4*).

Let every Christian assist at funerals with similar dispositions. Let him enwreathe the departed with the immortelles of good works and with a garland of the roses of prayer, more beautiful in the sight of God than any floral decorations that can be offered. If an address is to be made, let him not dictate what is to be said, but leave this to the pastor, who will avoid vain praise of the deceased, and rather remind his hearers of the duties, obligations and hopes of a Catholic, consoling them by the promise of resurrection in Christ, who is our leader and light in life, our consolation in afflic-tion, our hope in death, in whom alone true happiness is to be found. Thus will the departed soul receive con-solation and relief by the prayers of the attendants, and by the Holy Sacrifice and ceremonies of the Church.

Prayer

The two most efficient means of obtaining the grace of God for ourselves and others, and thereby gaining Heaven, are the Sacraments and prayer. We treat of of the latter here, and reserve an explanation of the efficacy of the former for the relief of the souls in Purgatory for a later paragraph.

As a means for our salvation prayer is most important. Our good or bad life depends chiefly on our good or bad prayer; hence on it depends also whether Heaven or Hell shall be ours, and whether we assist others, especially the souls in Purgatory, in gaining Heaven. We are bound to pray not only now and then, but every day. Exhorting us to prayer, St. Paul says, "Pray without ceasing." (*1 Thes.* 5:17). And St. Augustine remarks, "Who knows how to pray well, knows how to live well."

Prayer is the elevation of the heart to God, either to praise Him, or to thank Him, or to ask a favor of Him; hence its division into prayer of praise, thanksgiving and petition. When we raise our thoughts, our mind to God, we soar up to Heaven, the habitation of God's glory, leaving behind us the sordid cares of this world. Thinking thus of God—is this prayer? No! For prayer is an elevation of the *heart* to God; but we have not elevated our heart to Him, but only our *intellect.* It is in our heart that we experience joy, sorrow, trouble, desire, etc., hence we say, our heart is cheerful, or sorrowful. Now, if we think of God, and feel our heart replete with joy at His greatness, His goodness at His being our Father, if we feel sorry for having offended Him, if we ardently implore Him to grant us a particular grace, etc.—in a word, if in thinking of God, we employ not only our intellect, as we do when solving a problem, but elicit in our heart, mind and will affections and aspirations of love, joy, sorrow, desire, etc., because of His perfections, then we raise our heart to God, in other words, we pray. And if, while we thus raise our hearts to Him in holy love, joy, contrition, etc., we express these sentiments in words, or at least elicit them mentally, then we converse with God, we pray. Hence prayer is also called a conversation with God. In prayer to the Saints we raise our hearts to God at least indirectly, for we converse with God through them.

Hence, when we contemplate the glorious setting of the sun in a halo of gold and fire on a beautiful summer's eve; when we listen to the joyful strains of the feathered songsters in the air; when we feast our eyes on the abundant harvest of the fields, and gratefully remember the greatness and bounty of God, who made all this, and then say, "O God, how great, how beautiful Thou art! Oh, that I might truly love Thee!"—then we raise our hearts to God to praise Him; our prayer is one of praise. When, on beholding a poor crippled beggar, we think of the goodness of God, whose fatherly care has preserved us from misfortune, and say, "Good Father in Heaven, I thank Thee for the benefits Thou hast conferred on me!"—then we say a prayer of thanksgiving. And when we are in distress, so that we know not where in the world to turn for relief and help, and then, remembering that God knows our needs and can aid us, turn to Him, and say, "My dear Father in Heaven, help me in my distress!"—then our prayer was a prayer of petition. Hence, when praying we raise our hearts to God either to praise Him, to thank Him, or to ask Him for favors.

Our Divine Lord, exhorting us to prayer, makes use of language conveying a two-fold incitement, by which every Christian must feel moved and inspired to pray. He says, "Ask, and you shall receive!" (*John* 16:24). "Ask!" This word includes a command of the Lord, imposing on us prayer as an obligation to be fulfilled by all. And Jesus has the right to give us such a command; He prayed continually Himself, and knows the great efficacy of prayer. Therefore He calls our attention to the blessing and fruits of prayer, and joining with the command a promise as incentive. He says, "Ask, and you shall receive; that your joy may be full." (*John* 16:24). He commands us to ask, because He is our Saviour, who wishes us to be saved; and because He knows that only in answer to our asking—to prayer—shall we attain happiness and salvation—shall our "joy be full."

We have remarked before that it seems probably that God does not remit our punishment in answer to prayer alone, but that we must perform some work of satisfaction. If this be so, the same law applies to the remission of punishment which we are desirous of obtaining for others. Contemplating victims of the plague of leprosy, of famine, etc., our heart is filled with compassion for these unfortunates, and calls on God for relief and help. And remembering the torments of the souls in Purgatory, which by far exceed all sufferings in this world, we are impelled to raise up our eyes to Heaven imploring the release of our loved ones. Both sinners and the just are informed of these torments by faith; they fall on their knees and call for mercy to God, from whom alone comes relief and redemption. But this prayer for the faithful departed, besides being trustful of God's fidelity and mercy, must be meritorious, if it is to accomplish its purpose in every case and beyond doubt. For Jesus says, "If you ask the Father anything in my name, He will give it you." (*John* 16:23). Asking in the name of Jesus is asking that His superabundant merits may be joined to our prayer, and if this is done, nothing is impossible to our prayer, for nothing is impossible to God's omnipotence. "If you ask the Father anything in my name, He will give it you"; this promise of Jesus is our surety of being heard; for taken in the abstract, God is not bound to hear our prayer.

To obtain the hearing of our prayers, certain conditions must be observed on our part:

a) The person praying must be a member of the Church Militant; for with death the state of merit ceases; there is no increase of merit in the next world— neither in Purgatory, nor in Heaven or Hell.

b) The person praying must be in the state of grace. It is only in the state of grace that we possess supernatural life; without it our works are dead in the sight of God, and inoperative for Heaven.

c) Our prayer must be voluntary, proceeding from

our own free will. What is done by coercion, against our will, has no merit.

d) To be meritorious, our prayer must be addressed to God from a supernatural motive, for His greater glory.

Because the Saints in Heaven can no longer add to their merits, but can only intercede, their prayer, as was remarked before, has the effect of moving God to hear and receive more graciously the prayers of the living. A certain effective power may also be attached to the prayer of sinners, for God not infrequently hears them when they ask something agreeable to Him. In this case He hears the prayer solely on account of His mercy, not on account of the petitioner's merit. A sinner acting in the name of the Church, or obeying the injunctions of a person departed in the grace of God, adds an additional value to the intercessions, but these latter have a value corresponding to the merit of the person that gave the commission. The latter is the principal, the former only his agent.

Hence the prayer of the just in this world is one of the effective means of assisting the Suffering Souls in Purgatory. It receives its efficacy, like fasting and almsdeeds, from the qualification and ministry of the person engaged therein. Prayer partakes of the state of the person praying. Fervent and submissive prayer penetrates the clouds, and moves the Heart of God to mercy. Therefore St. Augustine calls prayer the "key of Heaven," which opens the closed gates of that sublime abode—especially to the souls in Purgatory.

God is well pleased with prayer for the Suffering Souls, and therefore we may rest assured that it will attain its object. If God hears our prayer when we ask for transitory things, how much the more so will He hear it when we pray for the deliverance of the Suffering Souls, whom He ardently loves and who are destined for and sure of enjoying with Him His bliss for all eternity. Hence St. Bernard touchingly remarks: "I will invoke the Lord with mournful lamentations, I will beseech Him with continual sighing. I will remember the departed in my prayers, hoping that the Lord will cast a pitying glance on them, and will change their torments into rest, their distress into ineffable glory. By such means their time of punishment can be shortened, their pains and torments mitigated." No less aptly does Thomas á Kempis observe: "Therefore let us pray for our dear ones, whom we shall follow in a short time, that hereafter they may remember us in our distress and sufferings; but let us always pray with fervent devotion and attention."

A most appropriate prayer for the faithful departed is the Rosary. The Blessed Virgin herself assures us through St. Dominic that "the release of the Souls in Purgatory is one of the chief effects of the Rosary." By this sacred prayer we continue to renew our invocation of Mary's benevolent Heart; we implore the Queen of the Holy Rosary and of all Saints to deliver the Holy Souls from Purgatory, or to vouchsafe them consolation in their torments. We do this on the assurance of our Lord Himself, who says: "Ask, and you shall receive." (*John* 16:24).

Blessed Alanus relates that many Brothers and Sisters testified under oath to having had apparitions of souls from Purgatory during the prayer of the Rosary. They appeared to them wearing the Sign of the Cross on their foreheads, thanked them for their prayers, and asked them to persevere in it; for except Holy Mass and indulgences there is, they said, no means so powerful to release souls from Purgatory as the Rosary, and a great number of souls were delivered by it every day. Mary is the Queen of all Saints: of those in Heaven, on earth, and in Purgatory. The Holy Souls suffer without being in condition to help themselves; therefore they are befriended in a special manner by the sorrowful Heart of Mary, the refuge of all her afflicted children.

A short but fervent prayer is sometimes of greater benefit to the Suffering Souls than a prolonged form of devotion which is wanting in attention. St. Jerome observes: "I prefer one psalm recited with devotion to the whole psalter said with distraction." Blessed Thomas Morus closed his daily evening prayer, which he said in common with his family, with a short prayer, viz., the psalm *De profundis*, for the souls in Purgatory. This is the Psalm selected by the Church as her prayer for the faithful departed; persons that do not know or cannot read it say in its place one *Our Father* after the *Angelus*, and say it also in the evening before retiring. A still shorter prayer of the Church is: "Eternal rest grant, O Lord, to the souls of all the faithful departed. Eternal light shine upon them; may they rest in peace. Amen." If we must content ourselves with a short prayer, let us select these, or some other indulgenced aspiration, to relieve the Suffering Souls.

A saintly bishop once dreamed he saw a boy draw a woman resplendent with light out of a deep well. Next morning he was surprised to see the same boy kneeling at a grave in the churchyard. He asked him what he was doing, and the boy replied: "I am saying an *Our Father* and the psalm *Miserere* for the soul of my poor mother." By this the holy man was convinced that this good child had release his mother from Purgatory; and concluded thence that prayer for the dead must be highly efficacious.

How graciously and quickly God hears our prayer for the departed is demonstrated also by the following revelations. In a vision St. Mechtilde once saw many souls ascending out of the depths of Purgatory and entering a beautiful garden next to Heaven. The Venerable Dominic of Jesus-Mary saw some souls go to Heaven while prayers for the dead were said in choir. The Venerable Lindmayer counted four hundred souls that entered Heaven through her intercession between January and March of 1691. Venerable Catherine Emmerich, whose suffrages for the deceased were extraordinary, released a great number of souls from Purgatory by her prayers. An Angel sometimes folded her hands, thus reminding her to pray for them, and when she let them sink from fatigue, he held them up, saying: "You must continue to pray." Would that this consideration might induce the reader to redouble his fervor in prayer for the Suffering Souls! Not an Angel, but Our Saviour Himself appears to us, sweating blood in His agony in the Garden, and exhorting us to fold our hands in prayer, saying: "Watch ye, and pray!" When, at the crucifixion of Jesus, all the elements conspired to wreak vengeance on a sinful world, when the earth trembled, the rocks split, the graves opened, the sun was obscured—Our Saviour raised His eyes to Heaven and showed by His example how to invoke the mercy of God for the distress of others. "And Jesus said: Father, forgive them!" (*Luke* 23:34). By this prayer He reconciled His Heavenly Father, saved the world from utter destruction, triumphed over death, and opened the gates of Heaven. Oh, how effective, how powerful was the prayer of the dying Saviour! How happy are we, how happy the Suffering Souls, if we unite our prayers with His prayer, and with His merits, thereby to open the gates of Heaven to them! United with the prayers and merits of the Crucified, remarks St. Chrysostom, our prayer is almighty, it obtains everything for which we pray, especially if the Suffering, but nevertheless Holy Souls in Purgatory are the object of our intercession. Hence St. Augustine observes that there is no occupation more wholesome and meritorious than praying for the dead.

Official Prayer of the Church for the Suffering Souls

The official prayer of the Church has an essential and particular efficacy of its own. It is more powerful to obtain graces and benefits from God than the prayer offered privately by individual persons, however pious and holy they may be. Whom will a king hear more graciously, the spouse of his beloved only son, or a stranger? The Catholic Church is the Spouse of Jesus Christ; she serves God truly and faithfully, and God dearly loves her. Therefore He graciously hears her prayer, hears it more graciously than the prayer of individuals, however pious they may be; for no private individual possesses such dignity, and is so beloved by God, as His Church. Moreover, suppose the king were inclined to refuse a petition: would he do so, except for the most urgent reasons, if his beloved only son and his whole court, his best and most trusted friends, supported it? Now the prayer of the Church is ever united with the prayer of Jesus Christ and His Saints; in other words, when the Church prays, our Divine Saviour prays with her, He supports her prayer, and all the Saints join in it, beseeching God to hear it. Therefore, if the petitions presented by the Church are conformable to the designs of God's Providence, which is undoubtedly the case when she makes intercession for the Suffering Souls, God willingly grants what she asks for.

This being so, in what veneration should we not hold, with what eagerness should we not bespeak the prayer of the Church for the Suffering Souls? If we were ill, or otherwise in distress, and some saintly man would promise to pray for us, would we not be greatly consoled? Would we not be inspired with renewed confidence in God's help? And if a holy man, whose prayer in some instances was rewarded by miracles, were to give us his blessing and say a prayer over us—how grateful and confident we would be! No obstacle would prevent us from seeking his presence and his blessing. But is the blessing and prayer of the Catholic Church not more powerful and effective than the prayer and blessing of the most saintly individual? And we are made partakers of this blessing and prayer when we employ, in a devout and trustful frame of mind, the means of grace offered to us by the Church. We must remember well that the obtaining of graces and benefits depends in a great measure on the good and devout disposition in which we employ these means. Hence when we have recourse to the prayers of the Church, let us do so in holy veneration and in the full confidence of receiving from God, for the sake of the prayers of the Church, whatever she desires for us, especially the relief and ransom of the souls in Purgatory, these holy spouses of Jesus Christ.

The Catholic Church is the great institution for our salvation, founded by Christ for the whole world and for all times. As such she has the sublime mission and task of continuing throughout the centuries Christ's work for the redemption of mankind, and to accomplish it by the conversion and salvation of all nations. It is the Will of God that all men should receive heavenly light and life through the Church by being led by her to the knowledge of truth and to life everlasting. For this end Our Lord dwells in and remains with the Church, living and operating in her "all days unto the consummation of the world." Therefore when God graciously hears our prayer, or the prayer of the Church, He hears it not for our sake, but for the sake of Jesus Christ, who is our Mediator and Intercessor, and who has merited for us by His life, Passion and death the hearing of our prayer. Except for the merits of Jesus Christ our prayer would be in vain, it would not be heard. For this very reason the Church closes all her prayers with the words, "Through Christ, our Lord," thereby proclaiming the important truth that to Jesus Christ alone we owe the hearing of our prayer and our salvation in general.

The maternal solicitude of the Church for the speedy release of the souls in Purgatory is demonstrated by her ancient practices. There is not a moment of the day when she does not accompany her Divine Spouse to the portals of Purgatory by interceding for these souls in Holy Mass. At the offertory of every Mass she prays: "Accept, O holy Father, Almighty and Eternal God, this unspotted host, which I, Thy unworthy servant, offer unto Thee, my living and true God, for my innumerable sins, offenses and negligences, and for all here present; as also for all faithful Christians, both living and dead, that it may avail both me and them unto life everlasting. Amen." After the Consecration a special commemoration is made of the dead: "Be mindful, O Lord, of Thy servants *N.* and *N.*, who are gone before us with the sign of faith, and rest in the sleep of peace." (Here particular mention is made of such souls as the priest intends to pray for; after which he continues): "To these, O Lord, and to all that sleep in Christ, grant, we beseech Thee, a place of refreshment, light and peace." No Mass therefore is celebrated without a commemoration of the dead in general or in particular. The solicitude of the Church for the release of the Suffering Souls is proved also by the rubrics, which on certain days permit the celebration of the Mass of *Requiem* in black vestments. Such days are for instance the Monday of each week, and the first day of each month, when no feast occurs. The Church selects the first days because charity urges her to come to the aid of the Suffering Souls as soon as possible. To further show her solicitude for them, she ordains a special formula of the Mass for the third, seventh and thirtieth day, and for the anniversary of a death. The general anniversary of all the faithful departed is celebrated on All Soul's Day, when as far as possible all the Masses are said in black vestments. On this day the universal Church makes a strenuous effort to secure the release of the Suffering Souls.

With the Mass of *Requiem* is joined, at funerals or at the cenotaph, the ecclesiastical absolution. The Church returns in spirit to the deathbed of the deceased, where the judgment struck terror into his soul. She invokes God's mercy and implores Him to grant eternal rest to the departed soul and to receive it into paradise in the company of the Angels. Then the coffin or cenotaph is sprinkled with holy water and incensed, the Church meanwhile reciting the Lord's Prayer and imploring God to refresh the soul with the dew of

Heaven and with celestial odors.

Besides the Holy Sacrifice and the absolution, the Church has ordained also the recitation of a special Office of the Dead. This is handed down to us from the earliest ages of Christianity, and gives evidence of the ardent charity and devotion with which the Church implores mercy at the throne of God and intercedes for her suffering children. The phraseology expresses the sentiments of the Suffering Souls, who as it were pray with and through the person reciting it. Everything referring to the latter is omitted, and the whole is concluded by intercessions, for instance, "Eternal rest grant to them, O Lord! May they rest in peace!" etc. In the Vespers we join in the yearnings of a soul assured of salvation, but beholding its felicity as yet in the far distance; knowing itself destined for the vision of God, but separated from Him till its stains are removed; knowing for certain that, once having entered the abode of bliss, it will join all the Angels and Saints in the praises of God's mercy. The versicles and responses are invocations replete with consolation, declaring these souls happy despite their torments, because their salvation is assured. The canticle and antiphon express the joyous confidence that the souls departed in the faith of Christ, but still in need of purification, will soon be admitted to the beatific vision of God. Already the Church hears them in the joyous strains of the *Magnificat,* and then falling on her knees she breathes forth the *Preces,* a series of invocations, which she closes with the Lord's Prayer. Then follows the 145th Psalm, to evince her confidence of being heard. Oh, how consoling to be permitted to call upon the Lord! He shows His mercy for the Suffering Souls, and admits them to the habitations of the eternal Sion.

In his book on the Suffering Souls, Ackermann relates the following: A nobleman once gave a considerable sum of money to the Superior of a Carthusian monastery to have prayers said for his deceased father.

When the assembled choir sang nothing but the words
Requiescat in pace!—"May he rest in peace"—he
expressed his dissatisfaction at receiving so short a
prayer in return for his money. The saintly Superior
told the brethren to write those words on slips of paper,
and putting the slips on one side of the scales, requested
the nobleman to put the money on the other side. This
being done, the nobleman was astonished to see the
money rising high, while the slips of paper when down
in the scales. By this miraculous occurrence he was
filled with confusion, and at the same time with consolation. Mention of this occurrence is also made in
the Conferences of Pope Benedict XIII.

Because the clergy perform their ecclesiastical ministry in the name of the Church, it is evident that
these prayers are not private ones of the priests, but
the official supplication of the Church. As such they
have a special intercessory value, by which their effect
is attained independently of the state of the priest's
conscience. Through the Sacred Heart of Jesus the
Divine Spirit continually impels the Catholic Church
to send up to Heaven her powerful supplications for
the souls in Purgatory. Contemplating the ineffable
yearning of the Church for the release of the Suffering Souls, and the great efficacy of her prayer, will you
not, Christian soul, follow the impulse of your heart,
and do your part for their deliverance by joining assiduously in these prayers? If you would but unite with
the congregation in the aspiration of the Church, "Eternal rest grant to them, O Lord!" etc.—this alone would
be a great consolation for the faithful departed.

In order to enable our readers to follow and join the
Church in her liturgical suffrages for the dead, we subjoin in the appendix a faithful translation of some
prayers, and only regret that it is impossible to convey in the vernacular the full import of these supplications so beautifully expressed in the official language
of the Church.

Let us, then, regard with this profound veneration

the prayer of the Church; let us have great confidence in its efficacy and use its formulas with devotion. We shall thereby insure for ourselves the blessings of God for this life and eternal happiness in the life to come.

The Blessed Virgin Mary and the Suffering Souls

One of the most beautiful narratives of Holy Scripture is the touching story of Esther. Belonging to the banished Jewish people, this poor virgin, on account of her beauty and virtue, was called to ascend the throne, and by so doing saved her people. In her we recognize an image of that other virgin, also descended from the Jewish people, poor, but of noble lineage, and selected by God to become the mother of Him who redeemed sinful mankind. In virtue of this sublime motherhood Mary became the Queen of Heaven, the Mediatrix of mankind; and to her therefore the Church applies the words spoken by Joachim, the high-priest, to the victorious Judith, "Thou art the glory of Jerusalem, thou art the joy of Israel, thou art the honor of our people." (*Jdth.* 15:10). Mary, like Esther, is the most fair among women, and to her are applied the words, "Thou art all fair, . . . and there is not a spot in thee." (*Cant.* 4:7). For this reason she found favor in the eyes of the divine King, so that He divided His reign with her, retaining for Himself omnipotence, and turning over to her the dominion of mercy. Esther, when appearing before the king, was attended by two servants, one of whom supported her, while the other bore her train; in like manner the Blessed Virgin Mary is served by Angels and men, whose Queen she is. Finally, as Esther became her people's helper and intercessor, so Mary became ours. Hence we hasten to her in every distress, saying, "We fly to thy patronage, O holy Mother of God! . . . Despise not our prayer." And whence is it that Mary is so sublimely elevated above all mankind, why do "all generations call her blessed?"

The angel Gabriel in his salutation tells us the reason: "Hail, full of grace!" he said to Mary.

Mary was "full of grace" before her birth. Before and in *our* birth we are devoid of grace, we are in the state of Original Sin. Mary, however, possessed sanctifying grace in the first moment of her conception, and possessed it to such a degree that even the shadow of sin and concupiscence was excluded from her soul.

Again, Mary ever advanced in grace; that is, she increased in merit from day to day, and therefore became more and more filled with grace. We admire the various Saints for their particular virtues, for instance St. Aloysius for his purity, St. Francis of Assisi for his seraphic ardor, etc. But what is the purity of St. Aloysius compared with that of Mary, the love of St. Francis compared with hers? It is the glimmering of a star compared with the splendor of the midday sun. As the rainbow unites all the colors gleaming in the individual raindrops, thus Mary unites in herself alone all the virtues of the Saints in a supreme degree. Hence she is called the Queen of martyrs, of virgins, of all Saints. Oh, what an ineffable wealth of grace she must have possessed at the end of her life! According to the general acceptation she lived over sixty years, and devoted her whole life to the pursuit of virtue: how greatly she must have surpassed in it all the Saints!

There is another reason why Mary was full of grace; *she brought forth the Author of all grace.* The Source of all grace, He who merited it for us by His death, *was her Son.* As He selected Mary for His mother and deigned to take human nature from her, it is obvious that he adorned her with more grace than all the Angels and Saints. Not for Mary's sake alone, not in order to adorn her alone with grace did Jesus become man, but for the sake of fallen humanity. All the graces we receive, we receive through Christ, but Christ we received through Mary. She is the heavenly aurora which brought to us the Divine Sun, Jesus Christ. Hence it is the Will of Our Saviour, that Mary should be our mediatrix. She was, as it were, the bridge over which Jesus passed in coming to us; hence she is also the bridge over which we come to Jesus in Heaven. As she has brought us Christ, thus she is also by her intercession to bring His grace to our immortal soul. There is therefore no need for Mary in Heaven first to merit deliverance for the souls in Purgatory; she received this grace while on earth, together with her dignity of Mother of God. She is, in truth, the bridge by which the suffering yet happy spouses of her Divine Son cross from Purgatory to Heaven.

The clients of this Mother most clement are indeed to be called happy, for she is their consolation and help not only in this world, but also in Purgatory. Besides promising that she would preserve from Hell those who devoutly wear her holy habit, the scapular of Mount Carmel, she added a second privilege, namely that of speedy release from Purgatory. This latter promise was made about seventy years after the introduction of the scapular. Mary deigned to appear to Pope John XII and recommended to his care the Order of Carmelites. Extending her maternal solicitude even to the next world, she promised to assist the souls of the members in Purgatory, to console them and to release them as soon as possible, particularly on the Saturday following their decease. The pope published this privilege in a Bull dated March 3, 1322. (Beringer, *Indulgences*, p. 711). The meaning of this promise is that Mary gives those who wear the holy scapular and fulfill the conditions prescribed, as much assurance of their eternal salvation as can be obtained during mortal life, at the same time declaring that if they are constant in her service and lead a Christian life, they shall also receive the grace of final perseverance. Simon Stock, the General of the Carmelites, when giving this holy habit to his brethren, addressed them as follows: "Preserve deeply impressed on your minds the memory of this bounty, and be intent on receiving strength in your vocation by the exercise of good works. Never relax in doing good, watch and pray without ceasing, that the promises of Heaven may be fulfilled, and may show themselves in their full splendor for the praise of the Most Holy Trinity, and for the honor of the Most Blessed Virgin Mary." The mere wearing of the scapular, then, does not make us partakers of the second privilege. The Blessed Virgin, appearing to the Venerable Dominic of Jesus-Mary, addressed him thus: "My son, though many wear my scapular, yet there are few that perform what is necessary to acquire the Sabbatine privilege." It was affirmed also by other supernatural revelations, that they who wear the scapular are released from Purgatory on the first Saturday after their death only on condition that they have fulfilled all the duties imposed thereby. A deceased Sister appeared to the Venerable Frances of the Blessed Sacrament and said, "There are few who receive the benefit of this privilege, because there are few who observe its conditions."

Mary is solicitous for the Suffering Souls in Purgatory because she is the Mother of pure souls. St. Bernardine remarks, "In this prison of the spouses of Christ she exercises, so to say, absolute sovereignty in mitigating their pains, and in delivering them from their sad imprisonment." Mary demonstrated her charitable and tender heart even in this life. "And Mary rising up in those days, went unto the hill country with haste," when she heard that Elizabeth in her age had been blessed with a son. She did this to express her affection and to offer her services. At the wedding feast in Cana her tender heart caused her to anticipate the embarrassment of the host. Now the distress of the souls in Purgatory is incomparably greater than that of either Elizabeth or of the married couple at Cana. Their torments are so great that all the sufferings of the sick, all the pains and torments of the martyrs since the beginning of the world added together do not in the least compare with those of Purgatory, because the former are but trials, while the latter are punishments. The pains of the Poor Souls are similar to those inflicted by the surgeon or executioner.

Hence Mary descends with truly maternal charity into Purgatory and eases its torments. St. Bonaventure applies to her the words, "I have penetrated into the bottom of the deep" (*Ecclus.* 24:8), and adds, in our Blessed Mother's name, "into the abyss of Purgatory, there to mitigate the pains of the Suffering Souls." St. Vincent Ferrer exclaims, "O how amiable and benevolent Mary shows herself to them that suffer in Purgatory; for through her they continually receive comfort and consolation." By her mediation the poor captives are released from their fiery prison. St. Bernardine remarks, "To Mary was given the power, by her intercession and merits, to release the souls from Purgatory, particularly those that were foremost in their devotion to her." St. Bridget one night was addressed by the Blessed Virgin as follows: "I am the Mother also of the souls in Purgatory. Their torments are continually eased in some manner through my intercession. For it pleases the Lord to remit in this manner some of the punishments which are their due by justice."

St. Thomas and nearly all the holy Fathers teach that the Blessed Virgin Mary comes to the aid of the Suffering Souls. The Church also, in the Masses of *Requiem*, prays that God may grant eternal bliss to the deceased through the intercession of the Blessed Virgin and all the Saints. In the same manner she prays toward the end of the Litany of all Saints. Why should our heavenly Mother feel less affection for her captive children than an earthly mother does for her offspring? Can we imagine that she will refuse her efficient consent for their deliverance from the fiery prison, when we remember that she gave her consent for the redemption of the world?

When Robert of Flanders was held captive by Stephen de Blois, the prisoner's mother was filled with sorrow at the thought of the gloomy abode of her son; and yearning to see him, she continually exclaimed, "Once more let me see my son! I must visit, I must see and console him." And her prayer was granted. Can we imagine that Jesus would refuse His Mother's prayer? She is *His* Mother and also the Mother of the Suffering Souls; and therefore it gives Him the sweetest pleasure to release them, or at least to mitigate the torments of those for whom she pleads. And she never ceases her intercession, for, says St. Liguori, "the less the souls are able to help themselves, the more she increases her benevolence and solicitude for them."

Therefore the Queen of Heaven rejoices at being invoked for intercession in behalf of the Suffering Souls; and the more assiduously we pray to her for this purpose, the more efficiently will she cooperate with us for their relief. The Venerable Boudon therefore teaches that we should not be content with invoking her intercession for the Suffering Souls, but that we should trustfully place all our good works and prayers at her disposal for their benefit. "For," he remarks, "no one can dispose of them more equitably, and moreover, we cannot give a stronger evidence of love for and confidence in her."

The Saints and the Suffering Souls

Mortal eye has never witnessed an apparition similar to that vouchsafed the Apostle St. John, and which he describes as follows: "And I saw, and beheld in the midst of the throne and of the four living creatures, and in the midst of the ancients, a Lamb standing as it were slain, having seven horns and seven eyes: which are the seven spirits of God, sent forth into all the earth. And He came and took the book out of the right hand of Him that sat on the throne. And when He had opened the book, the four living creatures, and the four and twenty ancients fell down before the Lamb, having every one of them harps, and golden vials full of odors, which are the prayers of the Saints: and they sang a new canticle, saying, Thou art worthy, O Lord, to take the book, and to open the seals thereof: because Thou wast slain, and hast redeemed us to God in Thy blood, out of every tongue, and people, and nation." (*Apoc.* 6:6-9). This is the sacred spectacle to which holy Church directs our eyes in order to excite us to holy desires of emulating the example of the Saints, and thereby to imitate their charity toward the Suffering Souls; for it is clearly demonstrated by their lives that there is no Saint in Heaven who neglected to come to the aid of the souls in Purgatory. The Saints did all in their power to atone for the faults of the faithful departed. They repaired their own derelictions of duty, satisfied their obligations, loved their enemies, forgave injuries, were patient in trials, sought voluntary suffering, gave alms, were intent on gaining indulgences, offered up their own merits—all for the souls in Purgatory. With these meritorious works they joined retirement from the world and its pleasures, made pious foundations, prayed unceasingly, received Holy Communion; and above all, they were solicitous to have the Holy Sacrifice of Mass offered up, or to assist at it for the repose of the Suffering Souls. Thus the Saints were continuously intent on offering suffrages for the faithful departed. In their prayers and good works they remembered, first of all, those whose state of grace at the time of their death remained doubtful, the greatest sinner, as long as he lives on earth, being subject to God's mercy; as also those who died in the fame of sanctity, the smallest faults being unable to escape the avenging justice of God. They trustfully interceded, knowing that their good works would be received by the merciful God, who revealed to St. Gertrude that it is not in opposition to His justice to release the Suffering Souls immediately from all torments, if He was asked in confidence to do so. For in this manner He intends to glorify at the same time His mercy and His justice.

The Suffering Souls are loved by the Saints in Heaven just as they were loved by them during their earthly pilgrimage, and even more so, because in Heaven the Saints know better their present misery and the ineffable glory for which they are destined; hence it is their most ardent desire to see them released as soon as possible. This love and desire impels them to pray assiduously for their eternal rest. We know this from the unanimous testimony of the theologians. St. Augustine and St. Thomas remark, "It is a recognized truth that the Saints in Heaven are very powerful to procure the release of the souls in Purgatory by their intercession." Holy Church herself announces to us that it is profitable and well to invoke the Saints for the relief of the souls in Purgatory, as she invokes them and the Angels in Holy Mass and in her liturgical prayers to assist them by their intercession. We may further instance this truth by what is related of St. Francis of Assisi: The Saint once appeared to one of his brethren and announced to him a privilege which had been granted to him by Christ. "I grant thee," the Lord had said to St. Francis, "that every year, on the anniversary of thy death, thou shalt be permitted to release all the souls belonging to thy Third Order, as also the souls of all thy devout clients detained in Purgatory, and in virtue of the stigmata with which I honored thee, to conduct them to paradise." From this we also see that God Himself gives testimony in favor of the invocation of the Saints, and that it is in accord with His Will that we should invoke them for the release of the Suffering Souls.

However, from this power of the Saints in Heaven in favor of the Suffering Souls it does not follow that God remits punishment in consequence of their intercession alone. On the part of the person wishing to aid the souls in Purgatory it is necessary for him to perform works of atonement in order to make his help effective. But in Heaven merit is no longer acquired. The more probable opinion of theologians favors the view that the souls in Purgatory are under penalty of severe divine justice; for otherwise the intercession of the Saints might obtain their release in a short time, and that of the Blessed Virgin in a moment. Hence the intercession of the Saints in behalf of the Suffering Souls is directed to the following objects: They pray:

a) that God may graciously receive the works of atonement and the intercession of the faithful on earth for the souls in Purgatory; and this prayer is a most appropriate one for the reason that the acceptance of the suffrages does not antagonize the demand of strict justice;

b) that God may by His grace inspire the faithful members of the Church Militant, in order that they may more assiduously intercede for the Holy Souls;

c) that He may reduce the time of their punishment by augmenting its intensity; this is a great favor, since one day in paradise before the time originally set is an immense gain;

d) that God may accept their own supererogatory atonement in suffrage for the souls in Purgatory.

The latter point is considered doubtful by many theologians, because the atoning merits of Christ and the Saints accrue to the treasury of the Church. It is moreover doubtful whether the Saints pray to Christ to apply His merits, in virtue of their intercession, to the Suffering Souls. For according to the order established by Christ, it is left to the ministers of the Church on earth to draw from the treasury of the merits of Christ and the Saints, after the faithful have performed certain good works. As a rule, therefore, Christ Himself will not draw on this treasury, at least He will not do so without some corresponding reciprocation; and the Blessed Virgin and the Saints in Heaven do not pray for anything that is contrary to the order fixed by Christ. Whether it be done in exceptional cases is beyond our cognition. Thus argues the learned Suarez.

How wisely God's Providence has ordered all things in order to draw us to Him! He precludes the possibility of our yielding to sloth, since we cannot rely solely on the mercy of Christ and the Saints in our suffrages for the Suffering Souls. The elect are to incite us to fulfill the Will of God. We pray and labor here below, and leave our good works in the hands of the Saints in Heaven, that they may offer them to the Almighty and invoke Him to receive them mercifully for His poor captive spouses in Purgatory.

This doctrine of the theologians is corroborated by Bl. Catherine Emmerich. She says, "The Suffering Souls receive no direct aid from Heaven; they obtain everything from the faithful living in this world." In Faber's works we find an observation, the sense of which is as follows: "Some authors have maintained that Our Lord does not desire to help the Suffering Souls without our cooperation, and that the Blessed Virgin cannot aid them except indirectly, because she is no longer able to perform works of atonement." St. Bridget makes a similar remark. Once she saw the Suffering Souls undergoing purification in Purgatory similar to gold being purified in a crucible, and heard an Angel saying, "Blessed be the mortal that hastens to the relief of the Suffering Souls. The justice of God demands that they either be purified in the flames of Purgatory, or that they be released therefrom by the good words of their friends." Then she heard a chorus of mournful voices, "O Lord Jesus Christ, just Judge, we implore Thee for the sake of Thy infinite mercy to turn away Thine eyes from our innumerable sins, and to regard the merits of Thy Passion and death. Imbue with Thy true love the religious, the priests and the faithful, so that they may hasten to our relief by their prayers, sacrifices, almsdeeds and indulgences. They can aid us if they wish; they can hasten our union with Thee, O God!" When St. Gertrude on a certain occasion was praying most ardently for the relief of the Suffering Souls, she was assured by Christ Himself, "It would not be in opposition to my justice to release them immediately, if you would confidently pray for this purpose."

By this consideration we should be impelled and incited to move God with greater zeal and by works of penance to be merciful to the Suffering Souls. Let us place our prayers and works into the Sacred Heart of Jesus, into His holy wounds, before His divine Countenance, imploring Him to present our supplications to His Heavenly Father. The Immaculate Heart of Mary, full of grace, is always ready to receive our supplications, ever inciting us to be merciful to the poor Sufferers. The Saints, particularly the holy patrons of the Suffering Souls, are solicitous for them, and pray to God to move charitable hearts on earth to bring them relief. Let us be intent on laying up spiritual treasures; let us confide them to the Saints in Heaven for the purpose of offering them to God's justice, that we may thereby honor those whom God desires us to honor. That God may spread more and more this work of mercy, let us pray with St. Augustine when he supplicates Heaven for his deceased parents: "Do Thou, O my God, inspire Thy children, my brethren; do Thou, O my Lord, inspire your servants, in order that all those who will read this may remember at Thy altar Thy handmaid Monica, with Patricius, her husband."

Let us draw from this the wholesome lesson conveyed in the following words of St. Basil: "Let us not take a limited view of God. He who permits the sun to shine in splendor, punishes also with blindness; He who lets the raindrops descend, permits also rain of fire. The former is bounty, the latter rigor; by the one He draws us to His love, by the other He inspires us with fear; so that it may not be said to us: Dost thou despise the wealth of His bounty, patience and mercy? Dost thou not know that the bounty of God leads to penance?"

The final act of charity performed by the Saints for the souls in Purgatory consists in conducting them into Heaven at the end of their purification. The Venerable Frances of the Blessed Sacrament saw the soul of Pope Gregory XV, after a brief Purgatory, ascend to Heaven surrounded by Angels and Saints. Most conspicuous among the latter were the five Saints canonized by him, viz., St. Theresa, St. John of the Cross,

St. Isidore, St. Ignatius and St. Francis Xavier. If we invoke the Saints now, we will merit thereby to receive the aid of their intercession; if we neglect now to esteem their help, they will deny it to us when we are most in need of it.

The Angels and the Suffering Souls

From the time of our birth, when we become wayfarers on the road that leads to our heavenly home, we are favored like young Tobias with a companion and guide. "Then Tobias going forth, found a beautiful young man, standing girded, and as it were ready to walk." (*Tob.* 5:5). As soon as we begin our pilgrimage, behold the Angel is there, though invisible to us, ready to guide and protect us. What the Lord promised to the people of Israel is done also for us: "Behold I will send my angel, who shall go before thee, and keep thee in thy journey, and bring thee into the place that I have prepared." (*Exod.* 23:20). Such is the service rendered us by our Guardian Angel on our way to Heaven. He goes before us showing us the way; he protects us from dangers, and finally conducts us to the place prepared for us in Heaven.

His power, by which he has an almost unlimited control of the visible world, corresponds with his sublimity and perfection. It is easier for our Angel to move and destroy this whole terrestrial sphere, than it is for us to give motion to a small globe. We know from the Old Testament that an Angel in one night destroyed one hundred and eighty-five thousand warriors of the Assyrian army, and it cost him less effort to do that than it would cost us to crush a worm beneath our foot. Besides, the velocity of these pure spirits is so great that an Angel can pass from one place to another in less time than is required for the human eye or thought to reach the object to which it is directed. For the angels are God's ministers, employed by Him to accomplish the eternal designs of His Providence; and Holy Writ is full of examples showing us that God sent His Angels to protect His servants. Thus an Angel led Lot forth from Sodom; an angel conducted Hagar in the desert and preserved her son Ismael from death; an angel brought food to Daniel in the lion's den, and saved the three youths in the blazing furnace; an angel fought at the side of the Machabees and put to flight their enemy. In the New Testament we read that an Angel gave warning to the Three Wise Men from the East to return to their country by another way; an Angel appeared to Joseph commanding him to take the Divine Child and His Mother to Egypt; an angel loosed the bonds of the prince of the Apostles and conducted him safely out of prison. Such is the power with which God has invested the guardian spirits of those that hear their warning, as He Himself commands, "Take notice of him, and hear his voice, and do not think him one to be contemned." (*Exod.* 23:21). They cherish a great love for us; they are intent on our welfare, assist us in distress, and relieve our necessities.

Sin, and sin alone, is capable of rousing against us the anger of our Angel. It is in his power both to punish us for sin, as also to reward us for our good deeds. "And woe to us," says St. Bernard, "woe to us, if we should provoke the anger of the Angels to such a degree as to cause them to deem us unworthy of their further presence and ministrations, so that we are compelled to weep and moan with the royal prophet: 'My friends and my neighbors have drawn near and stood against me. And they that were near me stood afar off: and they that sought my soul used violence.'" (*Ps.* 37:12). A punishment like this should make us fear and tremble.

In Holy Scripture we find many examples of Angels visiting sinners with the punishments they had incurred. An Angel killed seventy thousand by the plague during the time of David. An angel killed one hundred and eighty-five thousand in the camp of Sennacherib. An Angel punished Heliodorus for his sacrilege by covering him with sores. Angels pour the vials of God's wrath over a sinful world. Finally, the Gospel assures us that the Angels will go forth at the end of the world to separate the just from the wicked, and to cast the latter into the fiery furnace, where there will be weeping and gnashing of teeth. How dreadful, if the very Angels, to whose care we are now committed, should be the ones commissioned to execute this terrible sentence on us! Is this not a reason to fear their power? Should this thought not move us to fulfill with the utmost fidelity our duties toward our Angels?

If we but listen to and follow their inspirations, our Angels will be a most potent help for us in the hour of death. They will strengthen us against temptations; they will comfort us in our agony; they will conduct our souls to judgment; they will console them in Purgatory. They are not content with performing in our behalf all the services imposed on them by God, but desiring most ardently to see us truly happy, they are intent on obtaining for us from God all the graces and favors conducive to our eternal welfare. The Guardian Angels therefore pray for their clients at the throne of God; according to St. John's vision in the Apocalypse, they bear their tears and sighs into the Divine Presence; they unite their own supplications with those of their wards to move God more effectually to mercy. They exclaim, according to the prophet, "How long wilt Thou not have mercy on Jerusalem" (*Zach.* 1:12) and on this troubled soul? Now, God willingly hears the prayers of His servants and friends, and grants great favors to those for whom the Angels pray thus assiduously. The Angels, we may therefore be certain, are continually in attendance on the suffering souls of their clients in Purgatory; it is their most ardent desire to alleviate their torments. From Purgatory they come to this world to gather diligently the good works performed for the Suffering Souls; they inspire the faithful to pray for them, to labor for them. Ascending to Heaven with their harvest of suffrages, they descend thence into Purgatory to fill the Suffering Souls with consolation by announcing to them the abbreviation of their torments. Of the patriarch Jacob we read that he saw in his sleep a ladder reaching from the earth to Heaven, on which Angels ascended and descended. They ascend to present to the Almighty their petitions in favor of the Suffering Souls, and they descend to bring to the souls in Purgatory the favors which they obtained for them from God through the good works of the faithful on earth.

Boudon maintains that the Angels inform the Suffering Souls of the happenings in this world about which these Souls are concerned; that they reveal to them who are their benefactors, exhorting them to pray for their benevolent friends, in doing which these good spirits gladly lend their assistance. St. Augustine says, "The departed may be informed by the angels of things happening in this world, in so far as this is permitted by Him to whose judgment everything is subject."

However, it may also happen that certain Suffering Souls are deprived of the aid of their Guardian Angels, of the Blessed Virgin Mary and the Saints, because they were not devoted to them during their life on earth, or neglected to aid the Suffering Souls. Blessed Margaret Mary Alacoque saw souls in Purgatory who were sentenced to forego the assistance of Mary and the Saints, because during their life they had lived in discord with their superiors.

Confraternities for the Relief of the Suffering Souls

In the middle of the eighteenth century, the Danube, being blocked with ice, flooded a great part of Vienna, thereby causing great damage to valuable property and threatening the lives of many of the inhabitants. The force of the angry waters had already carried off barns, undermined houses, and threatened the lives of all the inhabitants of the suburbs Leopoldstadt and Rossau.

The lamentations and cries for help beggared description. Multitudes witnessed the heartrending scene, but no one dared to come to the aid of the unfortunates, the danger was so great. The news of the distress was brought to the imperial palace and to the ears of the emperor Francis. Scarcely had he been advised of it, when he hastened to the scene of disaster, and jumping into a boat, called out, "Who has the courage to save lives with me?" The emperor's word and example inspired all present, and soon boats and skiffs were manned with rescuers. All in danger were saved, not a life was lost. This was assuredly a royal deed of the Austrian emperor, and a heroic deed of those who joined him, worthy of being recorded on the pages of history and of being held up as an example to coming generations. But what spiritual lesson does this deed convey to us? First, that we ought not to shun danger, however great, when there is question of saving life; secondly, that we should not stand by unaffectedly when there is question of saving from the lake of fire the souls of our brethren. Therefore, let us demonstrate our fraternal charity by joining a confraternity for the relief of the Suffering Souls.

Terrified at the thought that, as Bellarmine expresses it, "but few just men will escape the exceedingly great pains of Purgatory, because only a very small number are admitted to Heaven through the supreme mercy of God immediately after their death," compassionate souls resolved to come to the aid of their deceased brethren by the extraordinary power of united prayer and other works of suffrage. The joint intercession, the increased devotion, the multiplied grace, the virtues and merits of brethren united in God, in a word, the charitable union for the relief of the Suffering Souls is a powerful means of moving the Heart of a God so full of compassion for His children in distress. As it is a holy and wholesome ministration of Christian charity to pray for souls departed in the faith of Christ and in His divine grace—souls that are, nevertheless, still subject to temporal punishment and unable to acquire merit for themselves—therefore numbers of Catholics have formed unions for the purpose of coming to the aid of their deceased brethren. By continual suffrage and sacrifice these zealous Christians, thus united, endeavored to release from the fiery prison of Purgatory as many souls as they could in the shortest time possible.

Hence they resolved, without binding themselves under pain of sin, to offer up for this end the Seven Offerings of the Most Precious Blood, or seven times the *Glory Be to the Father*, etc., or to say the Rosary, or some other prayer of their choice, with the addition, "Eternal rest grant to them, O Lord! May eternal light shine upon them, and may they rest in peace. Amen." If they are able they give every month a small pecuniary contribution as stipends for Holy Masses to be said for the Suffering Souls, or to be applied for the expenses incurred in the propagation of the Confraternity for the relief of the Suffering Souls. The members also give each other mutual encouragement in the performance of other good works for the relief of the Suffering Souls, for instance by assisting poor boys who have a vocation for the priesthood, by contributing to the conversion of the heathens, to the support of the poor and sick; they often visit the Blessed Sacrament, propagate devotion to the Blessed Virgin Mary, assist poor churches, etc. They incite one another especially to assist often at Mass, and to receive Holy Communion frequently. This latter is prescribed by the rules of the Confraternity, and one member is encouraged to it by the good example of the other. They are further encouraged by occasional meetings and special sermons, and by indulgences granted both for membership in the confraternity, as also for the performance of good works and the reception of the Sacraments as members thereof.

This Pious Union for the aid and relief of the Suffering Souls is founded on the faith in Christ, without

which faith there can be no true spiritual fraternity
of mankind. True, all men became brethren through
their creation by the same God, but they did not remain
what they were, namely obedient children of God. As
a result great misery visited mankind—hatred interiorly and war exteriorly. Then Christ came into the
world. "He came unto His own, and His own received
Him not. But as many as received Him, He gave them
power to be made the sons of God." (*John* 1:11, 12).
Once children of God, they are also brethren. Hence
Christian fraternity is founded on faith in Christ. With
St. Peter the early Christians exclaimed: "Thou art
Christ, the Son of the living God," and thus became
united with one another. "And all they that believed,
were together, and had all things in common. Their
possessions and goods they sold, and divided them to
all, according as every one had need." (*Acts* 2:44, 45).
They persevered together in prayer. This same faith
must animate us, the faith namely which shows us
God as the common Father of all men, and all men as
our brethren in Jesus Christ. This faith directs our
attention also to our departed brethren in Purgatory.
It speaks to our hearts, thus: "Behold these souls in
Purgatory, so severely tried and entirely helpless: they
are your brethren!" This faith, living and operating in
the souls of those who profess it, will naturally hold
them together in the bond of a truly Christian fraternity.

The charity of Christ unites the various members
of the Church. God Himself inscribed indelibly into the
hearts of men the command, "Thou shalt love God
above all things, and thy neighbor as thyself." But as
soon as man turned his eyes toward the forbidden tree
in paradise, Satan obscured this divine command and
replaced it with self-love. Inordinate self-love caused
all the misery that followed the fall of man; selfishness was the source of all his tears, of all the streams
of blood unjustly shed. Fraternal charity had vanished
from the world. Then Jesus came to reunite and

strengthen the disrupted bond of charity, as He Himself declares in His farewell prayer, "Holy Father, keep them in Thy name, whom Thou hast given me; that they may be one, as we also are." (*John* 17:11). This union He achieved by His divine love for us which He manifested by His death on the Cross. "Greater love than this no man hath, that a man lay down his life for his friends." (*John* 15:13). Who can view this love sacrificing itself on the Cross and close his heart to charity? Forsooth, only a heart of stone could do so! Where charity is enkindled in a heart, and especially where charity for our suffering brethren in Purgatory dwells, there is the true spirit of fraternity; and the more sublime and ennobled this charity is, the stronger is its bond, the more meritorious its ministry in behalf of the souls in Purgatory.

The Confraternity, moreover, must be enlivened with the spirit of Christ. Without spirit there is no life. When man opened his eye, ear and heart to Satan, the image of God in his soul was disfigured and concupiscence was enkindled. St. Paul portrays the miserable condition of man, saying, "All have turned out of the way; they are become unprofitable together: there is none that doth good, there is not so much as one. Their throat is an open sepulchre; with their tongues they have dealt deceitfully. The venom of asps is under their lips. Whose mouth is full of cursing and bitterness: Their feet swift to shed blood: Destruction and misery in their ways: and the way of peace they have not known: There is no fear of God before their eyes." (*Rom.* 3:12-18). Horrible thought, that man could thus debase himself! Christ by His death triumphed over sin, and diffused His Spirit into all that converted themselves to Him, according to His promise by the prophet, "I will pour out my spirit upon all flesh: and your sons and your daughters shall prophesy . . . moreover upon my servants and handmaids in those days I will pour forth my spirit." (*Joel* 2:28, 29). And this Holy Spirit brought forth abundant fruits, such as "charity, joy,

peace, patience, benignity, goodness, longanimity, mild-
ness, faith, modesty, continency, chastity." (*Gal.* 5:22,23).
Jesus lived and died for the welfare of mankind; this
same Spirit was transmitted also to His disciples, who
excluded no one from their charity. They even sacrificed their temporal possessions for the welfare of the
living and the dead. We read of the first Christians,
"And the multitude of believers had but one heart and
one soul: neither did any one say that aught of the
things which he possessed, was his own; but all things
were common unto them. . . . Neither was there any
one needy among them." (*Acts* 4:32, 34). On this principle of charity are founded the confraternities for the
relief of the Suffering Souls. All their prayers and good
works are directed to this end.

As long as this one faith, this one charity, this united
spirit of Christ animated all Christians and filled them
with the courage to lead a holy life, there is no mention made in history of special confraternities in the
Church. But when error and unbelief became rampant
in the world, when a worldly life gained entrance into
the Church, when immorality wrought sad havoc in
the Christian community, then it was that pious Christians formed themselves into a confraternity for the
purpose of resisting with all their might the impend-
ing evil which endangered so many of their brethren;
in a word, they combined for the purpose of combat-
ting the evil of sin, so that a pagan governor testifies
of the early Christians: "The Christians often come
together in their dwellings, and before they separate
they solemnly promise each other to abstain from murder, theft, intemperance," etc.

Confraternities for the relief of the Suffering Souls
are moreover a help against transgressing that spirit
of Christian moderation which the Church inculcates.
They keep before our eyes the torments of Purgatory;
they direct our attention to the needs of the Suffering
Souls, and dissuade us from worldly display at funerals, insisting that we should remember the souls of

the departed in prayer and by good works rather than to do homage to the world and to Satan by sinful extravagance at burials.

We are able to trace such a union or confraternity for the relief of the Suffering Souls as far back as the year 700 of the Christian era, namely in Mabillon's "Acts of the Saints of the Order of St. Benedict." In the lives of other Saints also we often meet with leagues of prayer which holy persons entered into for the purpose of helping one another in mitigating the torments of Purgatory. We find instances of this in the biographies of St. Boniface, the Venerable Bede, Abbot Eudberct of Wiremouth, and others. St. Boniface wrote to Optatus, Abbot of Monte Cassino: "We ardently implore that a bond of brotherly love unite us, so that the living offer prayer for each other, and join in prayer and in offering the Holy Sacrifice of Mass for the deceased, whose names shall be exchanged between us for this purpose."

In the *St. Benedict's Stimmen* of 1880 we are informed that as early as 1005 bishops, priests and clerics formed a league, the former binding themselves to celebrate a certain number of Masses after the death of a member, the latter to recite the psalter repeatedly. Emperors and kings, bishops and other persons of rank promised to give food to a certain number of poor, or to give a specified alms, and to have lamps and tapers lighted in suffrage for the dead. In our times also we find these confraternities throughout the Church, in villages and cities, for priests, religious and laymen. We now proceed to mention some of them for practical purposes, particularly such as deserve special recommendation on account of their extensive membership and their extraordinary privileges for the living and the dead.

The Archconfraternity of the Most Precious Blood was founded at the beginning of the nineteenth century by the Rev. Francis Albertini, who at a later period became bishop of Terracina, Italy, and died in the fame of sanctity in the year 1819. The members of this arch-confraternity offer up to our Heavenly Father the Most Precious Blood of Jesus Christ for the forgiveness of their own sins, for the needs of Holy Church, for the conversion of sinners, and for the relief of the souls in Purgatory. Pope Pius VII, in 1815, raised this pious union to the rank of an archconfraternity and endowed it with numerous indulgences. These latter were added to considerably in 1850 and 1852 by Pope Pius IX, and were confirmed anew in 1878 by the Sacred Congregation of Indulgences. A great admirer and propagator of this now widespread devotion and confraternity was the founder of the Congregation of the Most Precious Blood, the venerable Servant of God, Caspar del Buffalo. The altars of the archconfraternity are privileged *ipse facto* and forever. The members have a special share in all the good works and penitential exercises of all religious Orders and Congregations in the world. (Rescript of 1852.) All the indulgences are applicable by way of suffrage to the souls in Purgatory.

The Confraternity for the relief of the Suffering Souls, whose headquarters are in the Redemptorist church of St. Mary in Monterone at Rome, was raised to the rank of an Archconfraternity by Pope Gregory XVI. It is also endowed with many indulgences and privileges. It was founded in the church named in 1841, for the purpose of continually aiding the Suffering Souls by good works and sacrifices.

Other well-known confraternities for the benefit of the Suffering Souls are the following: The Archconfraternity of Our Lady of Intercession, at Rome; the Pious Union of Masses, at Ingolstadt, Bavaria; the Confraternity of the Perpetual Adoration, at Lambach, Upper Austria; the League of Helpers of the Holy Souls, in France, of which every Catholic can become at least an honorary member; St. Benedict's Society of Priests for the relief of the Suffering Souls, at Lambach; the Society of Priests and Association of Perpetual Masses, under the patronage of St. Joseph, for deceased priests, etc.

But Christian piety was not satisfied with uniting the faithful in unions and societies for the purpose of attaining more speedily the various pious objects aimed at. The devout members of the Church felt themselves moved to organize such unions or societies also for the purpose of combating some prevalent heathen custom, or as a means of oppugning more effectually some particular sin or vice. For instance, there were confraternities against unchaste jests and conversations, against forbidden marriages, against intemperance in eating and drinking, etc. The faith and charity with which the Church was animated in the past, are still living and operating within the Church of today. One of the most laudable Christian enterprises of the present age—a work highly beneficial to the deceased as well as the living—is the Society against Extravagance at Christian Funerals. This Society, founded in England, has been spread to some extent in our own country, the United States of America. God grant that this Society, productive of so much good, may grow more and more in strength and influence for the spiritual benefit of the living and the dead!

To surround death with excessive indications of sorrow and mourning shows a deplorable degeneracy of the Christian spirit. The Divine Founder of our religion, who sent His own Paraclete to be our Consoler, has robbed death of its sting. "Death is swallowed up in victory." (*1 Cor.* 15:54). It is the object of the Christian religion to bring consolation to mankind on this very point. The natural feeling of a Christian at the burial of one of his brethren ought to be joyous, buoyed up by the hope of a blessed immortality, by trustful confidence and resignation to the Will of God. O religion, truly divine, how consoling thou art to the just! What a wellspring of joy dost thou open to him by the promise of a blissful eternity! What could give us greater consolation than the hope of another, better life, where sin, sorrow and death shall no longer reign? And this is the goal to which we are led by complete and perfect abandonment to the Will of God. Whosoever truly desires to possess God, resigns himself fully to the dispositions of His Providence; he is discouraged at no trial, however severe; patiently he undergoes every probation. This resignation is the foundation of every virtue, it is a cause of true happiness; it is the virtue by which we attain to bliss here and hereafter.

The principal concern of a Christian in the hour of death should be the welfare of his soul and not the care of his body. His burial therefore ought to correspond with all these sentiments. But, alas! In our age the love of display at funerals has taken so deep roots that societies are founded for the purpose of providing the poor with the necessary means of gratifying at funerals this perverse sentiment of show and extravagance, thereby withdrawing the attention of the faithful from the soul of the deceased and directing it to the body. This is a perversion of the respect due to the dead, of which all those are guilty who ignorantly regard such extravagant demonstrations of mourning as tokens of honor and love. Real sorrow at the death of a member of one's family does not seek expression in a pompous funeral; therefore Christian burials ought to be models of simplicity. Such a society for the benefit of the poor ought to take for its aim to oppose all worldly display at funerals of this kind and to do away with costly monuments and unchristian symbols.

At burials the thoughts of a Christian should be directed to his last end; hence he should be more concerned about the soul of his deceased friend or relative than about his body. At the moment of its departure from the body the soul appears before God's judgment seat. Those who have departed in the state of grace, but whose works, though good, are yet found wanting in perfection, are sentenced to make atonement in Purgatory. However great our sorrow at parting from our loved ones naturally is, the thought that we can mitigate their sufferings is a truly consoling one, and calls our attention to the means by which this is to be done. Our very nature prompts us to pray for the deceased in general, and much more so for those who were dear to us in life. This sentiment, instilled into our souls by God, cannot be a false one; therefore alms and other works of suffrage for the Suffering Souls must be pleasing to God. But the most efficient means of relieving, consoling and releasing the Souls in Purgatory is the Holy Sacrifice of the Mass. The Society against Extravagance at Funerals directs its principal efforts to procure for the Suffering Souls a truly Christian demonstration of love and respect. The personal expressions of sorrow in which the relatives indulge are rendered sacred in a special manner by the renunciation of a pompous funeral. This renunciation is an alms much more acceptable to God than any charitable gift to the poor; for by it many are dissuaded from lavish extravagance, whereas the gift of charity lends temporary assistance only to a few persons.

Moreover, the members of the Society endeavor to make extraordinary sacrifices for the benefit of the Suffering Souls. What others spend in the service of the world, they devote to the assistance of the poor, to the conversion of infidels and heretics, to the relief of poor convents and religious Orders, and to Holy Masses for the dead. They carefully avoid sin and lead a godly life; above all, they do not indulge in impurity, regarding their bodies as temples of the Holy Ghost. They patiently bear the trials and ills of life. All this they do for the special intention of bringing consolation and aid to the Suffering Souls in Purgatory.

Is it not most honorable to belong to such a confraternity or society and to be able to think: "I do my part and have my share in all the good achieved by it, in all the blessings dispensed through its agency?" Is it not a most noble charity to pray daily for our brethren? Is it not consoling to think: "Thousands pray for me every day?" Can we thereby not hope to receive many more graces? And are the numerous indulgences so easily gained by the members of a confraternity not of immense value? By them we shall be relieved of a lengthy punishment in the next world, and at the same time we can relieve souls now undergoing it. What should we desire others to do for us after our death? We should ask, not that they make an extravagant display at our funeral, but that they obtain for us the suffrages of our brethren and the services of the Church. May God in His mercy imbue the hearts of the faithful more and more with such sentiments, and unite them in such confraternities for the welfare of the living and the relief of the Suffering Souls!

William V, Duke of Bavaria, ordered in his last will that at his funeral every kind of extravagant display shall be omitted. In particular he directed that no eulogy should be delivered, but in its place there should be a sermon on the art of dying well. He also ordered that before his interment in the church of St. Michael the funeral cortege should be preceded by the cross and a banner emblematic of death; that the bier should be attended by seventy old men and seventy old women in mourning, whom he had assisted in their poverty during life. He moreover forbade the erection of a monument, ordering in its place a plain cross with the inscription to be seen today: "Awed at Thy majesty I tremble for my sins; when Thou comest to judge me, O Lord, do not condemn me."

An example worthy of imitation was given also by the late Mr. Cooper, a lawyer in New York. In his last will he specified a small amount of money which must suffice to cover his funeral expenses, permitting no more carriages than were necessary for the members of his family. The sum thus saved was bequeathed to St. Francis Hospital and other charitable institutions.

The Efficacy of Holy Water in
Behalf of the Suffering Souls

The priest blesses water in the name of the Church, to be used for ritual purposes and by the faithful. The priest in reciting the form of the blessing makes the Sign of the Cross over the water, and mingles with it a little salt that has been previously blessed. The prayer recited is a petition that God may preserve those sprinkled with this water from the snares of Satan, grant them health of body and purity of soul, etc. Holy water is to remind us of the Sacred Blood of Christ, by which we are cleansed from sin, and whose prototype saved Israel from the Destroying Angel. It is moreover to exhort us that we should purify our souls by a chaste and pious life. Let us therefore remember how Jesus shed His Precious Blood amid excruciating torments to cleanse us from sin and to deliver us from the bondage of Satan; let us pray to be more and more cleansed in the Blood of Jesus, and to be preserved from future sins. And may God, through the death of Him who vanquished Satan by the shedding of His Blood, protect us in all dangers, and ward off from us all temporal and spiritual evils.

The prayer of the Church and the blessing of the priest are rendered efficacious through the merits of Christ. Hence the faithful and confident use of holy water is attended with great benefits for soul and body in life, and brings consolation to the souls of the faithful departed. The following are some of its effects:

a) It brings remission of venial sins to the souls in the state of grace.

b) By the devout use of it at least a part of the temporal punishment of sin is remitted.

c) It promotes the health of the body.

d) It puts to flight the evil spirits and guards us against their snares.

e) It prevents sickness and wards off other evil influences.

When we take holy water and sprinkle ourselves or our surroundings with it, the prayer of the Church ascends to Heaven, drawing down blessings upon us and on the objects that are sprinkled with it. The missionary, Father Alexander of Rodez, relates that his catechists wrought numerous miraculous cures by the Sign of the Cross and the sprinkling of holy water. Thus he once sent six catechists to a village sadly afflicted with sickness, and within a week they healed two hundred and seventy-two sick persons. Church history relates that holy water was also used to avert the plague of locusts. For instance Pope Stephen VI had the fields devastated by locusts sprinkled with holy water blessed by himself, when these voracious insects suddenly disappeared.

Holy water may be used not only for the purpose of benefiting persons present, but may also be applied with the intention of procuring its blessed effects for the absent, and especially for the Suffering Souls. In this case the prayer of the Church ascends to Heaven in favor of the person or soul intended to be helped. A drop of holy water is sometimes more effectual than a long prayer. Our prayer is often distracted and lukewarm; the prayer of the Church connected with holy water always pleases God, no matter when, where and by whom it is said—provided it be said in the name of the Church. Hence the Suffering Souls thirst for holy water, and could we but witness their yearning for a drop of it, we would certainly not omit to refresh them at least in the morning and evening and sometimes during the day with its sacred dew.

From the following private revelations we may conclude with what joy the Suffering Souls receive, and how yearningly they long for holy water. A stranger had been buried in the *Campo santo* at Rome. Seventeen years afterwards he appeared to the Venerable Dominic of Jesus-Mary, begging that the remains of his body might often be sprinkled with holy water, because thereby his soul would be refreshed. This same servant of God, as is customary with the Carmelites, had a skull always lying before him on his desk. One day he sprinkled this skull with holy water, when he heard a pitiful voice imploring him: "More holy water! More holy water!" The sprinkling of the holy water undoubtedly refreshed the soul and relieved its pains in the fiery prison. To the Venerable Sister Frances of the Blessed Sacrament there often appeared a deceased Sister begging that her grave be sprinkled with holy water, because her soul was refreshed thereby. The Venerable Lindmayer was frequently reminded by God to sprinkle the remains of the deceased with holy water, and she was accustomed, before retiring, to sprinkle the souls that appeared to her. Once she forgot to do so, when the souls continued to implore her till she rose from her bed and complied with their request.

The following is related by the learned divine Mendo in his life of St. Martin, canon regular of Liege, the manuscript of which is still preserved in the convent of St. Isidore: "There were many Saints who were privileged to enjoy the visible intercourse of their Guardian Angels; and this holy servant of God during his whole life was similarly attended by the soul of a priest from Purgatory." This soul revealed to him, among other particulars concerning the punishments of that state of purification, that the souls felt a great mitigation of the pain of fire as often as the faithful sprinkled with holy water the graves in which their bodies were buried, feeling its effects in about the same manner as when in life a person overcome by heat is refreshed with water.

With regard to the use of holy water the directions of the Church and the example of our ancestors are the unerring compass which we must follow. Hence, if we desire to be worthy children of the Church and of our glorious predecessors in the Faith, we must do as follows: As often as we enter a church, we ought to sprinkle ourselves with holy water, dipping our bare fingers into it and devoutly making the Sign of the

Cross. Thereby we drive away Satan, and excite ourselves to recollection in prayer. On Sundays we should assist at the sprinkling of holy water which takes place regularly before the parochial Mass. We should not omit to have holy water at home, preserving it in an appropriate vessel and in a decent place. In Catholic Europe there was a time when not a house was to be found in city or country, no matter how rich or poor the dwellers therein, where holy water, the crucifix and sacred images were not kept. Even today we find these indications of a true religious spirit wherever true faith has a home. The use of holy water is very ancient. Some are of the opinion that it was introduced by the Apostles. Its introduction in homes where its use was hitherto unknown, would go far to revive the spirit of faith.

If hitherto we have made use of holy water from custom, simply because we were thus trained, let us henceforth do so from a conviction of its usefulness and with due regard to its purposes. Convinced that we give great consolation to the souls in Purgatory by the devout application of holy water, can we regard it as troublesome to give a drop to them on leaving or entering the room? It is a commendable custom when using holy water to give one drop for ourselves and the loving members of our family to receive protection for soul and body; a drop for the dying, especially dying sinners, that God may be moved to grant them the grace of conversion; and a third drop for the Suffering Souls in Purgatory. Oh, how much of blessing and true welfare, of merit and grace we would obtain during the course of the year for our dear ones and for innumerable others by this easy practice, thereby gaining a great number of intercessors during life, in death, and for the time of our own purification in Purgatory! As often as we perform this service for the Suffering Souls, they will requite it by interceding for us with an ardor impossible to the most saintly persons on earth. And God willingly hears their prayer, it being the prayer of His elect, and vouchsafes an immeasurable amount of grace to their helpers.

Hence the devout Christian, who is zealous for the glory of God and intent on his salvation and on the release of the Suffering Souls, makes it a practice to use holy water often—at home as well as in church. He sprinkles himself on entering the church and on leaving it; he is careful to keep it at home, and sprinkles himself on rising in the morning, before leaving the house, and before retiring for the night. Many zealous Christians make it a practice to take holy water as they enter or leave a room, in temptation, danger of lightning, etc. Good parents bless their children with it every evening.

When using this salutary sacramental, let us pray that God, for the sake of our Redeemer's Blood, may grant to the souls in Purgatory refreshment in their pains and speedy relief. Behold how light and fleeting the vapor of steam: yet these few drops of diluted water are powerful enough to move enormous burdens! How small and inconsiderable is a gnat, how insignificant its sting; yet under certain circumstances such a sting may cause death! Now, if things so small and apparently so insignificant may cause death, why should not small things have saving properties? A drop of holy water possesses them. Oh, what comfort it gives to a Suffering Soul! Deodatus, one of the ancient Fathers of the desert, remarks: "As the flowers withering in the heat of the sun are refreshed by the rain, so also the souls in Purgatory—these flowers elect of Heaven, scorched by the Sun of eternal Justice—are refreshed by the devout application of holy water." Hence the cry of Dives in Hell: "Father Abraham, have mercy on me, and send Lazarus, that he may dip the tip of his finger in water, to cool my tongue: for I am tormented in this flame." (*Luke* 16:24). His request was refused. "But," says the learned Eck, "when the souls in Purgatory thus address us, saying, 'My brother in Christ, dip the tip of your finger in holy water and cool us, for we are tormented in this flame of Purgatory,' oh, do not refuse to do so, but grant them this consolation!"

The Burning of Blessed Candles Is
Beneficial to the Suffering Souls

God Himself in the Old Law ordained that lights should be used in His temple and at the religious rites performed there. For this purpose He gave the minutest directions: "Thou shalt make also a candlestick of beaten work of the finest gold. . . . Thou shalt make also seven lamps, and shalt set them upon the candlestick, to give light over against." (*Ex.* 25:31, 37). These lamps were to burn continually. "Command the children of Israel that they bring thee the purest oil of the olives, and beaten with a pestle: that a lamp may burn always, in the tabernacle of the testimony . . . And Aaron and his sons shall order it, that it may give light before the Lord until the morning. It shall be a perpetual observance throughout their successions among the children of Israel." (*Ex.* 27:20, 21).

Under the Christian dispensation the use of lights was retained not only when the sacred mysteries were celebrated at night during times of persecution, but also during the day. In the early Church those selected to take care of the lamps and candles were specially ordained for this purpose. This minor order of acolytes is still conferred by the Church. And because candles and lamps are used at divine service, the Church blesses them. The burning lamp or candle signifies Christ, the eternal Light, which we implore in our prayers to shine upon the departed. At the same time they are also a continual admonition for the living to remember their deceased brethren; they are an alms for the Suffering Souls symbolizing charity; for as the flame gradually consumes the blessed candle, thus charity reduces the torments of the purifying fire. St. Athanasius lays great stress on this pious custom. He says, "Though the deceased is buried in the earth, thou must not omit to burn oil and wax on his grave, for this is pleasing to God and merits great reward. Oil and wax are an offering, the Holy Sacrifice is a propitiation, and alms given to the poor is an increase of recompense."

The tombs, particularly those of the martyrs and Saints, were adorned even at the time of the early persecutions. Hence St. Thomas, with St. John Damascene, declared that oil was among the gifts offered in early times for the relief of the departed. In the middle ages the custom prevailed and in certain countries, for instance in Southern Germany, has descended to our times, the custom, namely, of burning lamps on the graves throughout the year, or at least during certain seasons of the year. The Church sanctions this pious practice by recognizing provisions for this purpose, and by burning numerous lights at all her solemnities. This custom is observed particularly in places of pilgrimage, in convents, etc., where a number of lamps are kept burning day and night during Triduums or Novenas for the souls in Purgatory. At St. John's Protectory, West Seneca, New York, there are often over three hundred lamps burning for this intention. In the basilica of Our Lady of the Sacred Heart, at Issodoun, France, over one hundred lamps are kept continually lighted; numerous lamps burn for this same devout purpose in the House of the missionaries of the Sacred Heart at West De Pere, Wisconsin; at Loreto, in Italy; at Einsiedeln, Switzerland, etc., in all of which places provision is made to satisfy the individual devotion of those who desire such lamps to be lighted on the altar.

Finally, examples are not wanting to prove that this pious custom is acceptable to the souls in Purgatory, and legendary lore knows of touching incidents showing that God Himself sometimes gave evidence of His approval of this practice. A lamp at the tomb of St. Thomas the Apostle continued burning during the fiercest storms, sometimes even after the oil was consumed. The same is related concerning St. Gregory and St. Constantine. The efforts of the evil spirit to extinguish the lamps of St. Genevieve, in Paris, were ineffectual; the symbol of virginity continued to shed its light. Boudon relates that a deceased person appeared to a relative and complained bitterly that the customary number of candles had not been offered at his funeral. Also, that pitiful moaning was heard in a house where it had been neglected one Saturday to light to customary "Poor Souls' Candle." A priest vouches for the following which he related to the author: A peasant of his acquaintance, in the Tyrol, attempted during three nights to steal fruit from his neighbor's orchard. Every time he came near the place, a light either came toward him, or moved in a circle around the house. Later he confessed his guilt to the owner, observing that the latter must have a vigilant guard. The man replied that he knew of no guard, except that it was his custom to burn a candle every evening for the Suffering Souls, and that these grateful spirits must have guarded his property.

Effect of Indulgences on the Suffering Souls

It is of faith, that if Christ had shed but one single drop of His Most Precious Blood, this would have sufficed for the salvation of all mankind. As He has shed all His Blood for us, and moreover, as all His labors and sufferings possess infinite value to atone for all sins and their punishment—where is the immense treasury thus merited for mankind? Surely, it was not the Will of God that it should, so to say, be lost or become unprofitable. Whom, then, has God entrusted with all these infinite merits of the Passion and death of Christ? They were placed into the treasury of the Church, to be always at the disposal of the faithful. The same is true of all the supererogatory merits and atonements of the Blessed Virgin Mary and the Saints. The works of Christ are satisfactory by reason of their own proper value, while those of the Saints are satisfactory only through the grace of Christ, which gives them their worth. The superfluous satisfactions of the Saints, or those which they did not need for payment of their own debts, are added to the merits of Christ, not by way of supplement, since His satisfactions are superabundantly sufficient, but by way of accumulation or fruit, or of interest accruing from His satisfactory merits. This is a consequence of the communion of Saints, whereby one member of the Church communicates in all the spiritual goods of the others, since they are members of one body, in organic union with its Head.

According to the doctrine of the Church, the *guilt* of sin and its *eternal* punishment is remitted in the sacrament of Penance. The *temporal* punishment due to sin however is not always remitted *entirely* in the sacrament of Penance, as is done in Baptism. This remaining temporal punishment, as long as it is not remitted, must be suffered either in this world or in Purgatory, before we can enter Heaven. Satisfaction for temporal punishment is made by the works of penance imposed in the sacrament of Penance and united with the merits of Christ, and is applied to us by the power of binding and loosing granted to the Church. By this same power works of penance are imposed on us outside the sacrament of Penance for the purpose of gaining indulgences. Finally, satisfaction is also rendered by voluntary works of penance, and by unavoidable sufferings borne with patience and resignation—all this in union with the merits of Christ.

An indulgence therefore is the remission of the temporal punishment due to sin which the Church grants to the faithful, provided they observe certain conditions. The entire temporal punishment is remitted by a plenary indulgence; a part of it only by a partial indulgence. The Council of Trent declares that "the use of indulgences is in the highest degree wholesome to the Christian people; that the Church was empowered by Christ to grant them, and has made use of this power from the earliest ages: and that because their use is approved of by the councils, they are to be retained in the Church."

By an indulgence the temporal punishment is remitted only on certain conditions; that is, the gaining of the indulgence is made dependent on the performing of certain specified good works. By the faithful performance of these works the temporal punishment is atoned for; or rather, to state it more exactly, the punishment is thereby counterbalanced. However, not every temporal punishment incurred by sin can be remitted by indulgences. For the temporal punishment of sin can be threefold: first, punishments of a natural order— for instance poverty, sickness, disgrace, etc.; secondly, punishments inflicted by Providence and to be undergone in this world and in Purgatory; thirdly, punishments fixed by the penitential code of the Church, by which she ordained certain penances for certain sins. To maintain that the punishments of the natural order are remitted by indulgences would be saying too much, for the natural consequences of sin can be removed only by divine interposition. An indulgence therefore can be nothing more than the remission of one or both of the two other kinds of punishment mentioned, because for the remission of these punishments no change of the natural order is necessary. These two kinds of punishment being inflicted by the Will of God, they must also be remitted by this same divine will.

We now come to the question: Who can declare that certain temporal punishments of sin are remitted? It cannot be denied that the Church of Christ has this power; but she has not the power to change the natural order established by God. When God has fixed a punishment, the Church cannot summarily declare this punishment to be remitted; she can only replace it by a punishment of some other kind. This she does by adding to certain penitential works to be performed by the penitent with scrupulous exactitude the infinite merits of Christ committed to her treasury, thus rendering them so valuable that they replace the punishment fixed by God.

To gain an indulgence the first rule to be observed is contained in the motto: "All for the greater glory of God!" If we were intent only on our own profit or that of the deceased, without regard to the glory of God, we would not gain the indulgence. We must seek our own salvation and that of others because it is the Will of God that we should. The more the love of God is increased in our hearts, the easier it will be for us to overcome our natural evil inclinations. If we have triumphed over every voluntary, conscious inclination to sin then we are in the condition requisite for gaining an indulgence. For to gain a plenary indulgence we must be without sin; not only without mortal sin, but without unrepented venial sin, yea, without voluntary, conscious inclination even to venial sin, which though venial is nevertheless sin. By a plenary indulgence we are delivered entirely from the punishment of sin, so that we would be admitted to Heaven immediately in case we should die right after gaining such an indulgence.

As often as we desire to gain a plenary indulgence, let us strive to fulfill with the greatest purity of heart the conditions that are prescribed. If we do not gain the indulgence to its whole extent, we may be sure that we will gain at least part of it.

The power of the Church to apply indulgences to the faithful departed is a consequence of the intimate union existing between the Church Militant and the Church Suffering. This is evident from the papal Bulls. Moreover, the doctrine that the living can come to the relief of the dead is clearly contained in Holy Scripture, and is handed down to us by the most ancient tradition. It is evident that if private suffrages relieve the Suffering Souls, the suffrages authorized by the Popes, and for which they granted an indulgence, must have the same effect. Heretics, for example Luther, Calvin, etc., deny that the Church has the power of granting indulgences applicable to the souls in Pur-

gatory. The Church has ever proclaimed the doctrine
that she can aid the Suffering Souls by indulgences.
St. Thomas Aquinas declares it to be a custom of the
Church to grant indulgences not only to the living, but
also for the benefit of the dead. Pope Sixtus IV condemned the doctrine of Osma, who maintained that
the Pope had no power to release the punishments of
Purgatory. Pope Leo IX declared it to be the continued
doctrine of the Roman Church, that the Pope had the
power of granting indulgences for the benefit of the
living and the dead.

Since, however, the Church on earth has no juris-
diction over the souls of the dead, she cannot apply
indulgences to them *in the same manner* as she does
to the living. To the latter she grants indulgences by
way of judicial sentence and absolution, to the former
she does so by way of suffrage. That is, the Church in
applying indulgences to the dead offers to God the satisfaction made by the good works of the faithful and
rendered meritorious through the merits of Christ; in
doing so she petitions the Most High that, in view of
the offered payment, He would deign in His mercy to
remit the whole or a part of the debt of temporal punishment still weighing on the soul of the deceased. In
granting an indulgence to the living, the Pope's act
may be compared to that of a man who gives the means
of payment into the hands of the person indebted,
thereby enabling him to release himself from prison;
in granting an indulgence for the dead, he may be said
to act like a man who offers payment of the debt to
the creditor, asking that in his mercy he might release
the prisoner.

It has always been the practice of the Popes to grant
numerous indulgences applicable to the Suffering Souls;
by the gaining of which indulgences we cede to these
imprisoned friends of God so much remission of temporal punishment as we would have obtained for ourselves. The charity of Holy Church for the souls in
Purgatory has always been the same; in her love and

compassion she continually invents new means and methods of assisting them. She has granted indulgences for various devotions, exercises, prayers, etc., in order that all her children might ever cooperate with her the more readily and willingly in the grand work of relieving and rescuing the Suffering Souls.

God does not always bestow the indulgence on that soul for whom we intend to gain it, especially if the soul be that of a Christian, who during his life in this world was negligent in gaining indulgences and relieving the Suffering Souls; for divine justice deals according to the words of Christ, "With what measure you mete, it shall be measured to you again." (*Matt.* 7:2). It is probable in such a case that God applies the indulgence to some other soul more pleasing to Him; and this soul will then be very grateful to the person by whose charity it is released from Purgatory. The same is due with regard to Masses said for a certain soul at a privileged altar with the intention that the indulgences granted in consequence of the privilege may be applied for the release of that soul from Purgatory. When the indulgence is refused to the soul for whom it was intended, God will probably grant it to some one of its relatives in Purgatory; or it may be given to a soul who in this world was assiduous in prayer for the Suffering Souls, but is now forgotten. This may sometimes be the case with poor persons, who during their life on this earth remembered the Suffering Souls by prayer and good works, but who, for want of means on the part of their relations, do not receive the benefit of even one Holy Sacrifice after their death.

St. Magdalen of Pazzi and the religious of her convent were confirmed in their zeal to gain indulgences for the Suffering Souls by the release of one of the Sisters, who after her death had to suffer in Purgatory for fifteen hours, and was then released on account of the indulgences gained for her by the inmates of the convent. She revealed to St. Magdalen that this speedy deliverance was due to the zeal she had herself manifested during life to gain indulgences for the Suffering Souls.

It was revealed to St. Bridget that many and great punishments are remitted on account of indulgences, so that whosoever departs this life after having gained a plenary indulgence before consenting to another sin, is admitted to Heaven the same as one dying in his baptismal innocence. At Venice there lived a pious priest who intended to make a pilgrimage to Assisi in order to gain the great indulgence of Portiuncula. Falling sick before he was able to do so, he requested a friend to gain the indulgence and apply it for his release from Purgatory in case he should die. Soon after he departed this life, but his friend postponed the gaining of the indulgence. One day the deceased appeared to him quite disconsolate, and asked him: "Why do you postpone so long the good work I so ardently implored you to perform? Go at least now, I pray, and gain the indulgence for me!" The friend did so, and the deceased appeared to him radiant as the sun, telling him that by the indulgence he had been released from Purgatory and was now on his way to Heaven.

As we may take it for granted that many of our relatives, friends, benefactors, etc., are in Purgatory, where they have to undergo severe punishment, who among us should not be most zealously intent on gaining for them as many indulgences as possible, thereby to release these poor captives from their prison?

Fasting for the Benefit of the Suffering Souls

Everybody in this world experiences in himself two conflicting powers, which are described by St. Paul as follows: "I am delighted with the law of God, according to the inward man: but I see another law in my members, fighting against the law of my mind, and captivating me in the law of sin, that is in my members." (*Rom.* 7:22, 23). Reason and religion demand that in this combat of the "inward man" we decide in his favor against sin. Our soul is immortal, the breath of God, His image. Our body is a handful of clay, soon to molder in the grave. What does it matter if the body, a food for worms, be made to suffer, if only the immortal soul be saved? Of what consequence is it, if the body die, if only the soul lives? St. Paul was the Apostle of the Gentiles, a light of the world, a vessel of election; nevertheless he felt it a necessary duty to bring his body into subjection. He says, "I chastise my body, and bring it into subjection: lest perhaps, when I have preached to others, I myself should become a castaway." (*1 Cor.* 9:27). Many Christians are filled with terror of their adversary, the devil, of whom St. Peter says that "as a roaring lion, he goeth about seeking whom he may devour (*1 Pet.* 5:8); but let them know that the devil himself with all his cunning and power is not able to injure their souls as much as they themselves may injure it by pampering their flesh. Let us bear in mind that the assaults of Hell are greatly weakened by the mortification of our flesh. If we hate Satan, then how much more should we hate our flesh, which is more treacherous than Satan! During mortal life the souls in Purgatory did not always have a due regard for the final results of vain pleasures, but often looked only to the momentary gratification of their senses. Hence they must now atone even for the least inordinate enjoyment of sensual pleasure.

In order to help the Suffering Souls, we must render satisfaction to God for the sins that offended Him. We must satisfy the demands of divine justice by corresponding works of atonement, works by which God is glorified, and man is deprived of some enjoyment in penalty for the sinful gratification in which he wrongfully indulged. Now it is manifest that God is glorified by every good work; whereas to fallen man every good work is troublesome and painful, so that the performance of such a work deprives him of some kind of gratification. Hence every good work has a propitiatory quality. As in prayer we consecrate our whole being to God, trampling underfoot the pride of life by the humility of supplication, so also do we by fasting deny ourselves in atonement for the rebellion of our flesh against the law of God. By fasting we chastise our body, refuse gratification to its appetite, give strength to our soul and pleasure to our whole spiritual being. Fasting is directed against the lusts of the flesh and the sins proceeding therefrom, against all forbidden pleasures and enjoyments. By fasting, therefore, we atone for the sins committed by and against our body. Instead of applying this atonement to ourselves, we can offer it to Almighty God in union with the fast of Christ in favor of the Suffering Souls.

To propitiate the offended majesty of God was the end for which St. John the Baptist performed such austere penance. Of His forerunner Our Saviour Himself said that "there hath not risen among them that are born of woman a greater" (*Matt.* 11:11); and yet "he was clothed with camel's hair, and a leathern girdle about his loins; and he ate locusts and wild honey." (*Mark* 1:6). Our Divine Redeemer Himself, "the Way, and the Truth, and the Life" (*John* 14:6), gives us an example of the efficacy and value of fasting. To prepare Himself for the great work of redemption He observed a fast of forty days and forty nights. To appease divine wrath and to obtain mercy for his people, Moses "fell down before the Lord as before, forty days and nights neither eating bread, nor drinking water, for all your sins, which you had committed against the Lord, and had provoked Him to wrath: for I feared His indignation and anger, wherewith being moved against you, He would have destroyed you. And the Lord heard me this time also." (*Deut.* 9:18, 19). This clearly demonstrates how efficient fasting is to obtain God's mercy. Christian soul, contemplate the torments of Purgatory! Let your heart be moved to compassion for the Suffering Souls. Follow the example of Moses, thereby to release these poor spouses of Christ!

Lysimachus, king of Thracia, while surrounded by his enemies, suffered severely from thirst. To obtain water he delivered himself and his army to the enemy, thus sacrificing his liberty and his kingdom for a drink. David, the royal prophet, acted differently. Surrounded by his enemies, and exhausted by the fatigues of battle, he exclaimed, "O that some man would give me water of the cistern of Bethlehem, which is in the gate!" (*1 Par.* 11:17). The water was brought to him by three captains of his army, who risked their lives in fetching it from the cistern. "And he would not drink of it, but offered it to the Lord." A soul thus master of its appetite and inclinations is capable of every virtue and will surely be rewarded by the Lord.

We might mention ever so many signal blessings which the Saints obtained by fasting and prayer; but we confine ourselves to two examples. The Blessed Cecilia, a Dominican nun, was accustomed to mortify herself in drinking, thereby to honor the sacred thirst of Our Lord on the Cross, and to quench the flames of Purgatory. After her death she appeared to one of the Sisters, and revealed to her that immediately on her entrance into Purgatory an Angel appeared bearing a golden vase from which he poured water into the flames, and then led her to Heaven. King Sancio having died of poison, the queen prayed day and night for the repose of his soul, and on Saturdays fasted on bread and water in honor of the Blessed Virgin Mary. Her husband appeared to her thanking her for her penitential suffrages, and begging her to continue them. After this apparition she persevered in fasting and prayer for forty days. Then she saw him again surrounded by heavenly splendor, and heard him address her with these words: "Now I am released from my torments. I owe it to you, my pious queen; may God bless you for it throughout all eternity."

In order that our fasting may be beneficial to the Suffering Souls, it is not enough for us to abstain from food and drink, but we must also refrain from com-

mitting sin. Our fasting, to be efficient for the release
of the captive souls from their prison, must be done
according to the spirit of God. Our Lord says by the
mouth of the prophet, "Is not this rather the fast that
I have chosen? Loose the bands of wickedness, undo
the bundles that oppress, let them that are broken go
free, and break asunder every burden. Deal thy bread
to the hungry, and bring the needy and the harborless
into thy house: when thou shalt see one naked, cover
him, and despise not thy own flesh." (*Is.* 58:6, 7).
Through the same prophet the Lord rejects fasting that
is not attended by self-denial. "Behold in the day of
your fast your own will is found, and you exact of all
your debtors" (meaning that stubbornness and want of
charity render our fasting useless); "behold you fast
for debates and strife, and strike with the fist wickedly.
Do not fast as *you have done* until this day, to make
your cry to be heard on high." (*Is.* 58:3, 4). If you desire
to relieve the Suffering Souls, the bonds of iniquity
that bind your soul must be loosed, your soul must not
be held captive by pride, avarice, impurity, envy and
other vices.

Let us, then, fast by abstaining from hatred, anger,
impurity, slander, etc.; in a word, let us fast by our
works. If you see a person in distress, come to his
relief; if your neighbor is prosperous, do not envy him.
Let your hands fast by keeping them from acquiring
unjustly what is not yours; your heart, by guarding it
against covetousness; your feet, by preventing them
from going to dangerous amusements. How often have
we neglected all this, and yet it is an essential condition if our fasting is to be meritorious for the Suffering Souls! Let us therefore remember the exhortation
of St. Augustine: "What will it avail us if we abstain
from wine, but are intoxicated with anger; if we abstain
from flesh meat, but like wild animals destroy the rep-
utation and good name of our neighbors?"

St. Francis de Sales relates that a mother released
her son from Purgatory by performing an heroic act

of charity. He had been murdered, and his mother not only forgave the murderer, but shielded him from justice. Her son was permitted to appear to her; and he told her that this charity had pleased God so much, that his whole punishment in Purgatory, which would otherwise have lasted for years, had been remitted to him. Count Hyacinth of St. Florent was executed during the French Revolution. His sister Hermania was so embittered against his enemies, that she refused the Sacraments and mourned excessively for her brother. On the fifteenth anniversary of his death he appeared to his sister, and complained of her heartlessness, whereas he had so tenderly loved her in life. "Your tears and despair," he said, "do not help me. I yearn for your prayer, that it may help me to atone for my faults." Hermania deplored her mistake, and for the first time offered up a prayer for the murderers of her brother that God might have mercy on him. She then continued in works of charity and mercy for twenty-five years, and at her death her brother appeared to her in heavenly splendor. The chronicles of the convent of St. Teudon relate that one of the monks, who died about the year 1250, was released from Purgatory by the patient suffering of a woman who meekly bore the harsh treatment of her husband. And who can estimate how many Suffering Souls were released by the self-denials of so many Saints, for instance St. Augustine, St. Thomas Aquinas, St. Malachy, St. Patrick, St. Bridget, St. Lidwina, St. Elizabeth, and innumerable others?

Let us, then, fast not only by abstaining from bodily food, but also in a spiritual sense, by mortifying our passions. Following the example of the Saints, let us bear all our trials and sufferings with patience and resignation, offering them for the relief of the Suffering Souls. Let us say as often as a misfortune or adversity befalls us, "I will bear it patiently and offer it up for the release of my dear father, mother, brother, sister and other relatives, thereby to open to them the portals of paradise."

Almsdeeds Release the Suffering Souls

We read in Holy Scripture: "Water quencheth a flaming fire, and alms resisteth sins." (*Ecclus.* 3:33). And: "Lay out thy bread, and thy wine upon the burial of a just man." (*Tob.* 4:18). Does Tobias here instruct his son to remember the dead by feasting? Not at all; but according to Lyranus he taught him to feed the poor and to do other works of mercy at the death of the just, for he said to him, "Prayer is good with fasting and alms more than to lay up treasures of gold: for alms delivereth from death, and the same is that which purgeth away sins, and maketh to find mercy and life everlasting." (*Tob.* 12:8, 9). Pope Benedict VIII after his death appeared to the bishop of Capua and said, "Know that I have died; and though I am in the state of grace, yet I am greatly tormented in Purgatory. Therefore I pray thee, tell my successor John to give alms to the poor, for then I shall be released from my insupportable torments." His request was fulfilled; and he was soon released from Purgatory on account of the alms distributed for his sake.

It is scarcely necessary to add, that alms given for the Suffering Souls help to atone for our own sins of extravagance, sins proceeding from the abuse of wealth; and that this is almost the only way of attaining salvation for those who live in affluence. "If it were not possible," observes St. Chrysostom, "to atone for our misdeeds by alms, we might have reason to complain and say, 'Oh, how happy we should be if the gates of Heaven could be opened by money, if we could purchase the glory of the Saints by means of our earthly possessions!' Now, my brother, this is very easy of accomplishment; therefore avail yourself of this privilege. Before you lose your wealth, hasten to place it at the disposal of the Suffering Souls, as the price of their eternal salvation. Perhaps you will lose it by the malice of man; perhaps your passions will consume it; at all events death will deprive you of it sooner or later; charity alone insures you against this misfortune and renders you its possessor forever. You will prevent the loss of your earthly possessions by consigning them to the tabernacles of God, where you will enjoy them for all eternity along with the souls released by means of them." Thus speaks the Holy Ghost in the *Book of Tobias:* "Give alms out of thy substance, and turn not away thy face from any poor person: for so it shall come to pass that the face of the Lord shall not be turned from thee." (*Tob.* 4:7). Eusebius, duke of Sardinia, devoted the tenth part of his revenue to the relief of the Suffering Souls; his charity even went so far, that he gave to the poor the annual income of one of his cities, thereby to succor the suffering spouses of Christ in Purgatory. Might we not follow his example by devoting to the same purpose part of the proceeds of a certain business undertaking, of the rent of a certain house, of the interest of certain outstanding capital?

We must remember that the surplus of our wealth does not belong to us, but to the poor; and that it is our bounden duty to make use of only so much of it as corresponds with our state of life. We must one day render a strict account of the use we have made of our possessions. But our Divine Saviour does not claim a great part of our wealth and property. He does not strike us with sudden death like Ananias and Saphira, who secretly retained part of the proceeds of their property. He is satisfied if we devote a small part of what we possess to relieve the Suffering Souls. It is His Will that the wealthy who spend on superfluous articles of dress sums of money sufficient to relieve a great number of poor, should also do something to clothe the Suffering Souls; that is, they should aid these Souls to enter into eternal glory by relieving in their behalf the distress of the poor. The punishment of Purgatory is inflicted on many a soul who during its earthly life was wanting in charity to the poor. Oh, let us therefore hasten to appease the wrath of God by charity! By so doing we will gain the grateful friendship of those whom we have relieved in their suffering and ransomed from their painful captivity. They will aid us in working out our own salvation.

But alas, how small is the number of those who practically recognize almsgiving as one of the essential duties of a Christian! Still there are some—devout Christians, mindful of the distress and misery of the Suffering Souls—who do not pride themselves merely in being persons of rank and wealth—no; but they consider themselves rather as being members of the Mystical Body of Christ, and as such, brethren of the Suffering Souls. Forsooth, how can a Christian enjoy true happiness as long as he is convinced that these just souls are suffering in a lake of fire? If he is not moved to compassion by this consideration, he is devoid of every human feeling, and acts contrary to the dictates of reason and religion. A man so regardless of a most sacred duty would be regarded as a bad citizen even by a pagan commonwealth; he would be despised for his meanness, hardness of heart and ignobility of character even by the votaries of the unchristian world; how must he then be regarded by the Church of Christ? As a monster unworthy of the name of Christian, disgracing the Faith he professes, the Sacraments he receives, the holy temple he enters; for they are all symbols of Christian concord and charity. In the next world, too, divine justice is meted out most rigorously to those who neglect the giving of alms for the relief of the Suffering Souls. "For judgment without mercy to him that hath not done mercy." (*James* 2:13).

According to this declaration of the Holy Ghost, what kind of judgment must he expect, who from miserly greed permits the soul of a relative or benefactor to languish for months, years, perhaps for centuries in the horrible torments of Purgatory? Such persons sometimes receive just retribution even in this world. Father Rosignoli relates that a splendid farm was ruined by a terrific storm, while the adjoining fields were spared. A soul from Purgatory thereupon declared in an apparition, that the owners had been thus visited in punishment for their ingratitude toward their deceased parents. A soul appearing to a relative, thus addressed him: "Ungrateful nephew, you had no compassion for the soul of your uncle. Remember your promise, man with a heart harder than stone! In consequence of your faithlessness I had to suffer indescribable torments in Purgatory. Today I enter into the bliss of the Saints; but you shall die, and in retribution for your neglect the whole time I still owe shall be added to your term of suffering." A few days later the man died, and went to receive his sentence at the tribunal of God.

Not only the wealthy; but also the poor are able to give alms, if they only have the good will. The Angels sang at the birth of Our Saviour, "On earth peace to men of good will." (*Luke* 2:14). Hence many good Catholics combine and unite their savings for the purpose of procuring Masses for the repose of the souls of the faithful departed. And in order to assist these souls the more effectually, they direct their efforts also to the conversion of non-Catholics, in the hope that thereby the prayers for the relief of the Suffering Souls may be increased more and more. They have not the mission to preach the Gospel to the heathen and unbeliever, but they pray for the Suffering Souls; they contribute something every month to assist poor students preparing for the priesthood, or for the support of Catholic schools or missionaries, poor churches, orphan asylums and protectories, etc.—all this for the purpose that the Catholic Church may become known to and loved by all nations. By the prayers of these charitable souls Our Lord is implored to show mercy to the captives in Purgatory, to release them speedily, to bless the efforts of the missionaries, to grant the grace of conversion to all unbelievers, and to protect all the members of their union. Their motto is, "All for the greater glory of God and of His Saints, and for the relief of the Suffering Souls."

God often rewards even in this world these efforts for the relief of the Suffering Souls, and gives a hundred-fold increase to these little almsdeeds. The Rev. Father James Montford, of the Society of Jesus, born in England in 1605, wrote a remarkable work on Purgatory. In this work the author mentions that the following incident was revealed to him in a letter written by William Friesen, a printer of Cologne: "On a certain holyday, when my place of business was closed, I was occupying myself in reading the manuscript of your book on 'The Souls in Purgatory,' which you sent me to print. While absorbed in the perusal of your work, a messenger came and told me that my youngest child, aged four years, showed the symptoms of a very grave disease. The child rapidly grew worse, and the physicians at length declared that there was no hope for its recovery. The thought then occurred to me that I could save my child by making a vow to assist the Suffering Souls in Purgatory. Without delay I repaired to a chapel and with all fervor supplicated God to have pity on me; and I vowed that I would distribute gratuitously one hundred copies of the book that had awakened in me such a hearty sympathy for the Suffering Souls. I promised that I would give the books to ecclesiastics and religious, thereby to increase devotion to the Holy Souls. I acknowledge that I had hardly any hope. As soon as I returned to the house, I found the child much better. He asked for food, although for several days he had not been able to swallow anything but liquids. The next day he was perfectly well, got up and went out for a walk, and ate as if nothing had ever ailed him. Filled with gratitude I was anxious to fulfill my promise. I went to the College of the Jesuit Fathers and begged them to accept as many copies of the work as they pleased, and to distribute them among themselves and other communities and ecclesiastics as they saw fit, in order that my benefactors, the Suffering Souls, might be assisted by further prayers offered in their behalf.

"Three weeks had not passed by, however, when another accident quite as serious befell me. My wife, on entering the house one day, was suddenly seized with a trembling in all her limbs. She was thrown to the ground and remained lying there insensible. Little by little the illness increased until she was deprived of speech. Remedies seemed to be in vain. The malady at length assumed such aggravated proportions that everyone thought she had no chance whatever of recovery. The priest who assisted her had already addressed words of consolation to me, exhorting me to Christian resignation. I turned again with confidence to the souls in Purgatory, who had assisted me once before, and I went to the same church. There prostrate before the Blessed Sacrament I renewed my supplication with all the ardor with which affection for my family inspired me. This time I made a vow to distribute two hundred copies of the book, in order that a greater number of persons might be moved to intercede for the Suffering Souls. I besought those who had already been delivered from Purgatory to unite their prayers with mine on this occasion. After this prayer, as I was returning to the house, I saw my servants running toward me. They told me with delight that my wife had undergone a great change for the better; that the delirium had ceased and that she had recovered her power of speech. I hurried in at once to assure myself of the fact: all was true. Very soon my wife was so perfectly recovered that she came with me to church to make an act of thanksgiving to God for all His mercies. Your Reverence may confidently believe me: God is my witness that all happened just as I have related it to you."

God does not so much regard the amount of alms given as He does the heart of the one who gives it. The poor widow in the Gospel (*Luke* 21:2-4) was able to give only two mites; the good thief had nothing to give but the resolve of a true conversion. Yet both

were acceptable to God. Our charity must be commensurate with our means. "According to thy ability
be merciful. If thou have much give abundantly: if
thou have little, take care even so to bestow willingly
a little." (*Tob.* 4:8, 9). If this be our rule, our alms will
be acceptable to God; the mite of the poor will be of
greater value in His eyes than the abundance of the
rich. But the will alone is not sufficient when the
means of helping the Poor Souls are at our command.
"And if a brother or sister be naked, and want daily
food: and one of you say to them: Go in peace, be ye
warmed and filled; yet give them not those things that
are necessary for the body, what shall it profit?" (*James*
2:15, 16). To every such Christian St. Paul addresses
the following words of exhortation: "Let him labor,
working with his hands the thing which is good, that
he may have something to give to him that suffereth
need." (*Eph.* 4:28).

Good Christians feel within themselves an ardent
desire to relieve the suffering of the Poor Souls; and
therefore they will do all in their power to satisfy this
desire. They often make the greatest sacrifices for this
purpose; and if they find it impossible to give material aid, they at least devote a part of their time and
labor to this praiseworthy object. This can be done for
instance by exhorting others to this work of suffrage.
And the number of those who offer to God all their
labors, sufferings and good works for a more speedy
relief of the Suffering Souls is by no means small.

Charity sometimes impels a man to endanger his
life for the benefit of his fellow-man. The same may
be done to promote the spiritual life of our fellow-men.
St. Catherine of Siena implored God to permit the soul
of her father to enter Heaven without undergoing the
punishment of Purgatory. When the Supreme Judge
declared to her that it was indispensably necessary
that His Justice should be satisfied, she offered to bear
the full rigor of her father's punishment. Her offer was
accepted; and thenceforth her life was one of contin-

ued suffering and trial. Yet, so many persons think that a small sacrifice, a prayer of some months' or years' duration, a suffering patiently borne, the Holy Sacrifice offered up once in a while during the year, should suffice to release their dear ones from Purgatory. St. Catherine of Genoa says of herself, that she was permitted to suffer the torments of Purgatory for the space of two years—to suffer so much of these torments as it is possible for any mortal to endure. It may not be possible for us to do this. But if we only have the good will, we certainly can devote some time to prayer for the relief of the Holy Souls; or we can do something for the house of God, for the poor, etc., in this intention. This will be a most acceptable alms in aid of the Suffering Souls, and a consolation for them and us.

A soul from Purgatory revealed the following to St. Margaret of Cortona: "Did men but know from what great torments charity towards the poor delivers us, and what great treasure is contained therein, they would give everything they possess to the poor and for pious purposes to gain our prayers." For this reason we often witness that zealous Christians bequeath part or all of their estate to religious institutions, corporations, and for other pious purposes. St. Theresa relates that a benefactor of her convent was delivered from Purgatory on account of his liberality. The Lord said to her: "My daughter, his salvation was in great danger; but he found favor with me in return for the magnanimous donation he made to you. But his soul will not be released from Purgatory until after the first Mass shall have been celebrated in the new convent." At the Communion of this Mass the Saint saw the soul of her benefactor gloriously entering Heaven.

Others are filled with such compassion for the Suffering Souls, that they are not content with praying for them once in a while, but consecrate themselves entirely and unreservedly to God's service for this purpose, either retiring to a convent or devoting them-

selves to missionary labors. Between 1850 and 1860 a
religious congregation of women was founded, called
the "Helpers of the Holy Souls." Their object is to pray,
suffer and labor for the souls in Purgatory. On rising
in the morning their first aspiration is, "My Jesus,
mercy!" Thus they gain already at early dawn an indulgence of one hundred days for the Suffering Souls.
They repeat this ejaculation every time they make a
genuflection before the Blessed Sacrament, and, interiorly, whenever one member meets another. They end
all their prayers with the words, "Eternal rest grant
to them, O Lord, and let eternal light shine upon them,"
which ejaculation they repeat on many other occasions.
When the clock strikes the hour, they say, "O God, we
offer to Thee for the relief of the souls in Purgatory
all the acts of love by which the Sacred Heart of Jesus
glorified Thee at this hour during His sojourn on earth."
Every day they recite the Office of the Dead, and after
Mass they sing the *De profundis*. All their religious
exercises are offered up for the souls in Purgatory.

Another religious congregation devoted to the interest of the Church Militant and the Church Suffering
is that of the missionaries of the Most Precious Blood
of Our Lord, well known in Europe and America. In
the United States of North America this Congregation
numbers about one thousand members, eighty-five of
whom are priests. Its members are divided into three
classes—Priests, Lay-brothers and Sisters. In their convents, of which there are about twelve, the Sisters
practice the Perpetual Adoration of the Most Precious
Blood for the relief of the Suffering Souls. There is no
hour of the day when these good religious do not invoke
divine mercy. When they meet they salute one another,
saying: "Praise be to Jesus Christ!" and apply to the
Suffering Souls the indulgence granted for this aspiration. The Sisters receive Holy Communion every day,
except on the day of their confession, and on extraordinary occasions even then. The Brothers of this Congregation receive Holy Communion four times a week,

and on all intervening feasts. The whole community labors and prays for the relief of the Suffering Souls, for the propagation of the Faith, for the welfare of the Church and in honor of the Most Precious Blood. Before retiring for the night the members recite for the faithful the psalm *De profundis* together with the prayer of the Church that follows it. During the night they relieve one another from hour to hour in praying before the Blessed Sacrament. Thus do these religious, as well as the members of some other Orders, devote their lives to God for the benefit of the Suffering Souls.

To remove a scandal, to repair an injury, to pay debts, in a word to make good whatever the departed souls failed to settle before leaving this world—all of these are most meritorious works by which the punishment of Purgatory may be softened and abbreviated. To the Venerable Dominic of Jesus-Mary there appeared the soul of an artist who had to suffer for an immoral picture, until it was destroyed by the agency of Dominic. The soul of a citizen of Pampeluna appeared to the Venerable Frances of the Blessed Sacrament after being released through her efforts from a debt not yet paid at the time of his death. The Venerable Servant of God, Brother John de Via, a Franciscan, was admitted to Heaven only after his brethren had recited the Offices which he had omitted during life. Pope Benedict XIII relates that a husband appeared to his wife, thanking her for paying his debts and saying, "May God reward you for your charity. I was in bonds and torments until you paid what I owed." A curate in Baden had an apparition in which he saw the soul of the parish priest burning in Purgatory; and he was informed that to release the soul from its punishment it would be necessary to satisfy the obligation of saying thirty-five Masses, for which the priest had received the customary stipend without having had time before his death to say the Masses. The curate said the Masses, and the soul appeared to him no more.

In consequence of these and similar apparitions it

came to be believed that the souls are detained in Purgatory until restoration is made of their unjust gains, or the scandal given by them is repaired. Regarding this belief it must be remembered that by incurring such a guilt man commits sin, whereby he renders himself liable to punishment. This punishment, to be endured in this world or the next, is proportioned to the guilt incurred. As soon as divine justice is appeased by means of the punishment endured, the soul is admitted to Heaven; there is nothing to debar it. It may be that the goods unjustly acquired have not been restored, or the scandal given has not yet been repaired; but the soul is no longer able to mix in temporal concerns; therefore, the guilt incurred being atoned for, there is no longer any obstacle to its admission to Heaven. The time of atonement, however, can be shortened by the vicarious discharge of such liabilities. Hence Benedict XIII remarks: "It must by no means be inferred that souls, whose debts remain unpaid, will be detained in Purgatory until the debts are paid for them; but only that they are released more speedily by the adjustment of their liabilities through the charity of the living."

Offering Holy Communion for the Suffering Souls Is Most Beneficial to Them

We read in the Book of Esther that Aman had planned the destruction of the entire Jewish people. Queen Esther bethought herself of a means to placate the king and to save her people. "And on the third day Esther put on her royal apparel and stood in the inner court of the king's house, over against the king's hall. Now he sat upon the throne in the hall of the palace, over against the door of the house. And when he saw Esther the queen standing, she pleased his eyes, and he held out toward her the golden scepter which he held in his hand. And she drew near and kissed the top of the scepter. And the king said: What wilt thou, Queen Esther? what is thy request? If thou shouldst even ask one-half of the kingdom, it shall be given thee. And Esther answered: If I have found favor in thy sight, O king, and if it please thee, give me my life for which I ask, and my people for which I request." (*Esther* 7:3). She then recounted to the king the danger which threatened her people, the Jews, and implored his help, which was granted at once. The same may be done by every compassionate soul for the souls in Purgatory. When the Christian, with sentiments of profound humility and ardent devotion, approaches the Lord's table, there to renew the divine espousal by receiving Jesus in the Most Holy Eucharist—then is his most favorable opportunity to appease His justice and to come to the aid of the Suffering Souls. It is almost impossible that Our Lord in Holy Communion should refuse our petitions for the Sufferers in Purgatory.

A pious couple at Straubing, Bavaria, proposed to receive Holy Communion together on a certain Sunday and to offer it up for the souls in Purgatory. While they were talking over their pious resolve they heard a knock at the door, and a pitiful voice cried out, saying: "Remember me at the banquet." It was a soul from Purgatory who thus begged a share in the spiritual profit of Holy Communion. St. Gertrude experienced great happiness in being able to release so many souls from Purgatory; but her happiness was at its greatest height on Communion days. One day she asked Our Lord for the reason. He replied, "It is unseemly that I should refuse your prayer for the souls in Purgatory on those days when you are espoused to Me in Communion."

Can you doubt, Christian soul, that the frequent and worthy reception of Holy Communion is a most excellent means whereby you can pay off all your own indebtedness, and that thereby you can also most effectually help the Suffering Souls? Take heed, however, to observe that we do not refer merely to frequent Communion, but to frequent Communion after a good preparation. Beware of deceiving yourself; there is an immense difference between the two.

By frequent Communion is understood its reception three or four times a week, or even every day, or nearly every day. The receiving of Holy Communion on all Sundays and feasts of obligation, recommended by the Council of Trent to all the Faithful, cannot be called frequent Communion when reference is made to priests, religious, seminarians and such as devote themselves zealously to perfection; but regarding those who can devote only a small part of their time to exercises of piety, it is regarded as frequent Communion. On the other hand, the custom of receiving Holy Communion every month, and on all the higher feasts, is not frequent Communion. To be Christians, to remain united with God, we must receive Holy Communion. In this respect the soul is similar to the body. In order to live we must take food, but it is not the food that gives us life; it only nourishes the body, giving it that strength which we possess when we are in health. We eat not because we are strong, but to remain or become so. Now mark well: Holy Communion is not a reward for holiness already acquired, but a means for acquiring it. Therefore the Council of Trent expressly declares that "the faithful ought to receive Holy Communion not only spiritually, but sacramentally, as often as they assist at Mass, in order that they may more abundantly receive the fruit of this Holy Sacrifice." How dear to Our Saviour must those souls become who receive Him often and worthily in Holy Communion! And how numerous are the favors to be gained thereby for the benefit of the Suffering Souls!

In Luxemburg, on the Feast of All Saints, the departed Soul of a pious lady appeared to a devout girl to implore her aid. The girl was in the habit of receiving Holy Communion frequently, and as often as she did so this soul from Purgatory accompanied her. When asked for the reason, the reply was, "Oh, you do not know what a torment it is to be separated from God! It is impossible to describe it. I feel myself drawn irresistibly to God, but I must remain separated from Him in punishment for my sins. This is so painful to me, that I scarcely feel the fire by which I am surrounded. To relieve the intensity of my torments God permitted me to come to this church to adore Him at least in His house on earth, until I shall be found worthy to possess Him in Heaven." She then ardently implored the girl to receive Holy Communion frequently, and to remember her every time. The girl did so and was privileged after a time to see this soul, resplendent as the sun, entering Heaven.

When St. John the Baptist, "greater than whom none hath risen among them that are born of woman," was about to baptize the same Divine Saviour who is present in the Blessed Sacrament, he trembled and said, "I ought to be baptized by Thee, and comest Thou to me?" (*Matt.* 3:14). After the miraculous draught of fishes Peter deemed himself unworthy of the presence of Our Lord, and exclaimed, "Depart from me, for I am a sinful man, O Lord!" (*Luke* 5:8). The centurion, imploring Our Lord to heal his sick servant, said, "Lord, I am not worthy that Thou shouldst enter under my roof: but only say the word, and my servant shall be healed." (*Matt.* 8:8). And we, poor sinners, should we deem ourselves worthy of receiving in our heart this Supreme Lord of Heaven and earth? But though we are infinitely more unworthy than St. John, who dared not touch Him, than St. Peter, who deemed himself unworthy of His presence, than the centurion, who trembled to receive Him under his roof—it is nevertheless Our Saviour's desire that we should receive Him, and often too, in Holy Communion. It is entirely within our power to attain that sanctity which He requires for the reception of Holy Communion: the state of grace, together with the sincere will to avoid sin and to serve God faithfully. "Mortal sin alone," says St. Thomas, "is an obstacle to the reception of Holy Communion." And Suarez remarks, "It is not taught by a single holy Father that it is necessary to be in the state of perfection in order to receive Holy Communion worthily and with profit." Most assuredly we must strive to receive our God, the Most Pure and the Most Holy, as worthily as possible; and therefore we must prepare ourselves with the utmost zeal and conscientiousness for the reception of this Sacrament. Hence St. Bernard observes, "Take notice how prudent the serpent is. Before drinking it relieves itself of all poison. Follow its example; before you come to the fountain of life, that is, before you approach to be nourished with the flesh and blood of Our Lord Jesus Christ, relieve yourself from all venom of sin, especially of hatred, anger, envy, lust and sinful thoughts." Favored souls, after receiving Holy Communion for the relief of the souls in Purgatory, often beheld these happy spouses of Christ go forth into glory.

St. Bonaventure observes: "Let charity and compassion for your neighbors urge you on to approach the sacred table; for nothing is so effectual as Holy Communion to obtain relief for the Suffering Souls." Our propensity to sin ought not to deter us from partaking of this sacred banquet, which is the true preservative against Purgatory. If we have the misfortune of often falling into sin, let us frequently take the strongest antidote against this deadly venom; that is, let us often approach the holy table to obtain favors for the Suffering Souls. St. Augustine remarks, "You sin daily; then receive Holy Communion daily." The Suffering Souls are famished with desire for Holy Communion, and by receiving it for them we can refresh them, as the following example will show.

The Venerable Louis Blosius, this pious and learned writer, relates the following: A servant of God was favored with the apparition of a soul enveloped in flames and suffering great torments for lukewarmness at the reception of Holy Communion. This soul addressed the servant of God as follows: "I beseech you for the sake of the love we bore to each other, to have the charity to receive Holy Communion once in my favor; but do it with devout preparation and great fervor. For then I confidently hope to be released from the terrible torments to which I was sentenced because of my tepidity towards the Most Blessed Sacrament of the Eucharist." The saintly man complied with this request, and soon after saw the soul admitted to the beatific vision of the King of Glory.

According to the doctrine of the Council of Trent, Holy Communion may be received in a two-fold manner; first, sacramentally, by receiving the sacred species in the Holy Eucharist; secondly, spiritually, by exciting in ourselves a true sorrow for our sins, and an ardent desire for Holy Communion, thus uniting ourselves in a spiritual manner with our Divine Saviour.

The holy Fathers say of the exercise of spiritual communion, that if well made, it will benefit our souls almost as much as sacramental Communion. Hence we ought to be very solicitous to make the acts of spiritual communion often, particularly:

a) When assisting at Mass at the Communion of the priest. If we are unable to assist at Mass, let us include ourselves at morning prayers in all the Masses of the whole world, and offer them up to God for His honor, at the same time communicating spiritually.

b) When visiting the Blessed Sacrament. Had we been with the shepherds at Bethlehem, knowing that the Child in the manger was our Infinite and Almighty God dwelling among us in poverty and lowliness, we would have fallen on our knees to adore Our Lord and God. The same Redeemer who was laid in the manger is present day and night in the Blessed Sacrament enclosed in the tabernacle. Oh, let us not be remiss in visiting Him and receiving Him spiritually; we will thereby enrich ourselves and the Suffering Souls with abundant grace, help and joy.

c) In the evening, before retiring, we ought to examine our conscience, make an act of contrition for our sins, and again excite in us the desire of receiving Our Lord, recommending to His mercy the Suffering Souls.

God Himself deigned to indicate to pious souls how pleasing the practice of spiritual communion is to Him. Appearing to the Venerable Joanna of the Cross, Our Lord said to her, that as often as she made the act of spiritual communion, He favored her with grace similar to that she received in sacramental Communion. Blessed Angela was wont to say, "I could not have borne the trials of life if my confessor had not instructed me concerning spiritual communion." She made the act of spiritual communion one hundred times every day. Once, when St. Raymond celebrated Mass, and had proceeded as far as the Communion, St. Catherine of Siena, who was present, felt an ardent desire of receiving the Holy Eucharist. And behold! When St. Raymond broke the saved Host into three parts, the small Particle, which the rubrics direct to be placed in the chalice, all of a sudden vanished to the great consternation of the holy man. He diligently sought for it, and not finding it, he was overcome with a great fear of having offended God. St. Catherine observing this informed him that she had miraculously received the missing Particle in response to her ardent desire of receiving Our Lord. A pious religious, who on account of illness was not permitted to receive Holy Communion, begged so persistently that the Blessed Sacrament, enveloped in the *corporale*, might be placed on his breast, that it was finally done. This ardent desire so pleased Our Lord, that He permitted the sacred Host to penetrate to his heart and the good religious thus received sacramental Communion in a miraculous manner.

Considering all this, should you not, Christian soul, often approach the holy table to receive worthily the Flesh and Blood of Our Lord? Or at least should you not often make the acts of spiritual communion? This is the Will of God, the desire of the Church. By so doing you will greatly benefit your own soul and bring consolation to the Sufferers in Purgatory.

The State of Grace Is Necessary to Make Good Works Profitable to the Suffering Souls

What is necessary on the part of the Suffering Souls to obtain the effects of our suffrages? The answer is easy. They are confirmed in grace and sanctity, and are at the same time united with the faithful on earth in faith and charity. As they still have to suffer temporal punishment which they cannot mitigate or shorten by their own merits, they stand in need of the atoning works of the Faithful on earth. If they receive no help from them, they must continue to suffer till the last farthing is paid. The disposition they showed during their life in this world exerts great influence on God in permitting them to experience the relief of vicarious atonement. Want of compassion and hardness of heart displease God. He punishes the Suffering Souls for this by depriving them of the works of atonement— the prayers, good works and Holy Masses—offered up for them by their brethren on earth. Thus teaches the learned Cajetan, and with him agree Thomas á Kempis, Hugh of St. Victor and other divines. On the other hand, those Christians who mercifully and compassionately come to the relief of these suffering, yet most worthy souls, by performing for their benefit all kinds of good works, may rest assured that God is supremely pleased therewith; and He will permit such souls in their turn, when in Purgatory, to receive speedily the benefit of the good works performed for them by the members of the Church Militant. This we know from many private revelations. Sister Frances of the Blessed Sacrament was often visited by souls bringing tidings of others that were not permitted to appear to her. One day a deceased Sister asked her prayers for four others who were not permitted to leave Purgatory. Another soul, in 1870, even refused to answer questions concerning certain deceased persons, because God did not permit it.

On the part of the faithful the following conditions

must be observed in order that their suffrages for the
Suffering Souls may be accepted by God:

a) They must have the intention of resigning the merits of their good works in favor of the Suffering Souls.
The fruit accruing from our good works remains our
property as long as we do not cede it to some other
person. Our intention may specify a particular soul to
whom we desire to apply our suffrages. If the soul for
which we supplicate is already in Heaven or in Hell,
God will give the benefit of our intercession to some
other soul according to the pleasure of His wisdom,
mercy and justice. If the works of suffrage are offered
for the relief of the Suffering Souls in general, the satisfactory fruit thereof is divided among them all.

b) The work performed must be one of atonement.
All good works are such; but they are not all equally
valuable as atonement. Their atoning value depends
either on the disposition of the person performing them;
or it may be inherent in the works themselves, as for
instance Holy Mass, indulgences and the prayers of the
Church.

c) According to the unanimous doctrine of all theologians, the good works, to be effective, must be performed in the state of grace. Nevertheless there is no
doubt that the atoning effect of such good works as
possess atoning power of themselves, are of benefit to
the Suffering Souls even though they be performed in
the state of sin; such works are for instance Holy Mass,
the personal or local plenary indulgence of a privileged
altar, the prayers and blessings of the Church.

The Suffering Souls receive no benefit of a good work
performed in the state of sin, when the value of this
work requires it to be performed in the state of grace.
If in such a case the petition of a sinner is granted,
this is not done because the work itself was worthy of
the favor, but solely and purely as a result of God's
mercy. But if the sinner acts as the minister of the
Church, or in the name of one actually in the state of
grace, then the good work has the same value that it

would have if the one ordering it had done the work himself. Thus teaches the Angelic Doctor, St. Thomas.

St. Chrysostom reminds us: "Of what benefit is your excessive weeping? Not tears, but good works aid the deceased." Charity is inventive; and, Christian soul, the true Follower of Christ is all charity. Mindful of the departed, he therefore says, "I will make good the deficiencies of the Suffering Souls." But sometimes our excessive love for the deceased prevents us from using the right means at the proper time. We do not reflect on the condition of our own soul, we do not examine our state of conscience before God, but are only concerned at the sufferings of our brethren and friends. We perform our good works too hastily, without first offering to God an humble and contrite heart; and thereby we expose them to the danger of being rejected. God will not despise an humble and contrite heart. In the holy Sacraments He has provided us with the means of acquiring such a disposition of heart. True contrition and the firm resolution of making use of this means will place us in a condition to render our good works and prayers acceptable to God. And if we receive the Sacraments in this spirit, Jesus Himself will be our intercessor with His Heavenly Father. Hence the words of the elder Tobias are applicable also to us, "Lay out thy bread, and thy wine upon the burial of a just man, and do not eat and drink thereof with the wicked." (*Tob.* 4:18).

A dying father entreated his son to remember him frequently after death. The son did so, praying often and performing many other good works for him. But after thirty-three years his father appeared to him surrounded by flames and complained bitterly that he had neglected for so long a time to come to his relief. "Is it possible," inquired the son in great consternation, "that all my prayers, alms, etc., have availed nothing for your relief?" "Know, my son," replied his father, "that all the good works you have hitherto performed were fruitless both for you and me, because you performed them in the state of mortal sin. Your Confessions were null and void, because you had no true contrition for your sins. Our Lord in His mercy permitted me to inform you of this for your own benefit and mine." The son was converted, made a sincere and contrite Confession, and was soon informed of the release of his father. "A contrite and humbled heart, O God, Thou wilt not despise." (*Ps.* 50:19). "God resisteth the proud, but to the humble He giveth grace." (*1 Ptr.* 5:5).

The Holy Sacrifice of Mass Is the Most Powerful Means of Aiding the Suffering Souls

The Holy Sacrifice of Mass has always been considered by the Church to be the most effective means of releasing the souls of the faithful departed from their torments. "Although we are sinners," says St. Cyrillus, "we nevertheless send up our supplications to God for the departed, not offering Him for instance a crown, but Jesus Christ Himself, who bled for our sins, and beseeching the bountiful and gracious God to be merciful to them and to us. We pray for all that have departed this life, because we confidently believe that the prayer at the altar will be most profitable to them." Although Holy Mass is the most powerful Sacrifice of propitiation, it is to be feared that it is not sufficiently appreciated by the faithful. The truth of this remark is evidenced by the negligence of so many in frequently and devoutly assisting at Mass, and by the deplorable fact that so many Catholics are remiss in having Masses celebrated for their deceased. A great many count those hours that they spend in assisting at Mass as lost and unprofitable. Others excuse themselves with the want of means, saying they cannot afford to give the customary stipend for a Mass. If they would but reflect on the real essence of the Most Holy Sacrifice and on the futility of their excuses, they would soon be convinced how grossly they deceive themselves.

Death has entered our home and claimed a victim.

A beloved father, a dear mother, an obedient son, a dutiful daughter, a near relative, a dear friend has departed this life after an illness of days, weeks, months or years. During this time we did our utmost to afford them every relief in our power. But now, after they have departed this life, now, when they are suffering the indescribable torments of Purgatory, we scarcely find time to pray for the repose of their souls. To spend a short time in the morning assisting at Mass for their benefit and to appeal to Heaven for their relief and ransom, for our own benefit and the greater glory of God—for this we have no time! Our dear ones are scarcely out of sight, and already we begin to forget them. We have time to speculate and labor for our advancement in this world, to promote our welfare, to add to our wealth, to enjoy pleasures of every kind— but the souls of our departed dear ones are forgotten for the very reason, because amid all these engagements we find no time to remember them in prayer and in the Holy Sacrifice. No time for prayer? No time to show yourself a Christian? No time to assist at the august Sacrifice of Holy Mass?! And yet there is no service of the Church more pleasing to our Divine Lord, no act more profitable to us and the Suffering Souls, than Holy Mass. All works of piety and charity are profitable to us and valuable in the sight of God; nevertheless they are human acts, and therefore full of imperfections. Holy Mass however is not a human act, but a Divine Sacrifice offered by the great Highpriest Jesus Christ Himself to the Most Holy and Adorable Trinity. This Holy Sacrifice is the most efficient means of procuring the speedy release of the departed souls; and we, who claim to be Christians, have no time to assist at it!

Livius relates that in the year 360 before Christ an immense abyss opened in Rome. Venomous vapors ascended from it and soon caused a great mortality, so that the city was threatened with destruction. To save it a young patrician offered himself in sacrifice. He bestrode his richly caparisoned steed and plunged into the mysterious depth which immediately closed over him. A heathen sacrifices his life for his fellow citizens—and Christians do not even find time to devote a half hour to the relief of their suffering brethren! When St. Louis, King of France, was informed that some of his courtiers murmured because he spent so much time in assisting at Mass, he rejoined: "If I should devote double the time to play and amusements, nobody would say a word." Christian soul, can you not devote as much time to Holy Mass as you do to play and amusements? Do not excuse yourself with want of time. Blessed Thomas More, Lord Chancellor of England, was overburdened with work, and yet he served at Mass every morning before entering on the duties of the day. Our Lord promised to St. Gertrude, "At the hour of death I will send to everyone so many saints to console and assist him, as he devoutly heard Holy Masses during his life." And we dare to call it unprofitable to assist at Holy Mass? We have no time for this Divine Sacrifice? Rather let us say we have no true conception of our holy religion, no compassion for the dead.

It is then greatly to be feared, that Holy Mass is not duly appreciated by a large number of the Faithful, despite its being the most precious treasure in the world; and as a consequence this Holy Sacrifice is not offered up in suffrage for the departed as frequently as it should be. It is greatly to be deplored that this treasure, by which we are able to quench the flames of Purgatory, is so to say hidden in the earth for many, and appreciated only by a few. Seemingly, poverty is the reason that so few Masses are offered for the faithful departed; but this excuse in many cases is a very flimsy one, for experience proves that it is not consonant with truth. Many of those who show great zeal in having Masses celebrated for the faithful departed are less blessed with the goods of this world, than many that neglect to do so. Many also, who excuse themselves with poverty, spend more for useless, if not sinful extravagancies, than would be sufficient to have a Mass said often during the year. This is particularly the case at funerals, when a great sum is spent for vain display, while the soul of the departed is forgotten, and even the ministers of the Church whose services were engaged are defrauded under pretense of poverty.

Another reason why so few Masses are ordered for the deliverance of the faithful departed is to be found in the silence observed on this subject in sermons. It is not our affair, nor do we intend to criticize the action of zealous pastors. They well know that the world has little intelligence for things divine, and therefore accuses the ministers of God of selfishness when they refer zealously and frequently to the subject of having Masses celebrated for the dead. It is an old practice of the enemies of the Church to call the alms fixed by ecclesiastical law as a condition for gaining an indulgence a barter; and they do the same with regard to the stipend fixed for the celebration of a Mass according to one's intention. To govern her actions the Church was never yet in need of the enemy's counsel. As early as in the apostolic age she condemned the barter of things spiritual for things temporal. "Keep thy money to thyself, to perish with thee," said St. Peter to Simon Magus; and he gives the reason for this severe reproof in the following words, "Because thou hast thought that the gift of God may be purchased with money." (*Acts* 8:20). The Church at all times condemned the practice of degrading her spiritual ministrations by even the semblance of venality. True, she permits her ministers to receive a fixed stipend for their spiritual ministrations; but at the same time she enjoins it on them most rigorously to abstain from all appearance of striving after worldly gain. The Council of Trent, renewing the former strict laws in this regard, ordains the following: "With regard to avarice, let the bishops forbid entirely every species of contract and stipulation concerning the obligation of Masses; also importunate and unseemly claims or rather exactions of alms and the like, savoring of the pest of simony or of sordid gain."

The strict injunctions of the Church, and the prejudices of a great number of the faithful, cause many zealous priests to observe silence concerning the obligation of having Masses celebrated for the deceased. They wish to avoid even the semblance of seeking their own profit, and therefore omit entirely the instructions that ought to be given on this important duty; for they speak of it but seldom or only in a general way. Praiseworthy as this may be in itself, it is a source of great spiritual damage to the faithful, living and dead. Hence zealous pastors do themselves, what they hesitate to recommend to their parishioners. They offer up for the faithful departed all the Masses not ordered for a particular intention. In 1869 a young priest accompanied his bishop to Rome. In a conversation the latter asked him whether in his daily Mass he also remembered the faithful departed in general and his friends in particular. The priest replied, "Certainly I remember my departed friends very often." The saintly bishop continued, "I did the same when I was a young priest. Once I fell sick and became so dangerously ill, that my life was despaired of. I received the Sacraments of the dying; and while preparing for death, I reviewed my whole life with all its faults of commission and omission. I became aware how much I had still to atone for, and pondered how few Masses and prayers would be said for me after death. Since my recovery I have made it a practice to be very assiduous in saying Masses for the Suffering Souls; and I rejoice every time I am able to do so." Christian soul, this is the disposition of every zealous priest; but many of them scruple at inviting the faithful to do what they themselves are so anxious to perform.

On the one hand a pious priest is most reluctant to exhort his people to anything in which he might seem to strive for his own temporal interest; on the other he is convinced that very many even among the more religiously inclined regard him as actuated by self-interest, every time he is obliged—and he cannot escape the necessity of doing so at least now and then—to mention money matters. It is obvious that the Masses which the faithful are exhorted to have said must be celebrated by a priest, and that he is entitled to the stipend. Hence there are many who imagine and even say that he speaks in his own interest, when he discourses on the benefits accruing to the Suffering Souls from the Holy Sacrifice of Mass. In doing so they make themselves guilty of a species of sacrilege; they impede the priest in the discharge of his duty as teacher of religion; they deprive the souls in Purgatory of relief and deliverance from their torments, and God of the glory and adoration which He would have received by their more speedy release. And, as a consequence of this want of charity, the pastors speak only in general on prayer for the Suffering Souls, and leave it to their hearers to draw inferences according to the greater or less degree of their piety.

Nevertheless there are also very good Christians who regard this matter in the spirit of the Church. In 1885 a newly ordained priest was appointed to the charge of Ph. in the State of Ohio. It was customary in this congregation to take up a collection on All Souls' Day for Masses to be celebrated for the faithful departed, and this was usually announced on the preceding Sunday with an appropriate exhortation. The young priest, reluctant to make the announcement, omitted the customary exhortation. A good old lady, fearing that the Suffering Souls would be deprived of the usual suffrages by the action of the priest, went to the sacristy after Mass, and begged to remind him of the omission. "I think I discern your motive, your reverence," she said, "You did not omit the exhortation from forgetfulness, but feared to scandalize the congregation. Now please do not let this consideration influence you. We know our religion better. A short exhortation will be of great benefit to the Suffering Souls. Therefore do not let your sense of propriety cause you to deprive the faithful departed of a speedy release."—By this incident the priest was taught to regard in future rather the interests of religion than considerations of popular favor.

O poor Suffering Souls! They that loved you in life might easily come to your aid; but they neglect to do so either from want of knowledge or of faith. Poor Sufferers in Purgatory! Your friends lavishly spend money on their mortal bodies, devoting themselves to pleasure and business, and excusing their heartless disregard of you with the flimsy declaration that your position cannot be so very distressing, because they always knew you to be righteous during your mortal career. O love devoid of charity, how long and painfully will you permit your dear ones to suffer in Purgatory?

Value and Importance of Holy Mass for the Release of the Suffering Souls

In our mortal state we are unable to comprehend the torments of the Suffering Souls; but the time may come when we shall be taught their intensity by our own dreadful experience. Hitherto, we have heard the doctrine of the Church, of the holy Fathers, and of theologians in general concerning Purgatory; we have seen that many souls had to suffer long for a venial fault, and that even Saints did not escape the purifying flames. The Venerable Catherine Palluzzi continued for a long time to offer up with great solicitude all her good works for the repose of the soul of her deceased father. Finally she thought she might cease her supplications, when Our Lord and St. Catherine appeared to her and conducted her to Purgatory, where to her great astonishment she beheld her father in the midst of a fiery lake, imploring her for help. She nearly fainted from compassion, and called on St. Catherine to aid him by her prayers. Then she turned to Our Lord Himself, saying, "I beseech Thee to impose my father's debt on me. I am ready to bear whatever Thou wilt impose on me to make atonement in his stead." In consequence of this magnanimous offer her father was released immediately, but she had to undergo great sufferings.

We firmly believe that our prayer, and still more the prayer and suffrages of the Blessed Virgin Mary and the Saints bring relief to the Suffering Souls. But what is the prayer of Heaven and earth compared with Holy Mass? In prayer a creature intercedes for a creature; in Holy Mass Jesus Christ, eternal God like His Father, makes intercession for us. Speaking of the value of this Holy Sacrifice, St. Alphonsus Liguori says, "As the Passion of Our Lord Jesus Christ was more than sufficiently powerful to redeem the whole world, so also is one Holy Mass powerful enough to save it." We have recourse to Holy Mass not for the purpose of renewing the redemption of the world, but to procure for the souls confirmed in grace the treasures of redemption. This august Sacrifice is undoubtedly the most powerful means to release the Holy Souls from their place of torment. This is solemnly declared by the Council of Trent, saying, "The œcumenical Council teaches that there is a Purgatory, and that the souls confined therein are assisted by the suffrages of the faithful, and especially by the Holy Sacrifice of the altar." St. Thomas Aquinas teaches, "There is no sacrifice by which souls are released from Purgatory, except the Holy Sacrifice of Mass."

By Holy Mass sufficient payment is offered to our Heavenly Father to cancel the indebtedness of the departed. Every soul in Purgatory is an elect child of God, confirmed in His grace and love; for every one became reconciled to Him by contrition, Confession and penance. But as they have not rendered sufficient satisfaction for all temporal punishments, they must suffer the penalty now. They incurred punishment by small daily offenses and faults, and are detained in prison for the purpose of purification. Our Lord warns us to beware of this prison from which we shall not be released until we shall have paid the last farthing. A just judge will scarcely release a prisoner who is confined on account of debt merely because he is implored to do so; but if the debt is canceled by vicarious payment, he will free the prisoner. The Suffering Souls, beloved spouses of Christ, writhing in excruciating torments, are unable as yet to attend the wedding feast already prepared for them, because the infinite justice and holiness of God demand a ransom. In the Holy Sacrifice of Mass our Divine Saviour offers Himself in ransom, and hence the holy Fathers teach that, "many souls go forth from Purgatory every time that Mass is celebrated."

St. Chrysostom says, "As often as Holy Mass is celebrated, the Angels of Heaven hasten to open the prison of Purgatory." In this august Sacrifice the Body and Blood of Jesus Christ, this infinite treasure of satisfaction, is offered to the Heavenly Father for the living and the dead. The Suffering Souls themselves have repeatedly given testimony of this. Thus we read that in the time of St. Bernard a deceased religious of Clairvaux appeared to his brethren, thanking them for having released him from a long Purgatory. When asked what had brought him the greatest relief in his torments, he pointed to the altars, saying, "Behold, there are the weapons of divine grace by which I was released. There is shown the power of divine mercy—in the saving Sacrifice of the Victim that taketh away the sins of the world." Convinced of this truth the Venerable Curé D'Ars one day addressed his hearers as follows: "Dear children, you remember the occurrence which I related to you of a saintly priest who prayed for a deceased friend. Very probably God revealed to him that his friend was suffering great torments in Purgatory. Knowing that there is nothing more effective to procure the repose of a soul than the celebration of Holy Mass, he proceeded to do so as soon as possible. Before consecration he took the host into his hands and addressed God with childlike confidence thus: 'Holy and Eternal Father, let us make an exchange. Thou dost hold captive the soul of my friend, and I have the power of changing this bread into the real Body of Thy Divine Son. Now, do Thou release my friend from Purgatory, and I will make to Thee an offering of Thy Divine Son, with all the merits of His Passion and death.' And behold, after Consecration, when elevating the sacred Host, he saw the soul of his friend surrounded with glory entering Heaven."

This saintly priest was well aware of the value of Holy Mass, this inestimable treasure of the Church, and acted most wisely in having recourse to this august Sacrifice rather than to other suffrages. St. Lawrence Justinian observes that one Holy Mass is to be deemed more valuable than all the penitential exercises of the whole world. He says, "Take the scales and place on one balance all the good works, viz., prayer, night-watches, fasting, almsdeeds, mortifications, pilgrimages, etc., and on the other only a single Mass, and you will find that the value of the one cannot be compared with that of the others; for in Holy Mass He is offered in whom dwells bodily the plenitude of divinity, as St. Paul observes, who possesses an immense treasury of merit, and whose intercession is all-powerful." The blood of Abel cried to Heaven for vengeance, but the Blood of Christ cries for pardon. We have a type of this in the Old Law, where almost all the sacrifices were offered in blood, as St. Paul says, "For if the blood of goats and of oxen, and the ashes of a heifer being sprinkled, sanctify such as are defiled, to the cleansing of the flesh: how much more shall the Blood of Christ, who by the Holy Ghost offered Himself unspotted unto God, cleanse our conscience from dead works, to serve the living God? And therefore He is the mediator of the New Testament." (*Heb.* 9:13-15). And the prophet Zacharias says, "Thou also, by the blood of Thy testament, hast sent forth thy prisoners out of the pit." (*Zach.* 9:11). And in Holy Mass this Blood still releases the prisoners from Purgatory.

Blessed Henry Suso made a compact with a brother

priest that if one of them would die, the other should for a year say two Masses a week for the deceased. When after a few years his friend died, Suso prayed most fervently for him every day, adding fasts and exercises of penance; but it was impossible for him at the time to say the promised Masses. After some days the deceased appeared to him with a sorrowful countenance and reprehended him sharply, saying, "Faithless friend, do you thus keep your promise?" Suso called his attention to the fervent prayer and numerous penitential works which he had offered up for him. The deceased replied, "Your prayer, though pleasing to God, is not powerful enough to release me from my torments." And striking the table before him with his hand, he cried out, "Blood! Blood! Blood is what we Suffering Souls stand in need of! The Blood of Jesus Christ which is offered up for us in Holy Mass is what will deliver us from our torments. If you had said the promised Masses I should already have been released from my fiery prison. It is your fault that I must still burn. Let me have the Masses, the Masses you have promised me!"

Christian soul! Let this cry of the Suffering Souls for the Blood of Jesus find a willing ear with you. Hasten to come to their aid by means of the Holy Sacrifice of the Mass. If we could but see with our mortal eyes how profitable and valuable a ransom Holy Mass is for the Suffering Souls, we would not refuse to have this Adorable Sacrifice offered up for their relief. But if you are not able to order a Mass for them, you can at least assist at Mass for this intention and influence others to do the same. Once, when a poor widow complained to a saintly priest that she was unable to have Masses said for her deceased husband, he counselled her as follows: "Then assist at as many Masses as you can, and offer them for the soul of your husband; for he will find relief more speedily by having many Masses heard for him, than by having only a few offered up for the same intention." This is a great consolation; for though it is more to have a Mass said than to assist at one, it is nevertheless a special comfort for the Suffering Souls if we offer up for them the Masses which we attend, and thus pour out upon them the Sacred Blood of Jesus. St. Jerome remarks on this subject, "The souls in Purgatory, for whom the priest celebrates Mass while the faithful offer up their prayers, are free from pain during the time Mass is said for them."

Mass Is the Renewal of the Sacrifice Of the Cross for the Consolation of the Suffering Souls

Holy Mass, celebrated with becoming faith and devotion, is the most sublime Sacrifice, and nothing in the world can equal in value this service of God. In the New Testament we have only one sacrifice, namely that sacrifice which was offered by Christ on the Cross for our redemption, the fruits of which are transmitted to us in Holy Mass. By His Sacrifice on the Cross Jesus Christ redeemed all mankind; by it everybody was made capable of participating in the merits of His Passion and death, and of receiving the grace thereby obtained for us. But how is this to be accomplished? To rational beings whose perceptions depend on their senses, an external, visible action is most suited for this purpose; and therefore the Holy Sacrifice of Mass was instituted. In it the bloody Sacrifice of Jesus Christ is renewed in an unbloody manner; in it Jesus Christ sacrifices Himself mysteriously. Whosoever is present at this Sacrifice stands as it were beneath the Cross of Christ; he is a witness of the sufferings and death of his Redeemer, and has full opportunity to participate in the merits of Jesus, and to offer himself and his whole being for God's greater glory in this world and in the next.

Holy Mass is essentially the same Sacrifice as that once offered on the Cross. Hence the Council of Trent declares: "In this Divine Sacrifice of the Mass there is contained the same Christ who offered Himself on the Cross in a bloody manner, the only difference being that in Mass He offers Himself in an unbloody manner." If we had no other declaration but this it should suffice to remove all doubt. For we must receive as infallibly true whatever the Catholic Church teaches and proposes to our belief, and we are not allowed to contradict it in the least. To prove that Holy Mass is essentially the same Sacrifice as that of the Cross, the Church adds the following declaration to the words quoted above: "For it is the same Victim, and the same Minister of sacrifice through the agency of the priest, who once offered the Sacrifice on the altar of the Cross; only the manner of sacrificing is different." This Sacrifice is not only a sacrifice of praise, but the Church regards it also as "a sacrifice of Propitiation for the living and dead." And hence she has at all times offered it also for the aid and consolation of the souls of the faithful departed.

By the sin of our first parents our Heavenly Father was so greatly offended, that the whole human race was sentenced to eternal perdition. The Son of God, knowing that only a victim of infinite merit could reconcile His Father, and moved by compassion for fallen mankind, resolved to offer Him such a victim. And this victim was no other than Himself. Behold, O Christian soul, the love of your Redeemer! The Son of God offers Himself as a Sacrifice of propitiation to the Eternal Father, and the Father accepts this Sacrifice from the hands of His Son, who "humbled Himself, becoming obedient unto death, even to the death of the cross." (*Phil.* 2:8). "He was offered because it was His own Will." (*Is.* 53:7). In order to accomplish this sacrifice, the Son of God became man and died to prove His infinite love for us. He concealed His divinity by taking to Himself a human body, in which He suffered the ignominious death on the Cross at the hands of His executioners. God permitted this and Jesus thus willed it for the sake of our redemption. He willed not the sin of those who clamored for His death, but it was His Will to die for us on the Cross. The sins of His executioners did not in the least detract from the infinite value of the Sacrifice of the divine Victim. "He was offered because it was His own Will."

God might have commissioned His priests to offer this sacrifice, as He commanded Abraham in the Old Law, "Take thy only begotten son Isaac, whom thou lovest, and go into the land of vision: and there thou shalt offer him for an holocaust upon one of the mountains which I will show thee." (*Gen.* 22:2). But He left it to His Divine Son to institute a ministry for the oblation of the unbloody Sacrifice, and He did institute it at the Last Supper with the words, "Do this for a commemoration of me." (*Luke* 22:19). In the Holy Scripture Christ is called "a priest forever according to the order of Melchisedech." (*Ps.* 109:4). From this it is evident that Christ, as "a priest forever," is to offer the Sacrifice not once, but repeatedly, "forever." Once He was both the Victim and the Minister of the Sacrifice on the Cross through the instrumentality of His executioners; but forever He is the Victim and the Minister of the Sacrifice on the altar through the instrumentality of His priests. And this is done because it is His Will that the living and the dead should participate in His merits.

To facilitate the offering of this Sacrifice He performed His greatest miracle: He hid both His divinity and humanity under the form of bread and wine, just as He had hidden His divinity by assuming a human body in which to suffer and to die. The first unbloody Sacrifice, which Jesus offered in the presence of His Apostles at the Last Supper, was not a mere type of the bloody Sacrifice which He accomplished the next day on the Cross, but it was the same Sacrifice; it was the same essence of His flesh and blood, of His divinity and humanity, only in a different form, under the appearance of bread and wine; it was the institution of the Sacrifice in the form in which it was to be offered to His Heavenly Father by the ministers of His Church until the end of time.

It is well known that the propitiatory sacrifices of the Old Law were accompanied by repasts. These were intended to symbolize the participation of the people in the sacrifices offered, and to signify in an impressive manner the reconciliation and renewal of friendship with God effected by means of the sacrifices. Our Divine Lord wished to retain this feature in His Sacrifice on the Cross as well as in that of the altar. Hence He Himself partook of the Last Supper with His Apostles and expressed His Will that they should follow His example; that is, they should permit the Faithful to partake of the Sacrifice as they had partaken of it with Him. This He commanded them to do by the significant words, "Do this for a commemoration of me."

St. Augustine calls the Holy Sacrifice of Mass "the sacrament of love, the revelation of unity, the bond of most intimate friendship." He remarks, "Christ was slain but once as the Victim of sacrifice, yet He is offered up for the people every day in the Sacrament or in Holy Mass." And St. Cyprian declares, "The passion of Christ is the Sacrifice which we offer." Thomas á Kempis says in the *Imitation of Christ*, "When saying Mass or assisting at it, this ought to seem to you so great, so new and joyful, as if Christ had just on this very day descended into the virginal womb of Mary to become man." O high dignity of Catholics, for whose salvation Christ every day renews His Incarnation in a spiritual manner! O great love for us poor sinners!

Not only for the living however, but also for the faithful departed does Christ grant His aid in Holy Mass. Though dissenters presume to deny this consoling truth, we are nevertheless assured of it by our infallible Church. Hence St. Chrysostom exclaims, "By no means do we celebrate the august Mysteries of the altar in vain; and not in vain and without fruit are our prayers."

Convincing as are the testimonials of the Church, of the Councils and the holy Fathers concerning the doctrine that Holy Mass is the renewal of the Sacrifice of the Cross on the altars of the New Law, our Divine

Saviour does not confine Himself to their authority, but confirms this truth again and again by miracles. For our Saviour is not compelled to retain the form in which it is His Will to appear in Holy Mass. It sometimes happens that He lays aside the form of bread and appears in the form of a child, of a man, or of blood, in order thereby to confirm or propagate the true Faith by a new miracle. For the twelfth time during Lent had Charlemagne advanced with his army against the Saxons to conquer them and have them converted to the Christian Faith. When Easter approached, he commanded his entire army to prepare with due devotion for the reception of the Sacraments on that feast. In order to witness the Christian service, Wittekind, duke of Saxony, disguised himself as a beggar and secretly entered the enemy's camp. He assisted at Mass, and was greatly impressed by the devotion of the Christian soldiers. He paid close attention to the celebrant, to whom all eyes were directed. At the Consecration he saw to his great astonishment a most beautiful little child in the hands of the priest; and at the same moment he felt his heart moved by a joy never experienced before. He now kept his eyes on the priest; and he saw that at Holy Communion the priest presented such a child to every communicant. To his further astonishment he beheld the child coming to some with all the indications of joy, to others with great reluctance. Later he related his experience to Charlemagne and asked for an explanation. On receiving it he was so affected that he asked for Baptism; and he took some priests with him to Saxony to convert the country.

A celebrated historian, a Benedictine of Monte Cassino, relates a remarkable occurrence in the life of St. Gregory the Great. A noble Roman matron had from devotion taken upon herself the task of preparing the altar breads and of bringing them to Church on Sundays. Once, when approaching with others to receive Holy Communion from the hands of the Pope, she began to laugh just as he was about to give her the Consecrated

Host with the words, "May the body of Our Lord Jesus Christ preserve thy soul unto life everlasting." The holy Pontiff withdrew the sacred Particle and placed It aside on the altar, where he stationed a deacon to guard It. After Mass the Pope questioned the matron about her unseemly behavior. She replied that she had laughed because the Pope had called the altar bread which she had baked herself the body of Our Lord. The Pope informed the assembled congregation of it, and exhorted the people to prayer. All present fell on their knees with him; and when he arose after some time and spread out the *corporale* in which the Consecrated Particle had been folded, his fingers were stained with blood miraculously exuding from It. The whole congregation thronged about him to view the miracle. Prayer was then resumed, and the sacred Host resumed its former appearance.

Now if God, for the sake of this mysterious Sacrifice, lifted the veil of unbelief from the souls of Wittekind and the Roman matron in so miraculous a manner, how much the more may we hope that He will disrupt the bonds of the Suffering Souls whom He loves so dearly! For we have already learned that this Holy Sacrifice is offered up not only for the living, but also for the dead. Who is able to describe how the Suffering Souls yearn for this Holy Sacrifice? St. Bernard relates that St. Malachy, Archbishop of Armagh in Ireland, had celebrated Mass for a long time for his deceased sister. Finally he ceased to do so. After thirty days he one night heard his sister's mournful voice telling him that she had waited for thirty days in the vestibule of the church for his help, but had received none. Then she appeared to him at the church door clothed in mourning. When he celebrated Mass for her again, he saw her inside the church, but still wearing a dark dress. He continued to offer the Holy Sacrifice for her every day until he saw her going to Heaven in great splendor in company with a great number of other released souls.

Holy Mass Is Essentially a Propitiatory Sacrifice for the Faithful Departed

Christian artists have illustrated very beautifully an idea of the holy Fathers, representing the Angels as gathering in golden vases the Most Precious Blood of Jesus Christ during its presence on the altar, and pouring it as a refreshing dew into the flames of Purgatory. By the power of this Blood numbers of souls are purified and then soar up into the realms of eternal bliss. By His Precious Blood our Saviour restored the honor of His Heavenly Father and brought redemption and salvation to mankind. In virtue of His divinity it was of infinite value and atoned for our guilt, immense as it was. The bond of charity, sanctified in this Blood, now bind us more intimately to God than before. The souls in Purgatory are souls ransomed and purified in the Precious Blood of Jesus Christ and bearing the indelible mark of His grace, souls for whom the Supreme Judge has already prepared the immortal crown of victory. The whole mystical body of Christ, the Catholic Church in all her three branches, is quickened and penetrated, sanctified and kept united with God by the all-pervading, supernatural power of the Most Precious Blood of Jesus Christ. This Blood is still being shed every moment on the altars of the New Dispensation; it is still being offered in Holy Mass for the benefit of both the living and the dead. Who, then, can doubt that the Suffering Souls in Purgatory receive consolation from this sacred oblation?

The Holy Sacrifice of Mass is a propitiation and atonement, in virtue of its very nature and by the ordinance of Christ. The Council of Trent teaches: "The Sacrifice of the Mass and the Sacrifice of the Cross are one and the same Sacrifice, because in both the Minister offering and the Victim offered are the same; the manner of offering them alone is different. Hence it is justly offered, according to the tradition of the Apostles, not only for the sins, punishments, atonements, and other needs of the living, but also for the departed in Christ who are not yet entirely purified." In Holy Mass we celebrate the work of our redemption: The Sacrifice of the Mass is in truth the unbloody renewal of the death of Christ; it is the representation and continuance of His Sacrifice on the Cross. The object of this Sacrifice therefore is to make us individually partakers of the various effects of the sacrificial death of Christ. This being its object, it must of necessity also make us sharers of the sin-destroying power of Christ's death; that is, it must make us partakers of the atonement rendered for us by Our Saviour's death on the Cross. In other words, the Sacrifice of the Mass must be a Sacrifice of Propitiation. The Holy Scripture frequently mentions, as being effects of the sacrificial death of Christ, the blotting out of sin, release from the curse of sin, destruction of its bondage, and reconciliation with God. Moreover Our Lord solemnly declared at the institution of Holy Mass, that His Body would be given and His Blood shed "unto the remission of sins." (*Matt*. 26:28).

Concerning the sublimity of Holy Mass, St. Alphonsus Liguori says: "The work of our redemption is renewed in every Mass; and this is done so effectually, that if Jesus had never died on the Cross, the celebration of one Mass would have procured for the world the same benefits that were realized by the death of Jesus on the Cross." St. Alphonsus declares that we are not allowed to entertain the least doubt concerning the aid given by the prayer of the Church and the Holy Sacrifice; and then he adds these words: "This ordinance has been delivered to us by the Fathers, and it is observed today in the whole Church—that this Sacrifice be offered up for all those who have died in the communion of the Body and Blood of Christ, and whose souls are remembered during the oblation." St. Monica's only wish at her death, her only prayer was, that her sons might remember her at the Lord's altar. St. Augustine relates that prayers were said and the Holy Sacrifice was offered for her after her death. St. Cyrillus of Jerusalem calls Holy Mass a Sacrifice of Propitiation, and adds, "For the departed, even though they be sinners (that is, even though they have died in venial sin), we offer our prayers to God. And not only our prayers do we offer for them, but we do infinitely more: we offer up Christ, the Victim for our sins, thereby to obtain from the God of mercy propitiation for ourselves and for them."

This propitiatory effect is inherent in the Sacrifice of the Mass itself; that is, it is produced in virtue of its celebration, without regard to the spiritual state of the celebrating priest, be he saint or sinner. If they, for whose benefit Mass is celebrated, are well disposed and capable of receiving its effects, they are sure of obtaining the fruit of atonement and release of punishment; and this is true, according to the doctrine of theologians, as regards both the living and the dead. Hence, to share in the effects of Holy Mass, the state of grace is necessary. For as long as a person is in the state of mortal sin and an enemy of God, he is not capable of receiving even the least remission of punishment. But the Suffering Souls are always in the highest degree capable of receiving the atoning effects of this Holy Sacrifice; for they are elect children of God, possessing an inalienable right to Heaven; they are just and holy souls, loving nothing besides God, and are consumed by a most agonizing thirst to be admitted to His beatific vision. God's wisdom, justice and mercy ordain to what degree their sufferings shall be diminished or abbreviated.

As a Sacrifice of Propitiation, Holy Mass therefore has the power, and by the ordinance of Christ it is its object, infallibly and directly and in virtue of its own efficacy to efface temporal punishment of sin. That this effect does not detract from the value of the Sacrifice of the Cross, but that its infinite power and efficacy is rather emphasized thereby, is obvious to everyone having a true comprehension of Catholic doctrine. The Church does not teach that by the Sacrifice of Christ

on the altar the treasure of redemption merited by His
Sacrifice on the Cross is increased or receives new value,
but that the unincreasable and inexhaustible price of
redemption paid for us through the Sacrifice of the
Cross is individually applied to us and made our own
in Holy Mass. Christ's treasury of grace ever remains
the same; but this grace is distributed and applied to
the souls of men in Holy Mass. And this will continue
as long as there are souls, here and in the next world,
capable and in need of salvation. Consequently the fruits
of the Holy Sacrifice of Mass are in general the very
same as those acquired by Our Lord on the noble tree
of the Cross. What was merited on the Cross for all
mankind is intended to be made the property of the
individual in Holy Mass; it is therefore a continual Sacrifice of Propitiation.

The Sacrifice of Mass possesses an infinite efficacy
which can neither be increased nor diminished by man,
because Jesus Christ is at the same time the Minister
and the Victim of the Sacrifice. For this reason it is a
means of obtaining from God the most sublime gifts,
in general and in particular. If Mass is celebrated for
the Suffering Souls, there is no doubt that one Holy
Sacrifice possesses of itself more power than is necessary to release at once all souls detained in Purgatory,
as the Council of Trent teaches: "The fruits of the bloody
Sacrifice on the Cross are distributed and received most
profusely through the unbloody Sacrifice of the Mass."

Can we be astonished, when reflecting on the propitiatory powers of Holy Mass, that by it many souls
are delivered at once from Purgatory? St. Nicholas of
Tolentino saw a great number of Suffering Souls in a
field, who all united in imploring him to celebrate Holy
Mass for them. After having done so for eight days, it
was revealed to him that the souls he had seen were
all released. St. Anthony of Padua relates: Blessed John
of Alverina once offered the Holy Sacrifice of the Mass
on All Saints' Day. At the Consecration, while holding
the sacred Body of Our Lord in his hands, he ardently

implored the Heavenly Father, by the Blood and the merits of His only Son, to release the Souls from Purgatory; and behold, he saw a great number of these holy souls, like sparks of fire escaping from a furnace soaring up triumphantly to the heavenly Kingdom!

Application of the Fruits of Holy Mass To the Suffering Souls in Purgatory

By His Passion and death on the Cross, Our Saviour redeemed us from sin; and when He ascended into Heaven, He left us the whole treasure of His merits and all the graces He had acquired for us. But these merits and graces must be applied to the individual souls of men, if they are to be saved by Christ's redemption. To make this application of Our Saviour's merits and graces is the office of the Holy Ghost. It is the Holy Ghost who communicates to every individual soul, till the end of the world, the merits of Christ's Passion and death, thereby rendering it susceptible and worthy of the redemption. Before His death, Our Lord therefore said to His Apostles: "It is expedient to you that I go: for if I go not, the Paraclete will not come to you; but if I go, I will send him to you." (*John* 16:7). To redeem us, to regain for us the grace lost by our first parents, to open for us once more the gates of Heaven— to procure for us all these blessings, Our Saviour had to die but once. After this one Sacrifice on the Cross He could return to His Father who had sent Him. But not so the Holy Ghost. His work of sanctification is not completed by one single act; it must and will be carried on continually till the end of time. One generation after another appears in this world; and of all these human beings there is not one born without the blight of Original Sin on the soul, not one who is free from the evil consequences of this sin. All these souls must share in Christ's redemption by having His merits and graces applied to them, if they are to attain eternal salvation. Now it is the Holy Ghost who must render every one of these souls capable of participating in the merits and graces of the redemption; that is, He must sanctify every individual soul to make its salvation possible. The Holy Ghost is therefore called the Paraclete, that is, the Consoler; and this He is in a special manner for the Suffering Souls who, being sanctified, languish to enter their heavenly abode.

The Most Precious Blood of Our Lord Jesus Christ is the means by which the Holy Ghost applies to us the graces of the redemption. In the Sacraments, that seven-fold stream of grace, the Precious Blood enlivens the Church, the Mystical Body of Our Lord. Hence the Precious Blood of Jesus Christ, that Blood which was shed on the Cross, and which is shed mysteriously in every Holy Mass, is the abode and treasury of the Holy Ghost. Among all the dispensations of grace for the direct sanctification of man, Holy Mass holds the first and most important place in consequence of its relation to the Sacrifice of the Cross. The Sacrifice of the Cross is the fountainhead of all grace, the general source of all spiritual aid; for in the Sacrifice of the Cross all blessings of Redemption have their origin, and from it all means of grace receive their power and efficacy. Now in Holy Mass this inexhaustible fountain of grace and salvation flowing from the Sacrifice of the Cross is transferred from the past to the present, from a distance into our immediate presence. For this reason and from this view Holy Mass may be called the cherished abode of the Holy Ghost; it may be regarded as the source of the means of grace, namely the Sacraments and sacramentals, by which the sanctification of individuals is accomplished. Holy Mass can therefore produce directly, or at least indirectly, all divine graces and blessings, not only for its minister, but also for those for whom it is offered.

In its relation to us Holy Mass aims at our sanctification and salvation; hence it is a means of grace, or rather the source of grace, by which the wealth of divine blessings is transmitted to us. The grace flowing from

Holy Mass is due principally to its character as a Sacrifice of Propitiation and Impetration. According to the Council of Trent, the propitiatory effect of Holy Mass embraces "sins, punishment and atonement." Christ offered Himself on the Cross as a Sacrifice of propitiation and impetation for the Redemption of the whole world. Before this Sacrifice there was no salvation; by it the price of ransom for the whole world was placed in the hands of the Heavenly Father. This reconciliation with God, effected for all mankind, is applied individually to man in Holy Mass. This Sacrifice appeases the just wrath of God, it disarms His avenging hand, and renders sinful man an object of divine favor and mercy. The effect of this propitiatory Sacrifice is to move God to condone, wholly or in part, the punishment incurred by the person assisting at Mass, or for whom it is celebrated. This remission of punishment is gained in virtue of the vicarious satisfaction or payment made to God by Christ; for in Holy Mass the price of atonement and propitiation is continually paid anew to the Heavenly Father, and this for particular persons, that He might avert from them the punishment they have incurred, and favor them with increased mercy. Holy Mass therefore draws down upon man grace to enlighten him, to impel him to turn to God in faith, hope, charity and contrition, and to receive worthily the holy Sacraments, by which he is sanctified interiorly and becomes again a child of God. This is expressed by the Council of Trent as follows: "Reconciled by the celebration of the Holy Sacrifice of Mass, Our Lord imparts the grace of penance, and remits sins and vices, however great they may be." And in the Gospel of St. John we read of the Holy Ghost: "He shall glorify me; because He shall receive of mine, and shall shew *it* to you." (*John* 16:14). Accordingly the Holy Ghost imparts the redemption of Jesus Christ individually to man by leading him to share in it.

Mortal sin is not blotted out directly and immediately by Holy Mass; and according to the opinion of most theologians, even venial sin cannot thus be effaced. We have seen however that this august Sacrifice effects a disposition by which we are drawn to reconciliation with God; hence we say that it leads us mediately and indirectly to pardon. The guilt of mortal sin is removed from man only by the infusion or restoration of sanctifying grace. This grace of justification, and consequently also the remission of mortal sin, is usually obtained, according to the ordination of God, only in the Sacrament of Baptism, or by means of the Sacrament of Penance, or by an act of perfect contrition made with the desire of receiving the Sacrament of Penance. The Sacraments are instituted for the direct justification and sanctification of man, and serve to originate and confirm the supernatural life of the soul. On the other hand sacrifice, as such and in the first place, is a service of God. True, Holy Mass is also a means of salvation, but it was not instituted primarily for the conferring of the grace of justification; hence it is not able of itself and without the help of some other means of grace to blot out and take away sin. And yet Holy Mass, according to the doctrine of the Church, is undoubtedly a means productive of atonement and remission of sin.

Fallen mankind was fully redeemed by the death of Jesus Christ on the Cross. Thereby it was made possible for every human being to be released from guilt; nevertheless everyone must individually apply to himself the means instituted for his purification. In Holy Mass the propitiatory Sacrifice of the Cross is renewed in favor of individual persons; but yet everyone must for himself offer up his heart to God in contrition and charity. If, despite the graces we receive, we continue in our wicked life and do not abandon sin, we shall die in it; and therefore St. Augustine observes, "God, who created us without our help, will not save us against our will and without our cooperation." This truth is illustrated by the crucifixion of Christ. We know that despite the tears and prayers of Christ on the Cross but few of the many thousands of sinners present at His death were converted and said, striking their breasts, "Indeed this man was the Son of God." (*Mark* 15:39). The rest remained obdurate and refused to avail themselves of the grace offered them.

Judas was a witness of all the miracles performed by Jesus, he was one of His chosen Apostles; and yet, like the malefactor who was crucified at the left of Our Saviour, he died in his wickedness. The Good Thief, also crucified with Jesus, died repentant and was received into Paradise. In like manner, the effect produced by Holy Mass is different according to the more or less worthy disposition of the person attending it. The better his disposition, the greater will be his share of the fruit and treasure derived from this Sacrifice. Hence it is necessary that they who assist at Mass do so in the proper spirit. Without our cooperation we will not experience the effects intended to be conferred by our Divine Saviour in this Holy Sacrifice. In a word, the effect depends on the spiritual disposition of the person assisting at Mass, or for whom Mass is offered. Those well disposed receive through this Sacrifice the grace to perceive and to be very sorry for their sins. A renowned spiritual writer says, "Holy Mass does not blot out sin, but excites contrition or a desire for contrition. This contrition is sometimes excited at the very time when Mass is celebrated; at other times it is granted later, yet as a result of this Holy Sacrifice. Thus it happens that many are converted by a special grace of God without being aware that they owe it to the efficacy of Holy Mass. Sometimes sinners are not converted at all, because they refuse the grace of God, or abuse it instead of cooperating with it."

What a consolation to know that our brethren deceased in the Lord are capable of receiving the atoning effects of Holy Mass! The Suffering Souls are in need of our help, because they have incurred temporal punishment, which they cannot mitigate or shorten by their own merit. But they are susceptible of our assistance, because they are in a state of grace, and are united with the faithful on earth in faith and charity. While Holy Mass is only an indirect means for the remission of sins, it is a direct means of obtaining remission of punishment, in virtue of the atonement made by Christ on the Cross, whose merits are vicariously applied to us. For on Calvary "He hath borne our infirmities and carried our sorrows . . . He was wounded for our iniquities, He was bruised for our sins: the chastisement of our peace *was* upon Him." (*Is.* 53:4-5). For our peace He suffered, averting from us the wrath of God. The merits of His Passion and death are applied to us for the remission of our punishment.

In the Suffering Souls God illustrates His justice and His mercy. Some theologians hold that the Suffering Souls all share in the fruits and suffrages of Holy Mass to the same degree; but the more prevalent opinion is, that the souls in Purgatory share in the fruits of Holy Mass according to the degree of worthiness they attained or aimed at in life. The defenders of this opinion declare that the disposition of departed souls can well differ; that there are special virtues, for instance a profound reverence for the Church's power of binding and loosing, great penitential zeal, charity for our fellowmen, especially for the Suffering Souls, and particularly a great fervor in assisting at Mass and in receiving Holy Communion, by which we gain during life a special claim to speedy help after death and to a particularly abundant share of the general and special works of atonement performed by the Church Militant. Souls who were insensible during life to the pitiful condition of the souls in Purgatory, will in their turn find no relief while suffering in this prison; they will have to pay their indebtedness to the last farthing, and this even in case prayers and sacrifices are offered especially for them. For the acceptance of these suffrages in behalf of those for whom they are intended depends entirely on the Will of the just God; and St. Augustine remarks, "Our suffrages for the deceased are not always distributed as we intend. Sometimes God makes the distribution quite differently, granting the merits of the good works which we perform for the departed to such of them as have deserved this privilege during life by their own charity for the Suffering Souls. 'For with what measure you mete, it shall be measured to you again.'"

As the state of the Suffering Souls always renders them capable to receiving the mercy of God, the Holy Sacrifice offered up for them is never ineffective; but their disposition towards it during life will affect the measure of this mercy. The better we are disposed when assisting at Mass, the greater will be the fruit we derive from it; therefore we must prepare our souls, purifying them by penance, withdrawing ourselves from earthly things, and inflaming our hearts with a desire for heavenly things. The propitiatory effect of Holy Mass is rendered so much more potent for us and for the Suffering Souls, the more earnestly we endeavor by our own efforts to appease the wrath of God. That we may be impelled to make these efforts, let us remember that the justice of God is infinite like His goodness and mercy; let us consider how displeasing to God and how culpable even the least sin and sinful inclination is; let us contemplate the rigorous and enduring punishments of Purgatory: then we will be penetrated with a wholesome fear of God's Majesty and a dread of His just and holy judgments. We will gratefully and diligently make use of the gracious hour of the Holy Sacrifice to wash our garments in the Blood of the Divine Lamb; and we will not fail to sprinkle with the same Most Precious Blood the Suffering Souls in Purgatory. "Blessed are the merciful, for they shall obtain mercy." (*Matt.* 5:7).

Having such a powerful Sacrifice of propitiation, possessing in Holy Mass the key of the treasury of the atoning merits of Jeus Christ—why should we permit the souls in Purgatory to continue to suffer? These souls must either undergo punishment sufficient to pay their indebtedness to divine justice, or the faithful must make vicarious payment by offering atoning merits for them till the last farthing is paid. These atoning merits are found superabundantly in Holy Mass. Segneri says very aptly, "The Sacrifice of the Cross is the general source of the remission of sins; the Sacrifice of Holy Mass is a particular source, by which the Holy Ghost directs the efficacy of the Blood of Christ to individual souls. The Passion and death of Christ have accumulated the treasury; in Holy Mass this treasury is distributed by the Holy Ghost. The death of Christ is a general treasury; Holy Mass is its key." These are consoling words, addressed to all who are truly conscious of their misery and weakness; they are a strong plea in favor of assisting diligently and devoutly at Mass. For when you assist at Mass, Christian soul, Christ gives you the key to His superabundant treasury; He permits you to open it, and to take away as much as your devout disposition enables you to receive. This treasure you can then devote to the relief of your dear ones in Purgatory.

Segneri continues, "Remark well, therefore, what is meant by celebrating Mass or assisting at it. It means that Holy Mass causes God, who is the God of all, to die again for me and for you all while assisting at the august Sacrifice, and this in such a manner as if He was dying to everyone separately." Thus does the Holy Ghost apply redemption and sanctification individually to the living, and to such of the deceased as are not yet sufficiently pure to enter paradise. Thus does the Holy Ghost sanctify souls to make them capable of entering the abode of bliss, but only such souls as are desirous of cooperating with His grace.

Catholics in general understand well the doctrine concerning the disposition necessary for obtaining the fruits of the Holy Sacrifice of Mass; hence they strive to become worthy of them by fulfilling well the duties of their state of life, by avoiding sin, by frequenting the Sacraments, by offering prayer and almsdeeds, by making novenas, etc. Knowing moreover that the Holy Sacrifice of Mass in virtue of its own efficacy, and prayer and other suffrages offered in the state of grace, never fail in their atonement for the souls in Purgatory, they do their utmost to come to the relief of these Holy Sufferers.

The Mass of Requiem

The loving solicitude of the Church for the relief of the Suffering Souls is demonstrated by the ancient ecclesiastical customs which have come down to us. Holy Mass was at all times her foremost means of relief. As observed before in the course of these treatises, the Holy Sacrifice is offered for the living and deceased members of the Church in general, and is also celebrated for certain souls in particular. For this latter purpose the Roman Missal has a special rite or manner of celebrating Mass. St. Thomas Aquinas observes, "The Church, even in very early times, prescribed certain proper Mass formulas for the various occasions on which she prays and offers sacrifices for the souls of the faithful departed, in order that the priest may make use of these formulas in Masses for the dead when no obstacle intervenes to prevent him from doing so. The objection is futile, that the fruit of the Mass is the same, whether the formula of Mass of the Blessed Virgin, or of the Holy Ghost, or that of *Requiem* be used: for true as it may be that the Holy Sacrifice, as such and in virtue of its own efficacy, obtains the same fruit in such cases; nevertheless the Mass of *Requiem* celebrated for the dead produces—for them—a greater fruit, because in it prayers are added to the Holy Sacrifice which have for their special object the relief and ransom of the faithful departed, for which reason they obtain a special fruit."

By prayer we can obtain every grace from our Heavenly Father; but no prayer, however fervent it may be, can obtain from God so sure and speedy a hearing as may be obtained through the Holy Sacrifice of the Mass. If we remember what has been said hitherto in these pages on the essence and value of Holy Mass, we will easily comprehend why Holy Mass is so effective a Sacrifice of impetration. In the Sacrifice of our altars Christ Himself implores His Heavenly Father with us for the fullness of all blessings. In Holy Mass Christ descends into the midst of His faithful, to unite the voice of His Blood, which cries to Heaven more powerfully than the blood of Abel, with the supplication of the Church of God on earth. And if God according to His promise grants us everything we ask in the name of His dearly beloved Son, why should we not obtain all the gifts of His mercy through this Holy Sacrifice? Christ obtains everything He asks for us; His Will never remains unfulfilled. And when He—our merciful and faithful Highpriest, our true Paschal Lamb—is mysteriously sacrificed on our altars: must we not believe that then, during those hours of grace, His intercession with God is all-powerful? Hence St. Chrysostom aptly remarks: "The holy Angels await the time of Holy Mass to intercede for us during it more effectually; and what we do not obtain during the time of Mass, we will scarcely receive at any other time." St. Alphonsus Liguori says, "Consider that God hears the prayer of the priest more willingly during Holy Mass than at any other time. True, He imparts His grace at all times when asked in the name of and through the merits of Jesus Christ, but during the time of Mass He grants them much more willingly; for then our prayers are sustained and reinforced by the prayer of Jesus Christ, whereby they receive immeasurably greater efficacy, because Jesus Christ is the Highpriest who sacrifices Himself in order to obtain grace for us."

Hence the Church not only offers the Sacrifice, but joins various prayers and ceremonies with this offering. Being the Spouse of Christ, the Church is always resplendent with sanctity. Therefore the Sacrifice, attended as it is with so many prayers and supplications, is graciously received from her hands by God and rewarded with abundant blessings. The entire sacrificial rite being performed in the name of the Church, it moves God most effectually to grant His favors to the living and the dead. For this reason the Church usually gives expression to our needs and desires in such a manner that we can easily discern what kind of favors she intends to obtain by Holy Mass, and for whom she intends to obtain them. The rite of the Mass of *Requiem* is so entirely and so exclusively adapted to the wants of the faithful departed, that prayers for the living are not allowed in it except in the Canon, which remains the same in all Masses. The liturgical prayers for the departed are productive of a special fruit which is added to the fruit essentially contained in the Sacrifice; and the whole is granted to the soul for whom the Mass is applied. The essential fruit of Holy Mass, which is inherent in it in virtue of its own efficacy, comes directly and solely from Christ's oblation of Himself, and is therefore entirely independent from the formula of the Mass.

According to St. Thomas a clearly expressed sentiment pervades the Masses of *Requiem*, which also indicates the grace obtained thereby; and these Masses enjoy greater privileges than other votive Masses. The fundamental sentiment of *Requiem* Masses, in which all their peculiarities are embodied, is the ardent yearning of the Church to devote all her prayers and the full fruit of the Holy Sacrifice to the release of the Suffering Souls. Our affectionate Mother the Church makes intercession for her departed children: will God, our Father, repulse her whom He Himself gave us for our Mother through His Divine Son? This loving Mother imitates the example of our Divine Saviour, who clothed the holy Sacraments in visible signs for the purpose of letting us share in the graces of redemption. Do we not conduct water and other fluids to their destination by means of pipes? Break the conduit and the current will cease to flow: reject the visible signs of the holy Sacraments and the means of grace will be denied to you. The rite of *Requiem* Masses is a form established by the Church to draw the grace of Heaven down upon the souls in Purgatory. If the formula of *Requiem* Mass is not used, the value of the Sacrifice will by no means suffer diminution; but the fruit of the Church's supplication will be wanting.

This being the chief sentiment of *Requiem* Masses, both priest and people join in them by praying in the name of the Church. In this supplication lies the special fruit of these Masses. Their whole rite is adapted to the end that this supplication may be made from the depth of the heart, so that the Suffering Souls may receive increased consolation also from the charity of the priest and of the faithful. Hence in *Requiem* Masses everything is omitted by which the benefits personally gained by those who assist at the Sacrifice are indicated: the water to be mixed with the wine is not blessed, nor is the blessing given to the people; deacon and subdeacon also receive no blessing. At the Introit the celebrant does not sign himself with the Cross, and incense is used only at the Offertory. At the Gospel neither incense nor lighted candles are used; the kissing of the book and the kiss of peace are omitted, also the prayer preceding the latter. At the *Agnus Dei* the Church supplicates for peace in the name of the deceased, for eternal peace. The psalm *Judica*, in which no reference is made to the departed, is omitted, as is also the *Gloria Patri*. But the Church gives full vent to her mourning and supplication in the touching strophes of the *Dies irae*. The *Requiem aeternam*, etc., and the Offertory are always recited in the plural number, to indicate that the souls of all the faithful departed share in the general fruits of the Holy Sacrifice, although its special fruits are reserved for the souls for whom it is offered in particular.

Christian soul! Cultivate a great esteem for these rites of the Church in the firm conviction that in all her beautiful ceremonies she is led by supernatural motives.

High Mass of Requiem

When the Holy Sacrifice is celebrated in the form of a High Mass, the fruit which comes to it by the prayers of the Church is increased. For the greater the solemnity with which the Church celebrates Holy Mass for the glory of God, the more pleasing to God and the more efficient is her prayer. Therefore she calls a greater number of persons to aid in the celebration of the sacred mystery, and invites all nature to implore God for the relief of the Suffering Souls. The three children in the fiery furnace (*Daniel* 3) invited all creatures, water, fire, heat, cold, light and darkness, hills and valleys, seas and rivers, etc., to bless the Lord. The soul of man honors God by sentiments of faith, hope, charity, humility, gratitude, submission, etc.; and it is the office of the body to express these sentiments by its attitudes, because the human body is the king of material creation formed by the Almighty's own hand. "And God created man to His own image." (*Gen.* 1:27). In man's body all material creation, so to say, does homage to God. This the Church acknowledges to the fullest extent. Hence she first sanctifies all nature, and then employs it for her purposes. At a solemn Mass the external accessories are of much greater splendor than at a private Mass.

At solemn High Mass the Church employs a greater number of ministering officials: deacon, subdeacon, acolytes; she employs more precious vestments and sacred vessels; the number of lighted candles is greater; there are incensations, singing and ringing of bells. All these accessories are for the greater glory of God, and to increase the devotion of the faithful. Hence the Church accords special privileges to the solemn High Mass of *Requiem*, so that it can be celebrated every day except on Sundays and higher feasts. How wise and compassionate is Holy Mother Church! Imitating our Divine Saviour she makes animate and inanimate creation serve her purposes. Jesus Christ sanctifies water in the name of the Tri-une God thereby to make us heirs of Heaven; He makes use of bread, wine, oil, etc., in the holy Sacraments to confer on us the graces of salvation. In the same manner Holy Church blesses and uses water, salt, incense, vestments, bells, etc., to make us share in the treasury of grace entrusted to her by Christ. Whosoever regards Christ as his Redeemer must needs have a firm faith in His infallible Church and cherish all her ordinances. Hence St. Cyprian aptly says, "Whosoever has not the Church for his Mother cannot have God for his Father." How sacred then must be the rites which the Church employs in the celebration of the august Sacrifice for the Suffering Souls, who were her faithful children on earth!

Christ delivered Himself substantially to His Church, not only to be her Oblation, but also that she might be able to offer herself in and with this Oblation of infinite value. She does this by living the whole life of Jesus Christ, in intimate union with this Oblation, through the entire course of every year. Guided by the Holy Ghost, she is intent on giving due expression to her faith by this Oblation as well as by her whole cult; and therefore she watches jealously over its purity. Hence the more solemn the ecclesiastical service, the more valuable and effective is the Sacrifice. This is demonstrated by the learned Pasqualigo. He answers the question whether a solemn and a private Mass are of the same value with reference to the Suffering Souls as follows:

"It must be admitted, *first*, that a solemn Mass in its character as a Sacrifice of impetration is more effective than a private one for the person for whom the Sacrifice is offered—offered as it is by the Church.

"It must be admitted, *secondly*, that a solemn Mass, offered by the Church as a Sacrifice of atonement for any individual, is more effective than a private Mass.

"It must be admitted, *thirdly*, that the Sacrifice solemnly offered is more effective than a private Mass in virtue of its own efficacy, as also in its character of a Sacrifice of propitiation, atonement and impetration."

In explanation of the last observation Pasqualigo adds that since Christ has left the Sacrifice to the Church for the purpose of applying the fruits of His Passion to the souls of men, its solemn oblation must in equity be productive of more abundant fruits.

Hence the greater the solemnity with which Holy Mass is celebrated, the more enhanced the majesty of the august Sacrifice becomes; and the greater is also the glory it gives to God, the more abundant are its blessings for the Church by whom it is offered. That fruit of Holy Mass which grows out of its own efficacy is the surest and most abundant, it is the essential and special fruit of the Sacrifice, because the value and efficacy of Holy Mass depend solely on the divine character of Christ and on the infinite merits of His Sacrifice on the Cross. But in order that the faithful may have a greater share in this fruit of the Sacrifice, the Church surrounds Holy Mass with the greatest solemnity possible; she adorns it with expressive ceremonies and sends her prayer to Heaven in suppliant chant. These accessories are not aimless, nor without signification; they are not made use of for the purpose of doing honor to man: they have a true value of their own. What incongruous ideas so many Catholics entertain concerning the solemnity of divine service! The increased ceremonial, the solemn Mass is not instituted for the entertainment of the congregation, or to foster the ambition of individuals, but for the purpose of moving God more effectually to grant the graces we implore; or in other words, to render the supplications and petitions of the Church more effectual.

Everything pertaining to faith and to the service of God, even the minutest detail, usage and custom, was regarded by the Venerable Catherine Emmerich as most sacred. She remarked, "Nothing is mere ceremony; all is essence and efficacy manifested by signs. All that is performed by the Church, even though her ministers through human frailty may be actuated by profane motives, is performed by the direction of the Holy Ghost. Animated confidence joined with simplicity changes everything into essence and substance."

St. Mechtildis often saw saintly Sisters of her convent released from Purgatory after the first Mass celebrated for them. Sometimes she beheld Christ, the Blessed Virgin and numerous other Saints surrounding the altar and offering up their merits. Some souls are privileged to assist at the Mass said for their release, and then go directly to Heaven.

What is more Profitable and Meritorious—to Have Masses Celebrated for Ourselves during Life, or after Death?

Many Catholics are solicitous to have a number of Masses celebrated after their death for the repose of their souls. For this purpose they save money and devise a portion of their estate in their last will and testament. This is good and praiseworthy, and persons intending this should by no means be disuaded from doing so; yet it is more profitable and meritorious to have these Masses celebrated during life. St. Leonard of Port Maurice exhorts us most earnestly to have Masses celebrated for ourselves during our lifetime rather than after our death; and he declares that one Mass before our death is much more profitable to us than many after it. He gives the following reasons: First, if we have a Mass said for us during our lifetime, we are the cause of its celebration and can assist at it, which latter is impossible after our death. Secondly, if a Mass is celebrated for us during our lifetime, and we are perhaps in the state of sin, we may hope to receive from God's mercy, in virtue of this Mass, the grace to perceive our sinful state, to be moved to true contrition, and to reconcile ourselves with God by a sincere Confession. True, God is not obliged to grant us this grace; for whosoever remains consciously in the state of mortal sin, is not capable of gaining supernatural merit. But as God is infinitely merciful, He usually grants to sinners who perform a good action the grace of true contrition for their sins. This grace or efficacy of Holy Mass cannot be obtained after death. For if we die in a state of sin, even thousands of Masses would not transfer us into the state of grace; we remain forever enemies of God and children of wrath.

Thirdly, Holy Mass can obtain for us the grace of a happy death, because in virtue of its being offered for us God will assist us with special aid to triumph over the enemy of our souls in that decisive hour. Fourthly, if Masses are said for us before our death, their merit will accrue to us after it, and we shall thereby either be preserved entirely from Purgatory, or our punishment will be mitigated and lessened. For by every Holy Mass we pay to God a great part of our indebtedness; and if we hear it with special devotion we moreover blot out many venial sins, so that we may reasonably hope to escape a great part of our punishment after death. But if we defer these Masses until after our death, we shall be obliged to wait for their celebration in case we are in Purgatory, and this waiting is most distressing and painful. Hence it is better that the benefits accruing to us from Holy Mass be obtained in advance, than to wait for them in the torments of Purgatory.

Fifthly, by ordering a Mass in our lifetime we make an offering to God of our money, inasmuch as we give the usual stipend or alms for the support of the priest, thereby depriving ourselves of some means of gratification. After death however we deprive ourselves of nothing; for then our earthly enjoyments have ended, and our means go to our heirs. By making bequests for Masses after our death, our action no longer includes self-denial; we give what death will inevitably deprive us of. Hence our offering cannot be so pleasing to God and so meritorious for us, as it would have been if we had made it during our lifetime. Sixthly, it is to be remembered that a person performing a good action in the state of grace receives a double reward. He receives a remission of part of the punishment due for his sins; and he merits a greater reward in Heaven. Thus a person having a Mass said for himself during his lifetime pays a part of his indebtedness to God, and merits a greater glory in Heaven; but when he defers the Mass until after his death, though he thereby pays a part of his indebtedness, his glory in Heaven is not increased. Even though thousands of Masses were celebrated for us after death, our heavenly glory would not be increased one degree; for in Heaven merits are no longer placed to our credit: a truth to be well remembered.

Finally, we ought to consider that by one Holy Mass celebrated for us during life more punishment is remitted to us than by a great number celebrated after our death. If we have offended someone and ask his pardon immediately, we may easily obtain it; but if we hesitate and defer seeking reconciliation till the matter is perhaps taken before the court, then one word spoken in our defense may cost us many dollars. Now we offend God often and in many ways during life: if we implore His pardon immediately and as long as we live, and manifest our willingness to atone for the offense by some good work—for instance by almsdeeds, acts of charity, a Holy Mass, etc.—this may suffice to cancel our whole indebtedness. But if we let our indebtedness accumulate until we appear before the tribunal of God, the penalty will be much heavier. In the next world the time of grace ceases, God judges everything according to the rigor of His justice; and accordingly every venial sin is punished so severely that many Masses will not suffice to cancel what one alone would have cancelled during our lifetime. If we have the misfortune of committing a mortal sin after having a Mass celebrated for us during life, we shall more easily receive the grace of true contrition and sincere Confession.

St. Bernard relates of a pious and wealthy merchant in Genoa, that the last will he had made was the occasion of most uncharitable remarks, because it contained no provision for Masses to be said for the repose of his soul. All his papers and business records were diligently searched to find an explanation how it happened that so devout a man could be guilty of neglecting so important a matter. To the great edification of all it was finally discovered that the deceased had caused thousands of Masses to be said for him during his lifetime. He had taken to heart the words of St. Bonaventure, "God values a trifling voluntary penance in this life much higher than a more severe but compulsory one in the next; just as a little gold is more valuable than a great lump of lead." Hence St. Anselm asserts, "To hear one Holy Mass devoutly in life is more profitable than to bequeath so much that thousands can be said after death."

And how much more meritorious will these Masses be, if we offer them for the relief of the Suffering Souls! "Blessed are the merciful, for they shall obtain mercy." (*Matt.* 5:7). Hence St. Paul exhorts us, "Let us go therefore with confidence to the throne of grace: that we may obtain mercy, and find grace in seasonable aid." (*Hebr.* 4:16).

What Amount of Punishment is Remitted by a Holy Mass?

It has been repeatedly stated in the course of these treatises, that the efficacy and value, that is, the internal efficiency of Holy Mass as a Sacrifice of propitiation and impetration, is infinite. The full price of our redemption, the inexhaustible treasure of atonement and merit gained for us by Christ on the Cross are offered by Him continually to His Divine Father for the purpose of applying them to mankind. The Holy Sacrifice of Mass therefore contains in itself superabundant atonement for the cancellation of all sins and punishments, an all-sufficient price for obtaining innumerable graces and spiritual favors. Hence the atoning value of Holy Mass is infinite. Nevertheless the efficacy of Holy Mass in its application to man is not unlimited, since even the efficacy of the Sacrifice of the Cross is limited to a certain extent, as the learned Suarez declares. The fruits of Holy Mass, in their application to man, are always limited as to their measure. Hence St. Thomas observes, "Althought the power of Christ in the Sacrament of the Holy Eucharist is infinite, yet the effect for which this Sacrament is ordained is limited. For this reason the entire punishment of those detained in Purgatory is not remitted by one Mass, and the priest offering this Sacrifice is not absolved from all debt of atonement which he owes for his sins. Consequently it may sometimes happen that several Masses are required before full satisfaction is made for a sin."

Moreover the Holy Sacrifice of the Mass does not always produce so manifold nor so powerful an effect as the person for whom it is offered is capable of receiving. Its efficacy is restricted to a certain measure, though in particular cases the effects may be greater or less. This is demonstrated by the fact that the Church usually offers the Holy Sacrifice repeatedly to obtain a favor, for instance the release of a soul from Purgatory, the conversion of a sinner, or bodily health. If Holy Mass would produce its full effect in every case, one single application of this august Sacrifice would be sufficient to obtain the desired grace. The blessings derived from Holy Mass do not result entirely from its essence, nor from the spiritual disposition of the person for whom it is celebrated, although the latter considerably influences the measure of the blessings: the reason of this limited efficacy of Holy Mass—mark it well, Christian soul—is to be found in the Will of Christ. And why did He so ordain? The renowned theologian Sporer answers, "Christ, the Son of God, willed and ordained that a Sacrifice should be offered to Him, and that it should produce a certain and limited effect of atonement and intercession, to be determined by Him and applied according to the capacity of those offering it, in order that this Sacrifice might be offered more frequently and more zealously."

St. Gregory relates that thirty Masses had to be said for a religious who had without permission retained a few gold coins. Constantia, a daughter of St. Elizabeth of Portugal, died soon after her marriage to the King of Castile. As soon as her mother was informed of her death, she hastened to join her husband who was in Cantarem. Presently a hermit asked for an audience; and he told them that their daughter Constantia had repeatedly appeared to him, stating that she had been sentenced to a long and painful Purgatory. But it had been promised to her that she would be released after a year, if Holy Mass was celebrated for her every day. The Queen conferred with her husband, and he deemed it advisable to do what had been asked of them in so extraordinary a manner. Besides the King considered it not more than proper that a Christian father should have Masses said for his deceased daughter. Hence they resolved to act on the suggestion of the pious hermit, and entrusted a saintly priest by the name of Mendez with the celebration of these Masses. At the close of the year, when the last Mass had been said, Constantia appeared to her mother, and told her that she had that day been released in consequence of these Masses, and that she was about to enter Heaven.

The faithful who take a personal and active part in the celebration of the Sacrifice, who assist at it with devotion and thus share in its celebration, thereby gain a special and particular fruit, either through the action and qualification of the ministering agent, or through the Sacrifice itself in virtue of its divine efficacy. It is generally held by theologians that this special and particular fruit of the Sacrifice is granted without restriction or diminution to all persons present during the offering of it, without regard to their number; every one individually receives the full and whole fruit of grace equivalent to his cooperation, his manner of offering, his piety and devotion.

But the case is different when we regard Holy Mass as a Sacrifice of impetration offered by the priest as Christ's agent. Here the question presents itself: Does the Sacrifice, when offered for many, procure for every one individually the full and whole fruit; that is, does it procure just so much fruit as it would if it were offered for him alone? Or is the fruit distributed in such a manner among those for whom it is offered, that their part becomes less in proportion to the number of those who share in it? The majority of theologians are of the opinion—and this opinion is sustained by interior and exterior reasons—that the fruits of the Sacrifice are distributed individually; and that they are therefore lessened in proportion as the number of participants increases to whom the priest by special intention applies them. This should not be forgotten when we cause the Holy Sacrifice to be offered for one or more souls in Purgatory.

The Holy Souls, helplessly suffering in Purgatory, are greatly in need of Holy Mass, thereby to receive from divine justice a lessening of the duration and intensity of their torments. The Church teaches that Holy Mass aids the deceased in a special manner, more so than all other suffrages. Holy Mass aids them more than prayers and indulgences, more than fasting, almsdeeds and night-watches, more than works of charity and piety offered for them by virtue of the communion of Saints. Holy Mass offered for them is never ineffectual.

Chapter 4

On the Motives for Helping the Suffering Souls

General Motives for Helping the Suffering Souls

THE joyous strains of the second Vespers of All Saints are hushed; the festive ornaments of the altar are removed; a catafalque is erected in its front. In black vestments the priest intones the Vespers of the dead. Has the cold hand of Death removed a dear member from the midst of the congregation? Is it a burial for which these preparations are made? No; it is the eve of All Souls' Day, the day on which the Church in maternal charity remembers in her prayers and in the Holy Sacrifice all those of her children who have passed through the portals of eternity, but who were not found pure enough to rest on the Sacred Bosom of their Lord; who are not yet permitted to stand before the throne of the Lamb, to take possession of the realms of bliss, but are detained in the debtors' prison to await their ransom, their release and admission to eternal glory. Thousands of faithful obey the call of Mother Church, and thoughtfully, sadly wend their way to divine service to remember the dead.

During our earthly pilgrimage we are often disquieted—not only by the thought, what shall we eat, what shall we drink, and wherewith shall we clothe ourselves, but also by solicitude for the welfare of our dear ones in the distance. Who of us has not observed the furrowed brow of a father, the scalding tears of a

193

mother, when a dear son or daughter takes leave of them to seek a way to fortune in the world? How will their children fare? What will happen to them? Will they remain steadfast in their faith, and avoid the snares of sin, the influence of bad company? Such are the thoughts that daily harass the fond parent's heart. And the children also may have to bear a heavy burden of mental trouble. When long silence on the part of their parents fills them with vague apprehensions for their safety, they are continually worried by the thought, "Why do they not write? Are they still alive and well? Are they perhaps sinking under the weight of advancing age?" These are their thoughts day and night; they follow them to their work and intrude themselves into their prayers.

But the solicitude for our dear ones reaches its highest point when our thoughts are directed to the condition of their souls in the other world. Our hearts are troubled, our minds feel oppressed when confronted with the question, "My father, mother, son, daughter, sister, brother has passed the confines of mortal life: in what state may their souls be in the world beyond? What was the sentence they received at the tribunal of the Supreme Judge? Is reward or punishment their lot?" Holy Writ informs us that nothing defiled can enter Heaven, and that even the just man falls seven times a day; are then our beloved ones in eternal torment? The heart recoils at the terrible thought!

Harassed by such doubts, a fond mother continued day and night to mourn the early death of a beloved son. But with all her tears it never occurred to her to come to the relief of his soul. It pleased Our Lord to show her in a vision the wrong she thereby committed. She saw a procession of youths who joyously wended their way towards a beautiful city. With straining eyes she sought her son among them, and finally discovered him plodding along dejectedly in the rear, impeded in his progress by the heavy folds of a wet garment clinging about him. Mournfully addressing her, he said, "Dear mother, this garment, which your tears have made so heavy, hinders me from keeping pace with my companions. Oh, cease your weeping; and if you really love me, assist me with prayer, alms, Holy Mass and other good works!"

Henschenius, in his life of St. Dionysius the Carthusian, also relates an instance of the impropriety of immoderate inquisitiveness concerning the state of the deceased. When this Saint was informed of his father's death, he sincerely mourned the deceased. At the same time, being anxious concerning his condition in the other world, he resolved to implore God to inform him of it. One day after Vespers, when he was devoutly engaged in prayer for this purpose, he heard a voice from Heaven, saying, "What does it profit thee that thou shouldst permit thyself thus to be led on by curiosity? Much better would it be if, instead of praying to know the state of thy father's soul, thou wouldst pray for his release from Purgatory in case he should be there. Thus thy prayer would be of assistance to him and thou wouldst gain merit thereby." Very much confounded at this reproof he thenceforth devoted himself with redoubled zeal to prayer for his father's release; and the very next night he saw him in terrible torments, calling on him for help. He continued offering his prayers and good works for him, till he had the consolation of being informed of his release. Moreover, from this time on he was an ardent helper of the Suffering Souls, and exhorted his brethren also to come to their relief.

These are private revelations concerning particular cases. But who will tell *us* what became of our dear ones, who departed this life with so many frailties? Our Holy Church consolingly responds to this inquiry: Mourn not as those who have no hope; for there is a middle state between Heaven and Hell, a place of purification, where according to St. Augustine all those receive salvation as if by fire, who have not sufficiently atoned for their sins. And Holy Scripture corroborates

her comforting doctrine by assuring us that "it is therefore a holy and wholesome thought to pray for the
dead, that they may be loosed from sins" (*2 Mach.*
12:46), "for the continual prayer of a just man availeth
much" (*James* 5:16), and "if you ask the Father anything in My name, He will give it you." (*John* 16:23).
Like an angel of consolation Holy Church assuages
our grief, saying, "Why mourn as those who have no
hope? If you desire that your loved ones enter the
glory of Heaven, why do you not aid them to attain it
by almsdeeds, fasting, the Holy Sacrifice and other
good works? These are prices of ransom acceptable to
God and a most powerful means of effecting their
release." "And making a gathering, he (Judas the Machabee) sent twelve thousand drachms of silver to
Jerusalem for sacrifice to be offered for the sins of the
dead." (*2 Mach.* 12:43). And the aged Tobias exhorted
his son: "Lay out thy bread and thy wine upon the
burial of a just man," for "alms deliver from all sin,
and from death, and will not suffer the soul to go into
darkness." (*Tob.* 4:11). And listen also to St. Ambrose,
writing to Faustinus, a nobleman who incessantly
mourned the death of his sister, "Cease your mourning. The Lord, in whose hand is life and death, deprived
you for a short time of your dearly beloved sister. Do
not weep for her. Rather pray for her that the Lord
may deliver her from the torments of Purgatory.
Enwreathe her with immortelles of good works and
with a garland of the roses of prayer. This is the most
beautiful tribute you can pay to her memory."

While the Church thus consoles us by her ancient
Faith and her scriptural doctrine concerning those that
died in the Lord, but who at their death had not yet
cancelled all their indebtedness "to the last farthing,"
a mistaken zeal for the glory of God may induce some
to oppose prayer for the Suffering Souls. The sentiment by which such persons are led may be expressed
in the following words: "As these just souls are sure
of their salvation and confirmed in the love of God, it

is much more meritorious to labor for the glory of God
by fostering the propagation of the Faith, by a fervent
devotion to the Sacred Hearts of Jesus and Mary, by
praying for the conversion of sinners, etc., than by
striving to obtain a speedy release for the Suffering
Souls." But this is not so. With Faber most theological writers maintain, that of all works of mercy and
charity the most exalted, pure and charitable is to aid
the Suffering Souls in Purgatory.

We read in the Annals of the Dominican Order that
a disciple of the great St. Dominic, a man of high
virtue, was remiss in his prayer for the souls in Purgatory. "Why trouble ourselves about their state?" he
said. "They are sure of their salvation; they are no
longer in danger of losing Heaven. I will rather labor
for the conversion of sinners, to lead back to God souls
whose salvation is still in peril, whose damnation is
humanly speaking inevitable because of their obdu-
racy of heart and depravity of mind. Hence I pray for
these unfortunates; I offer for them the Holy Sacrifice
of Mass; I do everything in my power for them—and
I do not doubt that I shall succeed." This line of reasoning is surely not logical; it rather betokens great
simplicity. And yet the good Dominican imagined that
it was not enough for him alone to act according to
this principle; but he sought also to influence others
to follow his example. Under the vain pretense of applying his charity to a better purpose he deprived the
Suffering Souls of the suffrages by which devout Christians would have willingly aided them.

But in this case God allowed the Suffering Souls to
leave their prison and to appear in menacing attitudes
to the one who had thus defrauded them; for it is God
Himself, who in His inscrutable mercy and justice created Purgatory, and who wishes the living to come to
the relief of the departed. The souls began to molest
the Dominican everywhere and at all times, filling him
with terror, announcing to him who they were and
why God permitted them to annoy him. Soon the good

religious was a changed man; and thenceforth he was filled with such charity for the Suffering Souls that he was most assiduous in his prayers for their relief. He offered the Holy Sacrifice for them as often as possible, and exhorted others in powerful sermons to help them. Never before were motives inculcated so effectually in defense of suffrages for the departed souls; and his success in convincing his hearers fully atoned for his former error.

History has not transmitted to us the arguments by which this zealous religious defended charity toward the Suffering Souls. Catholic theologians gather them from the Angelic Doctor St. Thomas, and from other great Saints and Doctors of the Church. They deduce the various motives for helping the Poor Souls from the very nature of this sublime charity; and accordingly they enumerate three classes of such motives—motives relating to ourselves, to God, and to the Suffering Souls. By a careful consideration of these motives we shall be led to esteem at their true value the exertions of fervent Catholics for the Suffering Souls; we shall refresh in our minds the memory of the departed; we shall feel impelled to greater exertions for their relief. These motives are to say to us repeatedly and with irresistible force: "Hasten to aid the Church Suffering, the souls in Purgatory!" For St. Chrysostom remarks, "It was so ordained by the Holy Ghost, who demands of us that we help them." Let us therefore make use of the effective means at our command, consisting of prayer, good works and Holy Mass. Let us never cease to implore our good God, the King of Glory, to release from their torments the Suffering Souls, and to make them members of the Church Triumphant, together with all the Saints in eternal bliss.

Motives Relating to God

One man has a strong affection for another. How will he show it? He will strive always and everywhere to please his friend, to gladden his friend's heart; he will endeavor to influence others that they also may love, praise and honor the person whom he himself loves. The same may be said as regards our love for God. If we truly love God, we will prove our love by being eager to do whatever we know is pleasing to Him; we will strive to promote His glory to the best of our ability. It was thus our Divine Saviour Himself manifested His infinite love for His Heavenly Father; for He said, "I do always the things that please Him." (*John* 8:29). And again, "The works that I do in the name of My Father, they give testimony for Me." (*John* 10:25). The purpose for which man was created is this: "Thou shalt love the Lord thy God with thy whole heart, and with thy whole soul, and with thy whole mind." (*Matt.* 22:37). In the Book of Proverbs we read, "The Lord hath made all things for Himself." (*Prov.* 16:4). The Lord Himself, through His prophet, says of man, "I have created him for My glory." (*Is.* 43:7). Man was therefore created for this sole end—to love, to serve, to honor and adore God.

"The greater glory of God"—this was the controlling motive of the Saints in all their actions. Our Lord Himself taught us to pray, "Hallowed be Thy name." And in the *Gloria* of the Mass the Church says, "We thank Thee for Thy great glory." Finally, to praise and glorify God is the chief occupation of the Saints in Heaven. The glory of God must therefore be the chief motive also in our works of charity for the Suffering Souls. And in fact we do promote His glory in a most efficient manner by hastening their entrance into Heaven, because there alone God is truly known, loved and glorified. A saintly servant of God was so affected by this consideration that he exclaimed, "I urge everybody who is zealous for the glory of God and strives to attain His pure love, to meditate on this truth. If St. Theresa and other servants of God declared themselves willing to suffer every possible pain to increase God's glory one degree, what should we not do and suffer for the release of the souls from Purgatory, when God's glory is thereby increased in millions of degrees?"

St. Anthony declares that the world is like a beautiful large book in which the glory of God is inscribed with flaming letters; for even inanimate creation contributes to His glory. But of what use is a book if nobody reads it? Man alone can read in this book of nature. For a man religiously inclined the whole world is animate; everything speaks to him, everything impresses his intellect and heart. To him "the heavens show forth the glory of God, and the firmament declareth the work of His hands." (*Ps.* 18:2). Every succession of day and night is a manifestation of God's wisdom and providence; every new year is an instance of His loving care for man. God, the invisible Lord of the universe, becomes visible to us in the greatness of His creation. His light shines in the stars of the firmament, His goodness grants us the splendor of the sun's rays; His bounty covers the earth with verdure and nourishing products, which He teaches us to gather and use. Who is it that instructs the bee to collect for us the sweetness of its honey, who covers the sheep with their fleece to provide clothing for us, who ordains that the cow shall produce milk for our nourishment? It is God. "And He said: Let us make man to our image and likeness: and let him have dominion over the fishes of the sea, and the fowls of the air, and the beasts, and the whole earth." (*Gen.* 1:26). For man therefore were all things created; to his heart all things should speak of the omnipotence, bounty and goodness of God.

While thus contemplating the beauties of God's creation, we are filled with gratitude; and we feel ourselves moved to exclaim, "How beautiful, O God, how full of perfection is Thy creation! How great is Thy bounty, how wonderful Thy providence regarding man! If even the contemplation of Thy works fills us with ineffable rapture, what must it be to behold Thee unveiled and in the splendor of Thy glory! Then we shall express our gratitude in hymns of thanksgiving, in which we shall be joined by all creation." St. Magdalen of Pazzi one day received an apple; and she was transported with joy at the thought that God had decreed from all eternity to let this fruit grow for her special delectation. Of St. Francis of Assisi it is related that one day, while taking his mendicant's meal of hard crust at a spring by the roadside, he wept for joy and gratitude to God. His companion could not understand how he could thus rejoice over their poor fare of bread and water; and he told him so. The Saint replied, "It is the love that God shows for us for which I am so grateful. From all eternity He has decreed that we should here receive this nourishment." Thus did the Saints recognize God's bounty in the least of His gifts; and thus did they thank Him for it. And we—where is our gratitude?

Oh, let us acknowledge the Lord's bounty! Let us unite in praising the Most High! But how dare we do so—we who are still slaves of the flesh, of our lusts, of our concupiscence and evil inclinations? And even if the fetters of this our bondage were broken, "How shall we sing the song of the Lord in a strange land?" (*Ps.* 136:4). How shall we worthily know, praise and love God, as long as we are exiled in this vale of tears? There is a means fully adapted to the attainment of our purpose. When the chief executive of a country comes to visit a place subject to his authority, the local magistrates engage artists to contribute by their services to give him a worthy reception; and though the magistrates do not personally conduct the celebrations, yet they receive the credit for them, since it was by their order that the celebrations took place.

The relation between God and ourselves is similar. The learned Bellarmine maintains, that what we do through another is regarded as done by ourselves. We have the privilege of engaging others to praise God in our name—namely, the souls in Purgatory. If then there is a question of glorifying God, of cooperating in causing His infinite Majesty to be worthily honored—is there a more appropriate and efficient means for the attainment of that end than to assist in populating Heaven with just souls? If we do the least for the release of a soul from Purgatory, we thereby augment God's ineffable glory; for a soul admitted to God's beatific vision becomes fully and clearly cognizant of His divine attributes—and instantly the soul is inflamed with a perfect, seraphic love of God, in which it will persevere throughout all eternity.

Let us imagine we saw a soul ascending from Purgatory to Heaven: who can describe the joy and exultation into which it will immediately break forth, how humbly prostrated it will adore God's supreme Majesty and perfections? Who can depict the ardor with which it will join in the incessant hymn of the elect, "Holy, holy, holy, the Lord God of hosts! The earth is full of His glory" (*Is.* 6:3); "to whom be honor and glory for ever and ever." (*Rom.* 16:27). Unspeakably great then is the work performed by him who aided the soul in its release and hastened its entrance into Heaven. He caused all these transports of love, gratitude, praise and glory to be offered so much the earlier to God's Majesty by the soul whom he helped to ransom. The souls released through our charitable suffrages are now enjoying the eternal bliss of Heaven; they will be our protectors, patrons and intercessors at the throne of Cod, where they join the heavenly host of Angels and Saints in unceasing adoration of the Most High— and this happiness they gained through our help. Must this our help therefore not be an object of infinite divine complacency?

Of course we do not refer here to that essential glory which is an attribute of divinity, and which God receives from His own infinite perfections; but to the accidental glory which He deigns to receive from His crea-tures. This glory, of which He is so jealous—"I am the Lord thy God, mighty, jealous" (*Ex.* 20:5)—by what means can we better promote it than by opening Heaven through our prayers for the admission of innumerable souls now suffering in Purgatory, souls who will praise and glorify His mercy throughout all eternity? He loves these souls, and they love Him; He ardently wishes to unite them with Himself; His Heart is moved with compassion by reason of their banishment; but His jus-tice—for as God He must be and is equally just and merciful—detains them in their prison until they shall have paid "the last farthing." He is like unto a father who declines the caresses of his son and banishes him from his presence until he shall have amended his ways by repentance and tears. The Suffering Souls are even now disciples of Christ yearning for the presence of their Master; but in His stern justice He repels them saying, "Nothing defiled is admitted into My presence." They are children of God seeking their Redeemer, but they can find Him only if the loving hand of Mother Church leads them to Him. They are famishing for His heavenly banquet, longing to partake in the Holy Sac-rifice of His Sacred Body and Precious Blood; but the sacramental species are no longer their spiritual nour-ishment.

What a joy for our Father in Heaven, what a delight for the Sacred heart of Jesus, when a friend, a medi-ator, equalizes by his atoning suffrages the faults and punishment of a soul in Purgatory, and thereby effects a reconciliation! It is in our power to be such friends, such mediators. We can obtain pardon for the Suffer-ing Souls. Though suffering the wrath of divine jus-tice, they are nevertheless our brethren in Christ; and God delights to hear our prayers for them.

During His sojourn on earth our Divine Saviour wept repeatedly. We have the authority of Holy Scripture for it, that He wept at least three times—at the tomb of Lazarus, over Jerusalem, and during His Passion.

Oh, what a most heartrending sight, to see the tears coursing down His sacred countenance! And yet the persons for whom He wept were sinful men; on the two occasions mentioned last they were His enemies and tormentors. How great then must be Our Lord's compassion for the Suffering Souls in Purgatory, who are confirmed in His grace and love! And He is compelled to make them suffer in their place of torment for weeks, months and years, perhaps for centuries! How He must yearn for mediators, who by their suffrages for these poor, beloved souls enable Him to temper His justice with mercy! For this purpose He places the full measure of His atoning merits at our disposal; and He Himself encourages us by His example.

From the blessed moment that "the Word was made flesh" the most Sacred Heart of Jesus began to pulsate in charity. Every one of these pulsations was an act of homage to God, more pleasing in His sight than all the worship offered by the creatures of His omnipotence in Heaven and on earth. And all these acts were offered up in favor of mankind. Whatever Jesus did on earth through the impulsive love of His Sacred Heart, whether manifesting His powers by miracles or giving an example of humility, teaching His saving doctrine or suffering for our Redemption—He did it all for our salvation. His every act was a new proof of His infinite love for us, a fruit of the tree of life, full of life-giving sweetness and nourishing sustenance. The ecclesiastical year presents to our view step for step the various manifestations of His love for mankind. At first we behold this love taking to itself the form of an infant, appealing to our affections, enchanting, ravishing us with sweetness—a love, which as yet appears to be lying dormant. "The goodness and kindness of God our Saviour appeared" (*Tit.* 3:4); and though He came among us a child, helpless and dependent, His condition is an earnest of the great work He came to achieve for us.

Next we behold Him in His wanderings, labors and

sufferings for mankind: His hands made callous by work, His brow streaming from exertion, His frame attenuated by the long fast in the desert, His sacred feet worn and stained with travel, His divine head with no place to rest upon, no house for a shelter. And now the plan of redemption is more and more developed. He no longer suffers for the love of us by His own divine action, but from ill-treatment at the hands of others, borne willingly, yea, rejoicingly for our sake. Now we behold torments, agony and death; the cords of life, strong yet tender, are ruthlessly severed; His filial devotion, His fraternal charity, His fatherly kindness—all these affections of His Divine Heart are wantonly assailed; the gratitude and veneration of an admiring populace are turned into bitter hatred. Contemplating His Sacred Body we see His head crowned with thorns, His hands and feet pierced with nails, streams of blood drawn forth by cruel scourging, His whole frame writhing in torments without number. And thus we behold Him commending His spirit into the hands of His Father. "It is consummated!" Our Redemption is accomplished. We see Him rise in splendor from the tomb, appearing to His disciples, instructing and consoling them, promising them to send the Paraclete; and then, taking leave from the scene of His labors and sufferings, He ascends into Heaven where the celestial spirits rejoicingly receive Him. Finally we are invited to celebrate in joyful gratitude, with all the pomp of ecclesiastical ceremony, that miracle of ineffable love, in which are centered all the wonderful achievements of His life, from His appearance on earth as a helpless Infant to His atoning death as the Victim of our redemption—namely that mystery of divine love, the Most Holy Sacrifice of the Altar.

In unceasing love, gently but powerfully, mildly but irresistibly, did the Divine Heart of our Saviour pulsate from the first moment of His earthly life; it pulsated lovingly in the Child and in the Man, in the manger and on the Cross, when Mary nestled Him in

her chaste bosom, and when the Beloved Disciple rested
on His Divine breast. For every motion of human affection His Divine Heart found an expression: it was the
source of the tears He wept over unrepentant
Jerusalem, of the drops of blood that exuded from His
pores during His agony in the Garden, of the streams
of blood that gushed forth from His four great wounds
on Calvary, of that blessed fountain of regeneration
which was opened in His sacred side by the soldier's
spear. His very death—what was it but the offering of
His last remaining drop of blood for the Redemption
of mankind? And He did and suffered all this for love
of you, for love of me, for love of us all! We were captive in the bonds of God's enemy, and He released us.
But He released us in a manner that necessitates our
cooperation. We must follow His example. "For unto
this are you called: because Christ also suffered for
us, leaving you an example that you should follow His
steps." (*1 Ptr.* 2:21). And as we were captive and helpless before the advent of Christ, thus also shall we
again be captive and helpless in Purgatory, unless the
Church Militant comes to our relief and assistance.

Let us illustrate this condition by an example taken
from the Gospel. At the pool of Bethsaida lay a man
"that had been eight and thirty years under his infirmity." (*John* 5:5). His limbs were lamed with palsy;
without aid it was impossible for him to move. "And
an angel of the Lord descended at certain times into
the pond; and the water was moved. And he that went
down first into the pond after the motion of the water,
was made whole, of whatsoever infirmity he lay under."
(*John* 5:4). And this poor, sick man, behold him so
yearningly anxious to be healed, hearing the movement of the waters, seeing the Angel descend—and yet
he is so helpless! So many passers-by, but no one to
assist him! One by one the companions of his misery
have been healed: they went their way rejoicing, but
him they forgot. Hear him bemoaning his sad conditions: "I have no man, when the water is troubled, to

put me into the pond." (*John* 5:7). Alas, no pitiful heart, no ministering hand to come to his aid! And for thirty-eight years he languished thus! This is the picture of a soul in Purgatory.

Such a soul is in a helpless condition, unable to do anything for its own relief. Suffering, suffering! Our Lord pities the miserable condition of these souls; He desires to receive them into His glory, and to reward their faithfulness in His service; but His justice demands full satisfaction, and their release must be delayed till payment of the last farthing has been made. And now, behold the mercy of our Saviour: He does not send an angel to Bethsaida; He goes Himself to do for them what is in His power; He descends upon our altars. If at this moment the Suffering Soul were to come to Him while the cleansing flood of His atoning Blood is sparkling in the consecrated Chalice—truly, its release would be assured, the soul would be permitted to fly to the bosom of its loving Spouse. But, alas! of itself it cannot come; it is captive, unable to move. Our Saviour cannot loosen its bonds, because His justice demands satisfaction. To the yearning question, "How long dost Thou turn away Thy face from me?" (*Ps.* 12:1). comes the sorrowful answer, "Until the last farthing shall have been paid, either by thy own suffering, or by the suffrages of thy brethren and friends."

Hence Our Lord commissions the Church to exhort the faithful to be merciful and charitable towards the Suffering Souls. The Holy Souls behold their brethren on earth going to the fountain of salvation; they see so many of their suffering brethren ascend to Heaven, because some merciful hand has applied to them the saving flood of the Holy Sacrifice; and this or that soul—alas!—is forgotten, and cannot leave the place of torment. Why?—Hear the mournful answer, "I have no one to come to my assistance." And sorrowfully our loving Saviour inquires of mankind, "What is there that I ought to do more, and have not done?" Forsooth,

what more could He have done? One single petition of
a confident heart would suffice to lessen the distance
between God and the captive soul. St. Gertrude had
prayed long and fervently for a soul that apparently
had departed this world in a sad condition. At length
she was permitted to see it in its torments. On imploring the Lord to grant it full pardon, He replied, "My
justice would not prevent Me from releasing it immediately, if thou wouldst confidently ask Me. For by My
omniscience, which penetrates the future, I invested
this soul with the necessary dispositions to receive the
benefit of thy charity." Accordingly even a prayer may
suffice to appease divine justice and to release a soul
from captivity. Wonderful love of God!

"Now there was a certain man sick, named Lazarus,
of Bethania, of the town of Mary, and Martha, her sister. Now Jesus loved Martha, and her sister Mary, and
Lazarus. When He had heard therefore that he was
sick He still remained in the same place two days:
then after that He said to His disciples: Lazarus our
friend sleepeth; but I go that I may awake him out of
sleep. His disciples therefore said: Lord, if he sleep,
he shall do well. But Jesus spoke of his death, and
they thought that He spoke of the repose of sleep.
Then therefore Jesus said to them plainly: Lazarus is
dead. Let us go to him. Jesus therefore came, and
found that he had been four days already in the grave.
And many of the Jews were come to Martha and Mary
to comfort them concerning their brother. Martha therefore as soon as she heard that Jesus was come, went
to meet Him, but Mary sat at home. Martha therefore said to Jesus: Lord, if Thou hadst been here, my
brother had not died; but now also I know that whatsoever Thou wilt ask of God, God will give it Thee.
Jesus saith to her: Thy brother shall rise again.
Martha saith to Him: I know that he shall rise again
in the resurrection at the last day. Jesus said to her:
I am the resurrection and the life: he that believeth
in Me although he be dead shall live: and every one

that liveth and believeth in Me, shall not die forever. Believest thou this? She saith to Him: Yea, Lord, I have believed that Thou art Christ, the Son of the living God, who art come into this world. And when she had said these things, she went and called her sister Mary secretly, saying: The Master is come and calleth for thee. She, as soon as she heard *this,* riseth quickly, and cometh to Him. And seeing Him, she fell down at His feet, and saith to Him: Lord, if Thou hadst been here, my brother had not died. Jesus therefore, when He saw her weeping, and the Jews that were come with her, weeping, groaned in the spirit and troubled Himself, and said: Where have you laid him? And Jesus wept. The Jews therefore said: Behold how He loved him. Jesus therefore, again groaning in Himself, cometh to the sepulchre. Now it was a cave: and a stone was laid over it. And He cried with a loud voice: Lazarus, come forth. And presently he that had been dead came forth." (*John* 11).

The Son of God weeps with the sisters at the death of their brother, and then calls him to life again! Behold the efficacy of Martha's faith, of Mary's love! Except for this faith and love of his sisters Lazarus would have remained in his grave till the day of general resurrection. Our Saviour graciously heard the prayer of these sisters: and so also will He today hear our intercessions for our departed loved ones.

This wide earth of ours is our Saviour's Bethania— an abode of sorrow and mourning, but nevertheless a place of happiness and bliss, because in it is a house in which He dwells and makes His abode, His Holy Church. There He remains, expecting our fervent prayers for the release of the Suffering Souls. "Behold I am with you all days, even to the consummation of the world." (*Matt.* 28:20). The members of this His Church are united in faith and charity. If one of our brethren or sisters dies, what does it avail to weep? Our Church is animated with the faith of Martha in Him who solves the bondage of death; with the love of Mary, who sheds tears at the feet of Jesus, and makes her weeping the expression of her confiding prayer. And as the sisters led our Saviour to their brother's tomb, thus also does the faith, the love of the Church bring Him to the graves of our departed ones. The sisters of Lazarus prayed for their deceased brother and thereby effected his resurrection from the prison of the tomb; the prayer of the Church effects the release of our dead from the prison of Purgatory. Without Martha's faith and Mary's love, Lazarus would have moldered in his grave; without Catholic faith and charity, innumerable souls would remain in Purgatory to the end of the world. Faith and charity are combined in prayer for the Suffering Souls, and thus the glory of God is promoted.

Should not these motives of the glory and love of God be a mighty incentive for us to come to the relief of the Suffering Souls? Let us remember how greatly we are indebted to God's mercy for the innumerable benefits conferred on us every moment of our life. By aiding the Suffering Souls for the love of God we can show our gratitude at least in some measure; and if we know our duty, we will surely not neglect so easy, so consoling a means to prove ourselves grateful. Sometimes, in moments of affectionate, fervent and grateful sentiment—they are, alas, so few and fleeting!—we are sorry at not being able to glorify God like those apostolic men who gained whole nations for God and the Faith. To help the Suffering Souls is to exercise an apostolate, which is almost if not fully as promotive of God's glory, and nearly if not quite as fruitful for Heaven, as are the most zealous labors of missionaries. Here we behold a multitude of just souls in need of spiritual aid. Their want is not that of faith, but of atonement; our object is not their conversion, but their attainment of Heaven. For this purpose we are not obliged to cross oceans, to penetrate wildernesses, to learn foreign languages; a prayer, an alms, a Holy Mass may be sufficient. Moreover we need not fear for their final perseverance; by our suffrages we insure for them the everlasting enjoyment of God and Heaven.

Consider now, Christian soul, the greatness of this work of charity and gratitude; consider how well pleased God will be with the prayers and good works of those who offer them in satisfaction, to release the Suffering Souls—how pleased He will be if the admission of such a soul to the Beatific Vision were thereby hastened even for one hour. Remember the words of Our Lord, "Amen I say to you, as long as you did it to one of these my least brethren, you did it to Me." (*Matt.* 25:40). Our Lord Himself revealed to St. Gertrude that these words apply in a special manner to the Suffering Souls. Dionysius the Carthusian quotes her, saying: "As often as you release a soul from Purgatory, the Lord is so pleased thereat as if He Himself had been released from prison by you; and in due time He will reward you most graciously for this charity." Who among us will refuse any longer to follow the footsteps of Our Lord who suffered for us? The glory and love of God, and the gratitude we owe Him, are most powerful motives, which should ever impel us to devote our lives to the release of the Suffering Souls.

Motives Relating to the Suffering Souls

On the 30th of May, 1889, I was about to start for the East to visit a friend, and to prepare a class of first Communicants for the reception of the Blessed Eucharist. I felt an inexplicable oppression of mind, an apprehensive fear of starting on my journey, so that I had to be reminded repeatedly that there was no time to lose. During the following night on the train, between the 30th and 31st of May, I was very restless. The next morning, however, on leaving Pittsburgh, I became calmer. Resigned to the Will of God, I was prepared for the worst. Before evening my unusual disquietude was explained: I became a witness of one of the greatest calamities of modern times, the Johnstown flood. After the bursting of the reservoir, the river Conemaugh continued to rise with appalling rapidity, until the angry waters had torn away bridges, outhouses and telegraph poles, undermined the railroad tracks and threatened destruction to the main part of the town. The flood struck Johnstown toward five in the evening; and the inhabitants had been warned to fly to the hills for their lives. Thousands were intercepted in their flight and found a watery grave.

No pen can describe the heartrending scenes that followed. The masses of water destroyed everything in their way. Thousands had sought safety in their houses; but the raging waters surrounded them, undermined the foundations, swept away the buildings together with their unfortunate inmates, men, women and children, till the great stone piers of the railroad bridge impeded their progress. Here they stuck fast and were exposed to the fury of the destructive element, until they fell to pieces and spilled their inmates into the yawning gulf. Hundreds sank to rise no more; and still the mass of wreck and ruin continued to increase, until it was three quarters of a mile long and between thirty and sixty feet wide, rising high out of the water. About fifteen hundred people were imprisoned here, some caught between the ruins, others free and able to move about in the debris.

To add to the horrors of the situation, fire broke out among the ruins. At first it burned slowly, the curling smoke apprising the dazed spectators on the shore of the new danger threatening their parents, brothers, sisters, relatives and fellow citizens. Soon the lurid flames greedily devoured whatever was in their reach, and lighted up the darkness in ghastly splendor. Horror of horrors! They attack the mass of living, moving, writhing humanity. Cries for help rend the air. Helpless misery everywhere—on the burning ruins the terrified victims of water and fire, on the shore a mass of people frantic because there is no way to aid the sufferers. Some of the latter escaped the flames to find death in the water, or were crushed in the debris; and thus the sad spectacle continued until the seething mass was engulfed in darkness beneath the bridge.

An adequate description of these horrors cannot be given. And now, O Christian soul, consider: if the Suffering Souls in Purgatory were to appear before us on such a burning pile to move us to mercy: if they were to appear in their bodies, as they once lived here on earth, and if we saw them surrounded by flames, themselves one seething mass of fire—who among us could repress his tears on witnessing their sad condition, on hearing their lamentations?—As the helpless victims of the Johnstown disaster called for help, thus also do the Suffering Souls implore our aid. "To you we have recourse," they call, "on you, fathers, mothers, sons, daughters, relatives, friends, neighbors, on you we call for aid, and for the sake of a vain pleasure you forget our torments! Remember, we are in a place where we have to atone for every evil thought, for every idle word, in a fire which, though not everlasting, in every other respect resembles that of Hell."

The disaster of Johnstown was appalling. But, oh, how would the souls in Purgatory congratulate themselves if divine justice would not demand more of them than what the victims of that calamity had to undergo. The difference between suffering in this and the next world is great. Here on earth God punishes us as our Father, even when He fulfills the word of the royal prophet, "I will visit their iniquities with a rod: and their sins with stripes." (*Ps.* 88:33). But in the next world God punishes us as our Judge. "For He will render to a man his work, and according to the ways of every one He will reward them. For in very deed God will not condemn without cause; neither will the Almighty pervert judgment." (*Job* 34:11, 12). In this world we can satisfy the justice of God as it were by way of compromise; in the next world we must atone according to the rigor of His judgment. In the world beyond we must suffer not only what all sinners have to suffer in this world, but also the punishment that sin deserves in its aspect as a rebellion against God. We must suffer punishment not only for sin, but we must also atone for all the graces which sin prevented us from receiving. We must moreover suffer not only for all the injustice and malice toward others, with which sin is so often fraught, but also for the offense and insult thereby offered to God.

God is so great, man so insignificant; God offers us so much, sin so little; God loves us so tenderly, and we offend Him so boldly! Considered from this view it is easy to measure the suffering of a soul in Purgatory: it is commensurate with the disparity between the infinite majesty of an offended God and the perishable trifle for which the soul offended Him; the disparity between the infinite goodness of an offended God, and the base ingratitude of a creature that once despised Him. As this disparity is inconceivable to us, the torments of Purgatory are also inconceivable; and hence we should have pity on the souls that must suffer these torments.

By sin God was offended, and Purgatory resulted as one of the means to satisfy divine justice. "It is a fearful thing to fall into the hands of the living God." (*Heb.* 10:31). God often punished sin in a most dreadful manner even in this world. We find a proof of this in the people of Israel, who were attacked in the desert by venomous serpents; in the boys that were torn by wild beasts because they had ridiculed the prophet Eliseus; in Ananias and Saphira, who fell dead because they had lied to the Apostle. If God punishes sin thus severely in this world, how will He punish it in the next? And we should have no compassion, no pity, no heart for the souls in Purgatory?

Purgatory is moreover the place of punishment for the elect. We read in the lives of the Saints how severely they punished themselves for the smallest faults. They fasted rigorously, and scourged themselves till they drew blood; they were assiduous in all kinds of austerities and never rested in their labors—and this they did not merely for a few days or weeks, but for years, and in some cases for almost a hundred years. Can we read the lives of the holy hermits Anthony, Hilarion, Pelagius and others without shuddering at the austerities they practiced? Can we remember the penitential code of the early Church without astonishment at its rigor? And yet in those days public scandals were of rare occurrence. If the Church, who is a loving Mother, imposed such severe penances on her dear children to preserve them from the torments of Purgatory—what then will God demand of a soul in the place of atonement, if despite all the opportunities and graces offered it was remiss in rendering satisfaction to divine justice?

The Saints chose the most excruciating pains and sufferings in this world, even praying to obtain them: but we know of no instance that a saint ever desired to undergo the sufferings of Purgatory, or viewed them with that callous indifference so often to be found among Christians of our day. They rather regarded them with dread and terror, and suffered in this world for the very purpose of escaping suffering in the next. If even the Saints, who loved suffering and regarded martyrdom as a blessing, trembled at the thought of Purgatory, we may conclude how great the difference must be between the sufferings here and hereafter. Let us therefore believe the holy Fathers when they tell us that one day in Purgatory is a punishment more severe than a hundred years of the most austere penance in this world.

Purgatory is a middle state between Heaven and Hell, and the soul is affected by the proximity of both. At all events it is painfully affected by the proximity of Hell. For like Hell, Purgatory is a state of bondage and captivity. According to many theological writers, it has the darkness and desolation, the flames and fire of Hell; it has everything that Hell has to terrify us, except despair and everlasting duration of punishment. If we should see someone in a fiery furnace, we would do our utmost to get him out of it, even if he was our greatest enemy. This was illustrated at the horrible calamity of Johnstown. Parents, children, relatives and friends stood on the shore anxious to save whomsoever they could. Now, as regards the Suffering Souls, we *can* help them. What have they done to us that we *do not* help them, that we permit them to suffer on, though in life they were perhaps our most intimate friends? Besides we must remember the terrible pains of sense which the souls in Purgatory suffer; also that most intense pain resulting from their deprivation of the Beatific Vision of God. They languish, they yearn to see their God; and they are banished from His presence. They are near to Him, and yet so far away. They seek Him and find Him not. They are attracted to Him and feel themselves repulsed. They sigh continually for Him and are not heard. What a torment, what inexpressible suffering! And yet we have no compassion on them!

Alas, these Poor Souls are in the debtors' prison, and are unable to do anything for their own release. Their time of merit is over. Their day is past, the night has befallen them. Their cry for mercy is unheard, as far as they themselves are concerned. Their tears no longer blot out their misdeeds. For them there are no longer the Sacraments, indulgences, means of grace. No longer can they atone for their faults by good works, prayer, fasting and almsdeeds in virtue of Christ's redeeming Blood. "For the time hath its end" (*Dan.* 8:19); that is, their time of merit is past. For them the time of suffering has come. And how long must they suffer? Who can know? Who can tell? It is the pious custom of the Church to pray for the departed centuries after their death; by this she conclusively proves that she believes, or fears, that these souls, so long since departed, are still suffering. These souls then cannot do the least for their own release. They cry to us for relief, they call on us for help. We *can* help them and we do not! We know that they are undergoing the punishment inflicted by divine wrath; we know that works of atonement are necessary for their relief; we know that they suffer the most excruciating torments in their helpless condition— and yet we refuse to help them! Have we hearts of stone?

The Suffering Souls in Purgatory, knowing that of themselves they can not cause any change in their deplorable condition, and that we can do so much for them, continually implore us to come to their aid by applying to them the merits of the life, sufferings and death of Jesus Christ from out of the treasury of the Church. But as they cannot without God's special permission draw our attention personally to their needs, the Church does it in their place both by means of her many pious practices for their relief, as also by calling our attention to their pitiable state. Hence the Venerable Catherine Emmerich observes: "Oh, these Poor Souls have so much to suffer because of their negligence, because of their former want of piety and zeal for God and their neighbor. How shall they be aided except by atoning charity, which offers up for them those acts of virtue which they neglected during life? And how they yearn for this charity! For themselves they can no longer do anything. But they also know that no good thought, no sincere desire offered up for them by the living, is without effect. Yet how few care for them! If anybody prays for them, suffers for them, gives alms for them, they immediately experience relief."

Since we know, and know by faith, how great the torments of these just souls in Purgatory are, should we not be moved to compassion for them? We cannot endure to see a living creature tormented, and can we be so insensible to the sufferings of these friends of God as to regard them with indifference, so unfeeling as to refuse to mitigate them? When Our Lord saw the sick man at Bethsaida, who suffered for thirty-eight

years because he had no one to place him into the
water, His Heart was moved to pity; and He passed by
the other sick and healed this one, who was unable to
help himself. The condition of the souls in Purgatory
is similar. Will the example of our Divine Lord not
impel us to help them?

Grateful love for our deceased is so deeply imprinted
into our hearts, that there are only few who are insensible to it. We even find that after death our love
increases for those who were dear to us in life. Their
loss makes us feel their worth more keenly. And those
whom we neglected during life—we miss them when
they are no longer among us. We have even a kindly
feeling for those in their graves, of whom we had reason to complain during life. Their defects are forgotten, and we remember only their virtues. These
sentiments were implanted into our hearts by our loving Creator as a connecting link between this world
and the next, by means of which we remain in contact
with Himself and His elect, and even with such of the
latter as do not yet enjoy His Beatific Vision. He, the
Father of mercies and God of all consolation, loves them
Himself and cheers them with the hope of release and
bliss after His justice shall have been satisfied and
their purification attained. They are His elect, objects
of His love; and hence our charity should extend to
them. "A gift hath grace in the sight of all the living,
and restrain not grace from the dead." (*Ecclus.* 7:37).

Who are the souls for whose speedy release we should
offer our prayers, the Holy Sacrifice of Mass, and good
works? They are souls that once inhabited a frail human
body like our own, a body created by God and now
moldering in its grave or in the bottom of the deep.
Like ourselves these souls had to engage in combat
against temptations of the flesh, against the evil influence of the world and the devil. Like ourselves they
feared death, and even now they are open to the influence of pain and joy. Like ourselves they are Christians, ransomed by the same Precious Blood of a dying

God-Man; perhaps they dwelt with us in the same community; at all events they shared with us the same holy Sacraments and means of grace; perhaps they were our best friends, to whom we are indebted for many an important service. Moreover, our Faith enjoins us to extend our charity not only to those that were dear to us in life, or to whom we are indebted for their good will toward us, but to all men; hence our charity must embrace also all souls that are in need of our prayer and help.

Again, gratitude and justice must impel us in a particular manner to this charity. Who are the Suffering Souls, whose pitiful condition appeals to us? Perhaps a dear father, once so solicitous for your welfare, earning bread for you by the sweat of his brow, laboring for your success in life, and perhaps suffering now for the very reason that he had too much regard for your welfare and therefore neglected his duty towards the poor. Ask him why he is thus suffering, and he will answer you with the sick man in the Gospel, "I have no one to help me!" Perhaps the Suffering Soul is a fond mother who brought you forth to life, who loved you with her whole heart, who spent herself for you; and now perhaps she has to suffer for the very reason that she was too fond of you, and therefore neglected to correct your faults, thinking that the virtues with which she imbued you were sufficient to conteract them. And now listen to her plaintive cry, "I have no one to help me!"

Or perhaps it is the soul of your pastor and spiritual guide that appeals to you for help. During life he conscientiously followed the advice of St. Paul, "Preach the word: be instant in season, out of season: reprove, entreat, rebuke in all patience and doctrine." (*2 Tim.* 4:2). But because greater perfection is demanded of the priest than of the rest of the faithful, and because neglect of duty is more reprehensible in him than in others, he is sentenced to purification in the fiery furnace; and because the faithful had so high a regard for his virtue, they neglect to pray for him; his chances of relief and deliverance are the smaller, the greater the esteem in which he was held. He helped so many others in life and in death, but was perhaps remiss in his duty towards the dead. And now, alas, he joins the mournful chorus, "I have none to help me!"

Perhaps your brothers and sisters, so dear to you in life, one heart and one soul with you in consequence of the same training, the same bent of mind, are in that fiery furnace; or it is your teacher who spent himself for your mental and moral improvement, sowing the good seed of religion and virtue into your heart; or they are relatives and friends, who with you bore the burden and heat of the day, taking upon themselves a great part of your share, ever ready to help, console and encourage you. Alas, you give them cause to join in the mournful plaint, "I have no one to help me!"

Or perhaps it is the soul of one, who in the opening bloom of life was most dear to you and was about to become one with you for life in the sacred bond of Matrimony; but the grim reaper Death suddenly swung his scythe—the blooming flower drooped and withered and was laid away to await the Angel's call to resurrection; and the soul which you so often tried to fathom to its depth, in whose love you found the supreme joy and happiness of your life—where is it now? Your own wealth of affection was too sensual, it called forth a like sentiment in your beloved, and your affianced's soul is undergoing punishment for a fault for which you are to blame. You cover the grave with flowers, you rear a splendid monument—and that is all! Listen, hear the mournful cry, "I have no one to help me!"

Or the soul is that of a faithful servant, who spent his best years and gave his sincerest efforts in serving you, even so far as to neglect the service of God. It is a soldier who laid down his life in defense of his country, in consequence of which you enjoy the blessings of peace. They also swell the mournful dirge, "I have no one to help me!"

How can you, how dare you neglect these and all the other Suffering Souls not mentioned in this hasty sketch? Their plaintive cry is voiced by holy Job, whose sufferings were nothing in comparison to theirs: "Have pity on me, have pity on me, at least you my friends, because the hand of the Lord hath touched me." (*Job* 19:21).

Oh, that we could see our suffering friends atoning for their faults in the deep abyss and fiery furnace into which Divine Justice has cast them! Oh, that we could hear their plaintive cries for help, their mournful reproaches of our neglect and hardness of heart! Children would hear their parents cry to them in the words of the prophet, "I have brought up children, and exalted them: but they have despised me." (*Is.* 1:2). Hence St. Leonard of Port Maurice justly censures all hard-hearted Christians as follows: "What are you about? Are you children or are you brutes and monsters of cruelty to remain unmoved at the bitter plaints of your father, of your mother? There are instances of tigers exposing themselves to certain death in defense of their young, of reptiles casting themselves into the flames to save their brood from burning: and you will not descend into Purgatory to save your poor father, your suffering mother from its painful flames? You are so hard of heart as to refuse to lend them a helping hand by the performance of a good work for their relief? Go, then, if this be so, go and tear down from your walls the pictures of your parents and cast them into the fire, rejoicing that while the originals are burning in Purgatory through your fault, their pictures may share their lot."

Heartless child, your parents have reason indeed to address you thus, "I loved my children so dearly; I ever had their welfare at heart, and they so soon forgot me! They still eat my bread; they owe to me whatever they possess, and yet it no longer reminds them of me!" And the forgotten friend exclaims with David, "If my enemy had reviled me, I would have verily borne with it. And if he that hated me had spoken great things against me, I would perhaps have hid myself from him: but thou, a man of one mind, my guide and my familiar, who didst take sweet meats together with me!" (*Ps.* 54). "You, my friend, who promised me on my deathbed to remember me, have so soon forgotten me! You feel compassion for malefactors suffering for their crimes, but for the soul of your friend you feel no pity! Unfaithful friend, mercy shall not be shown to you, because you showed none to me!"

Christian soul, answer candidly; it is the Church that asks you the question, the Church whose Faith you profess and whose Sacraments you receive: Is it really true, have you so shamefully neglected your departed dear ones? The souls of these departed ask this question; the souls of those that have a rightful claim on your gratitude and affection.—You are silent?—But in the depth of your heart you sigh: "Alas, it is true!" The tears start from your eyes and course down your cheeks in acknowledgment of your fault. And indeed, you have reason to weep scalding tears of repentance: it is dreadful to neglect for weeks, months and even years to say even one "Our Father" for the Suffering Souls, for those who during life were so fervent, so persevering in their prayer for us. It is awful not to have contributed even a mite of good works for the relief of those who must languish in prison till the "last farthing is paid." O Catholics, where is your faith and your practice of the Faith? Where is your charity and its practical demonstration? Where is your heart and its sentiment of compassion?

Oh, do not, in proof that you did *not* forget your departed ones, call attention to the pompous funeral display you ordered, to the costly casket, the profusion of flowers, the imposing monument. Vanity of vanities! It is help, *help* they need, relief for which they cry in the words of Joseph in Pharaoh's prison: "Remember me, when it shall be well with thee, and do me this kindness: to take me out of this prison." (*Gen.* 40:14).

This is the touching prayer of your father or mother, your brother or sister, your husband or wife, your friend or benefactor.

Pray, oh, pray for their release from the gloomy prison, that they may rejoicingly enter the heavenly court to partake of the banquet of God's elect, there to welcome us after our own death. This is our hope, our prayer, our supplication—that the greater our sorrow was at parting, the greater may be our joy at that heavenly reunion. To meet again! What a charm this assurance has for the human heart! Witness the gloom, the sorrow cast over a home, because a dear son is about to take his leave. The father's tears start unbidden while he says the parting words; the mother's heart is rent asunder and she will not be comforted—again and again she holds her child in fond embrace; brothers and sisters repress the outburst of their sorrow to spare their parents, but their trembling lips can scarcely say the dreaded word, "Farewell!" "Farewell, to meet again!" the answer comes. The scene is changed. A gleam of sunshine pierces through the lowering clouds. "To meet again!" The smile of hope dispels the gloom of parting.

How different, how bitter, when the assurance and conviction are expressed that the parting from our dear ones is forever! The aged father's life is fast ebbing away. "It is towards evening, and the day is now far spent." (*Luke* 24:29). He assembles his children around his dying couch, and in a weak but most impressive voice reminds them of his instructions during life; he warns them of the dangers of disobedience and neglect of duty. Amid loud sobbing they listen to his parting words. And now his voice is hushed—is stilled in death.

The loving husband sees the wife of his bosom slowly wasting away. He does whatever is in his power to ease her pains, but physicians and their remedies avail no longer. Her earthly doom is sealed; in the strong arms of him to whom she confidently trusted her life's happiness, she yields her spirit to God. But why pro-

long these heartrending scenes? Few there are who
have not experienced this sorrow. But one ordeal
remains to be undergone: the mortal remains are con-
signed to the grave.—Farewell! Farewell!—Though lips,
from sorrow, cannot say the word, 'tis indelibly engraven
on the heart.

Farewell forever in this vale of tears! And yet, "We
mourn not as those who have no hope." "Farewell to
meet again in Heaven!" O beauty of our Heaven-given
religion! O sweetness of its hope and consolation! To
meet again in Heaven! "And I heard a voice from heaven,
saying to me: Write: Blessed are the dead, who die in
the Lord!" (*Apoc.* 14:13). "I am the resurrection and
the life: he that believeth in Me, although he be dead,
shall live: and every one that liveth, and believeth in
Me, shall not die forever." (*John* 11:25, 26). Why then
mourn our dead excessively, if we have this consoling
promise by the word of Divine Truth? You may weep
at the death of your loved ones; 'tis but natural to do
so, and Jesus Himself wept at the tomb of Lazarus.
But why be disconsolate? We shall meet them all again.
Thus Holy Church bids us to hope and pray; thus Holy
Writ assures us: "For the trumpet shall sound, and the
dead shall rise again incorruptible." (*1 Cor.* 15:52). "How
do some among you say, that there is no resurrection
of the dead?" (*1 Cor.* 15:12). To meet again: O happy
thought, consoling assurance!

To meet again! What ineffable joy is contained in
this hope! Our Lord Himself assures us: "You now
indeed have sorrow; but I will see you again, and your
heart shall rejoice; and your joy no man shall take
from you." (*John* 16:22). When our dear ones after a
long absence return home again, we ask ourselves how
we can welcome them with the most pleasant surprise. And if we can do nothing in this respect, we at
least remove everything that might displease them.
And how well pleased is the returning member of the
family at seeing that his own love him in word and
deed, and that they spared no sacrifice to render the

meeting a happy one.

Now, what shall we do to render happy those of our loved ones who returned to their true home, who passed through the portals of eternity? Many of them are still undergoing punishment for their unatoned faults. Could we only see them, we could not but give them proof of our sympathy. Or would you not make use of the means of relief placed at your disposal? Would you refuse them your help, and thereby demonstrate your disregard for them? If so, they will not meet you in gladness when you enter the portals of the next world; they will give their welcome to those who were more charitable than you. You often remark, "Oh, that they were still living, they to whom I owe my being! Dear mother, could I but see you once more! Dear friends, whose intercourse and loving kindness is so pleasant a remembrance, oh, that I could show how grateful I am to you! If you were still among the living, I would do everything in my power for you." Christian soul, if these are really your sentiments, you can now show your gratitude. Faith tells you plainly and unmistakably what to do for your dear ones. If they have departed this world without having fully atoned for all their faults, they are now in torments compared with which all suffering in this world is as nothing. They call for your help. "Have pity on me!" Come to their aid, assist them to enter their heavenly home as soon as possible.

Faith describes to you the instinctive desire of every soul parted from its body to reach its ultimate destiny; and it shows you conclusively how this desire is the source of the most intense pain. The attainment of this their supreme good is denied by divine justice to your dear ones; they are detained in their abode of misery and separation from God, and nothing remains to them but to lament and sigh, "When shall I come and appear before the face of God?" (*Ps.* 41:3). "When will the happy hour arrive when we shall possess our supreme and infinite good, enjoying the beatific vision of our God, and with it everlasting bliss? O beautiful gates of the heavenly Jerusalem, if our present suffering is not sufficient to open you to us, let it be increased until we shall be permitted to pass through you!" "Be ye lifted up, O eternal gates!" (*Ps.* 23:7). Alas, the gates are not opened, the blessed hour is delayed, the beatific vision is denied. Hence the ceaseless yearning, the unrequited desire of love, the painful straining toward the attainment of its object, incomprehensible to us until we shall be able to comprehend its source. "Give me a loving soul," says St. Augustine, "to understand what I intend to convey." "When shall I come and appear before the face of God?" You must either pay "the last farthing" of your debt yourself, or payment must be made for you by your friends on earth. "Have pity on me, have pity on me, at least you my friends!"

Now you realize to a certain degree the condition of your loved ones in eternity; and you know that you are able to assist them. Will you delay your help and retard their entrance into our heavenly home, where they will joyously receive you? If you find a suffering stranger whose distress is relieved by no one, you have him taken care of and receive his sincere gratitude for this fulfillment of your Christian duty. But your dear ones in the other world—shall they alone be denied your aid? Oh, no! Your meeting with them after this life is to be a joyous one; they shall conduct you into heavenly bliss!

We related in a former paragraph that, according to a private revelation of Sister Frances of the Blessed Sacrament, the soul of Pope Gregory XV was surrounded by Saints at its entrance into Heaven after a short Purgatory, and was principally attended by the five Saints he had canonized in 1622, viz. SS. Theresa, John of the Cross, Isidore, Ignatius and Francis Xavier. Let us do our share and have the attendance of our loved ones in the same manner. It will be granted to us, if we hasten their release by our good works. What a joy to behold those meeting us as Saints, whom we so dearly loved on earth! Or shall they go and meet other benefactors?

Christian soul, are these motives on the part of the Suffering Souls not sufficiently powerful to move our hearts to compassion, and to invite us to procure their speedy relief? Their misery is beyond doubt; it is beyond our comprehension; it concerns our friends and benefactors, at all events those who are our brethren in Christ. Oh, let us hear their pitiful cry for help; let us renew our zeal for them from the unselfish motives of fraternal charity, of good example; let us pray for the repose of the immortal souls of the faithful departed; let us have the Holy Sacrifice of Mass, this most effectual means of speedy relief, offered for them; let us offer for them our own devout assistance at it; let us charitably aid the poor and distressed for this intention, and deny ourselves for them by fasting and other works of penance. Let us unite these our good works with the infinite merits of our Lord Jesus Christ, humbly imploring Him to receive and offer them to His Heavenly Father for the relief and speedy release of the Suffering Souls. If we do it in this spirit and manner, we may rest assured that we shall be heard.

Chapter 5

Gratitude of the Suffering Souls

The Suffering Souls Show Their Gratitude by Praying for Their Benefactors

OUR Divine Redeemer exhorts us, "Make unto you friends of the mammon of iniquity; that when you shall fail, they may receive you into everlasting dwellings." (*Luke* 16:9). The souls of the faithful whom we deliver from the depths of misery and lead to supreme bliss by means of the "mammon of iniquity," become our most grateful friends and incessantly implore God to shower upon us His choicest blessings and bounties. We cannot but believe that they will remember us in Heaven with the greatest gratitude. Or would we dare to accuse the Saints of that base ingratitude which we sometimes experience at the hands of men here below, where, alas, ingratitude is nothing unusual? Our Divine Saviour Himself experienced it. "Were not ten made clean, and where are the nine?" (*Luke* 17:17). Since and before that time ingratitude was and is still of daily occurrence here on earth. But in Heaven where nothing defiled enters this vice has no place. There charity reigns supreme, and base ingratitude is banished forever.

From this we may conclude with what gratitude all those souls will intercede for us, whose admission to Heaven we have hastened by our suffrages. As gratitude demands that benefits be returned with benefits—will they permit that our prayers which obtained

228

for them so great a boon shall surpass theirs in fervor? As we came to their aid so charitably when they were unable to do anything for their own relief, will they desert us of whose needs they are so well aware? As wayfarers on earth they observed the law of Christ—they loved even their enemies, doing good to them that hated them; and now that they are in Heaven, will they not love their most active friends, to whose charity they owe the hastening of their bliss, and prove this love by constant intercession for them? St. Alphonsus Liguori says, "Whosoever comes to the aid of these distressed souls, so dear to Our Lord, may confidently hope to be saved; for if such a soul is released through his prayer and good works, it prays incessantly for his salvation, and God will not refuse to hear His spouse." Bishop Colmar of Mayence, a great friend of the Holy Souls, remarks: "If I could know for certain that I had the happiness of releasing one of those souls, all my dread and fear of eternity would vanish; I should regard my salvation as assured. For such a soul could not witness me going to perdition without imploring mercy for me so fervently that the Lord would grant me His mercy."

The Suffering Souls in Purgatory do not wait until they arrive in Heaven to give evidence of their gratitude to their benefactors. Even while suffering the most dreadful torments they are anxious to return their charity; and hence they pray incessantly for the spiritual and temporal welfare of those who succored them. It is true St. Thomas teaches that the state of the Holy Souls is a higher one than ours, because it is no longer possible for them to commit sin. But their state may also be considered as being lower than ours, on account of the punishment they are obliged to suffer. Being in a state of suffering they are in a position rather to receive than to give help. The members of the Church Suffering can no longer acquire merit, nor can they effectually make intercession for others. They must render atonement to Divine Justice "to the last farthing." A drowning, a burning man's thoughts are centered too intently on his own dangers to be drawn to other occurrences around him. Thus the Suffering Souls are wholly occupied with their torments: "Have pity on me, have pity on me, at least you my friends, because the hand of the Lord hath touched me." (*Job* 19:21). And as the souls in the prison of Purgatory do not as yet enjoy the vision of God, and are therefore not aware of our thoughts, desires and prayers, they are not in a position to act as intercessors for us, but they rather have need of our prayers.

This is the doctrine of St. Thomas. But as the Church has not dogmatically declared for or against this doctrine, the question, "Can the souls in Purgatory, while in the state of suffering, intercede for us with God?" is an open one. Theologians are divided on it, and the Church tolerates the opinions of both sides. And if we ask the religious sentiment of Catholics in general, this question is confidently answered with, "Yes!" Most commentators of St. Thomas declare that his doctrine does not conflict with this opinion. According to the opinion of the Angelic Doctor—and his opinion is the general one—the Suffering Souls are not official intercessors for the Church Militant in the same sense as are the Saints in Heaven. Their position is not that of intercessors, but of beneficiaries for whom we ought to intercede; our position, as far as gaining merit and helping them in concerned, being preferable to theirs. Our prayer, addressed to God in the state of grace, is always heard, according to our Saviour's own declaration, "If you shall ask Me any thing in My name, that I will do." (*John* 14:14). These words were addressed to the living, not to the dead.

According to St. Thomas it is the Will of God that the inferior should be assisted by the superior. Since it is true that the souls in Purgatory, by reason of their captivity, are in a state inferior to ours, it might seem, because of this inferior state, that they cannot pray for us. But as they are also in a state superior to ours, since they are beyond the possibility of committing sin, does it not follow that they *can* pray for us? It is not necessary that they should possess every claim in order to be entitled to pray for us; it is sufficient that they possess one. Hence some followers of St. Thomas call the doctrine that the Suffering Souls can pray for us the common one. For as far as this second reason is concerned, they can be our intercessors the same as the Saints in Heaven, because they are in the grace and favor of God. Our motive of praying for the Suffering Souls should be rather a desire to help them, than to receive their help. It should be our principal object to pray for their aid and deliverance, rather than to obtain their assistance. But their condition is no obstacle to their prayer for us. Gregory of Valencia maintains that the souls in Purgatory pray for the Faithful in general, but particularly for those who were very dear to them on earth. Bellarmine, Suarez, Sylvius, Gotti, Jungmann and many others are of the same opinion.

The renowned theologian Scheeben remarks on this question: "The souls in Purgatory being confirmed in charity, it seems not only probable, but evident that they actually pray. That is, they present petitions to God in favor of the Church Militant, and particularly in favor of their benefactors; otherwise their charity would be powerless and inert. If here on earth we should and do pray for others, how much the more is it not to be expected of those Holy Souls! The state of grace, on which the intercession of the Suffering Souls depends as on its fructifying principle, is the very principle on which the prayer of all other just souls depends for its efficiency. Every just soul is a beloved friend of God. As the souls in Purgatory are no less friends of God than the just on earth, it would be a deflection from the order of grace if their charity were disregarded and unrequited in the very acts which are especially pleasing to God. This deflection becomes still more apparent if the communion of Saints is taken into consideration. This communion being the uniting bond of the Mystical Body of Christ, its unity must of necessity be like that of any organic body. This unity requires that every living member of the whole communion, each in his way, shall contribute by his ministrations to the welfare of the whole body; that consequently no living member shall act as the mere recipient of the benefactions of the rest, without himself being useful to the others; and particularly that he shall not receive favors from the other members without making a return to them by grateful reciprocation."

Continuing his argument Scheeben adds: "This last mentioned motive of gratitude is of special import. Its principle is recognized, because it is a doctrine universally taught in the Church that the Suffering Souls, at least after their entrance into Heaven, efficiently remember at the throne of God those whose benefits they received. But why should their gratitude remain sterile and ineffective till then? Is it not true that the Holy Souls are no less dear and pleasing to God in Purgatory than they will be later in Heaven? Would not their prayer in many instances be too late, especially as regards graces to be obtained for their benefactors while these latter are yet on earth? And would not the motive to pray for the Suffering Souls be greatly weakened—the motive arising from their gratitude toward their benefactors—if these Souls could pray effectually for their liberators only after they are released from Purgatory? Hence the practice of invoking the Holy Souls is well sustained and authorized. First, confidence in the gratitude of these Sufferers is revived, and with it our zeal to help them. Secondly, this practice leads us to consider them not only as Suffering, but also as Holy Souls, whose sufferings are not merely punishments, but also immolations; these souls are consumed by flames of holy love even more than they are by the flames surrounding them. Thereby our compassion for them receives increased sacredness, and makes us sharers in their pure and perfect penitential spirit, a spirit so strong and fervent that it cannot be equaled anywhere on earth."

True, for the Church Suffering there is no longer any time for action, but only for suffering; no longer any time for gaining merit, but only for bowing submissively to the Will of God and paying indebtedness to His Divine Justice "to the last farthing." But this places no obstacle to our intercession for the Souls in Purgatory.

The sinner is separated from Jesus Christ, the source of supernatural life; he is a dead member of His body. Hence he cannot gain merit for Heaven. "And if I should distribute all my goods to feed the poor, and if I should deliver my body to be burned, and have not charity, it profiteth me nothing." (*1 Cor.* 13:3). The sinner therefore has no merit of his works, however good they may be in themselves, even if he should give all his possessions to the poor, or suffer martyrdom. But though gaining no merit for Heaven by his good works, the sinner may obtain through them the grace of conversion. God does not owe him this grace. If He imparts it to him, it is granted not as a merit, but as an effect of divine mercy in reward for the good disposition shown by the good works he performed in cooperation with active grace. How effective good works are for conversion is demonstrated by Cornelius the centurion, "a just man, and one that feareth God" (*Acts* 10:22), whom God led to the true Faith on account of his good works. It is proved by the conversion of the Ninivites: "And God saw their works, that they were turned from their evil way: and God had mercy with regard to the evil which He had said that He would do to them, and He did it not." (*Jon.* 3:10). And of Manasses we also read: "He did evil before the Lord . . . And after that he was in distress he prayed to the Lord his God: and did penance exceedingly before the God of his fathers. And he entreated Him, and besought Him earnestly: and He heard his prayer, and brought him again to

Jerusalem into his kingdom, and Manasses knew that the Lord was God." (*2 Par.* 33:2, 12, 13).

Though Manasses was a sinner, God heard his prayer: can we imagine that His living Heart will refuse to hear the prayers of the Holy Souls, who forget their own sufferings to be mindful of the sufferings of others? Even though these Souls cannot effectively pray for themselves, will God reject their prayers when they pray to preserve their brethren from the flames of Hell, and if it so please Him, also from the purifying flames in which they themselves are confined? Can we imagine that God hears the supplications of sinners, but refuses to hear those of His beloved spouses? God undoubtedly hears them and grants their petitions—not because He is bound to do so by His promise, or because their prayers are meritorious; but simply because He loves these Souls. The Suffering Souls, then, can present our needs to God by way of intercession; and God in His mercy and love deigns to hear them, though He does not always grant their petitions. On earth we can rely on God's promise that He will grant our prayers; the Saints in Heaven can rely for the hearing of their prayers on God's complacency and on their merits; the Suffering Souls must rely on God's love for them.

Concerning the prayer of the Suffering Souls for the living, St. Augustine in his treatise on the care for the dead writes as follows: Holy Scripture testifies that sometimes the dead are sent to the living, while on the other hand St. Paul was transported from among the living into paradise. When Saul beheld the camp of the Philistines, he was much afraid and sought consolation with the Lord. "And he consulted the Lord, and He answered him not, neither by dreams, nor by priests, nor by prophets." (*1 Kgs.* 28:6). And he went to the woman of Endor, who called up for him the spirit of Samuel. "And Samuel said to Saul: Why hast thou disturbed my rest, that I should be brought up? And Saul said, I am in great distress: for the Philistines fight against me, and God is departed from me, and would not hear me, neither by the hand of prophets, nor by dreams; therefore I have called thee, that thou mayest show me what I shall do. And Samuel said: Why askest thou me, seeing the Lord has departed from thee, and is gone over to thy rival? For the Lord will do to thee as He spoke by me, and He will rend thy kingdom out of thy hand, and will give it to thy neighbor David: because thou didst not obey the voice of the Lord, neither didst thou execute the wrath of His indignation upon Amalec. Therefore hath the Lord done to thee what thou sufferest this day. And the Lord will also deliver Israel with thee into the hands of the Philistines: and tomorrow thou and thy sons shall be with me: and the Lord will also deliver the army of Israel into the hands of the Philistines." (*1 Kgs.* 28:15-19). Thus Samuel proved Saul's protector as in life so also after death, even enabling him to prepare for death by announcing it to him for the very next day.

Judas the Machabee also, renowned for his solicitude for the dead, was visited by apparitions from the other world. "Nicanor being puffed up with exceeding great pride, thought to set up a public monument of his victory over Judas. But Machabeus ever trusted with all hope that God would help them; and he exhorted his people not to fear the coming of the nations, but to remember the help they had before received from Heaven, and now to hope for victory from the Almighty. And speaking to them out of the law and the prophets, and withal putting them in mind of the battles they had fought before, he made them more cheerful. Then after he had encouraged them, he showed withal the falsehood of the Gentiles, and their breach of oaths. So he armed every one of them, not with defense of shield and spear, but with very good speeches and exhortations, and told them a dream worthy to be believed, whereby he rejoiced them all. Now the vision was in this manner: Onias, who had been high priest, a good and virtuous man, modest in his looks, gentle in his manners, and graceful in his speech, and who from a child was exercised in virtues, holding up his hands, prayed for all the people of the Jews. After this there appeared also another man, admirable for age, and glory, and environed with great beauty and majesty. Then Onias answering, said: This is a lover of his brethren, and of the people of Israel: This is he that prayeth much for the people, and for all the holy city, Jeremias the prophet of God. Whereupon Jeremias stretched forth his right hand, and gave to Judas a sword of gold, saying: Take this holy sword a gift from God, wherewith thou shalt overthrow the adversaries of my people Israel." (*2 Mach.* 15:6-16). This apparition of two just souls to Judas Machabeus and his victory over the enemy are regarded by some interpreters of Scripture as being the reward he received for the twelve thousand drachms of silver he had sent to Jerusalem for sacrifice to be offered in atonement for the sins of those who had fallen in battle.

Even the reprobate are concerned for the salvation of their relatives. When Dives was refused the cooling drops of water which he craved in his torments, he besought Abraham to send Lazarus to his father's house: "For I have five brethren, that he may testify unto them, lest they also come into this place of torments." (*Luke* 16:27, 28). And Abraham listened to his prayer, explaining to him that they had Moses and the prophets, whom if they did not hear, neither would they believe even if one should rise again from the dead; which argumentation seems to imply that if they had not had Moses and the prophets, he might have sent Lazarus to them. Now, if Onias and Jeremias, who as yet did not see God from face to face, could pray to Him and had their petitions granted; if even reprobate sinners, for whom the time of merit was past, could implore the mercy of Heaven—why, then, should the souls in Purgatory be denied the privilege of praying for the living? Richard of Mediavilla proves the probable truth of this doctrine as follows: "Prayer is a work of charity. If the souls in Purgatory prayed for us during their mortal life, when not yet confirmed in grace, they will do it so much the more, now that they are confirmed in grace. True, their prayers, like our own, may not always be heard, because the Holy Souls do not so clearly discern the counsels of God as do the Saints in Heaven. Nevertheless their prayers benefit many, yea, all of us, provided no obstacle be placed on our part. It follows therefore that the souls in Purgatory effectually pray for us, notwithstanding the fact that their time of merit by works is past."

Concerning the comparisons made between persons in their death agony and the Holy Souls in their agony of suffering, they are in all respects inadequate and therefore inadmissible. The reason is this: The souls in Purgatory suffer indescribable torments, yet they suffer so patiently and with such resignation to the Will of God, that they experience neither worry nor terror. Being assured of their final salvation, their pains are no obstacle to their love of God or their charity for man. Though in a state of terrible punishment, they are nevertheless convinced that He who punishes them regards both them and us with paternal complacency. Therefore they are resigned in their own sufferings and they remember our needs in their prayer. If like our Lord Himself many of these souls were able even in this world to preserve perfect equanimity and peace of heart amid the many tribulations, persecutions and sorrows that they had to bear, they will not lose their composure in the torments of Purgatory, where despite their terrible suffering they have the consoling assurance of being confirmed in the grace of God. Even in this life devout souls follow the example of Our Lord, who prayed for the salvation of the world amid the tortures of His crucifixion—they remember their friends and enemies in their prayers: why should they not be permitted to do so in the next world?

The condition of souls separated from the body cannot be compared with the condition of souls united with the body. If the body experiences pain, the spirit also is affected thereby. Hence Aristotle remarks, that the heart of a sick man is continually disconsolate and in pain. In illness we are scarcely able to formulate a good thought or an act of resignation to the Will of God, as Holy Scripture testifies: "For the corruptible body is a load upon the soul, and the earthly habitation presseth down the mind." (*Wis.* 9:15).

In proof of what we have just said let us adduce the sayings of some of the holy martyrs. St. Stephen exclaims, "Behold, I see the heavens opened, and the Son of man standing on the right hand of God . . . Lord Jesus, receive my spirit . . . Lord, lay not this sin to their charge." (*Acts* 7:55, 58, 59). St. Tiburtius protests, "I ardently desire to shed my blood for Him who for love of me died on the Cross. I do not fear the glowing coals; for me they will have the coolness of dew and the fragrance of roses and carnations." St. Lawrence addresses his tormentor, "Thou hater of the Christian name, thinkest thou to terrify me by these torments? Know that if these be torments, they are so for thee, not for me; for I rejoice in having to endure them. For a long time I have desired nothing more ardently than to be seated at this banquet and to partake of this delicious repast. For me the flames are a refreshment; they retain their heat to scorch thee for all eternity without consuming thee. Behold, my flesh is sufficiently done on one side; turn it over and feast on it."—Hundreds of other examples might be cited in proof of the fact that divine grace can gain the mastery over bodily pain.

If then the martyrs rejoiced during the most cruel torments, we have so much the more reason to conclude that the souls in Purgatory, freed from the bondage of the body and enjoying the full liberty of the spirit, may suffer great torments and nevertheless enjoy peace of mind. While suffering intensely, they may yet experience great supernal consolations; they may receive favors from God by their prayers and they may be in a condition to make magnanimous and heroic acts of love for God and man. To comprehend still better this peace of soul in the midst of the most excruciating torments, we must contemplate the sacred humanity of Our Lord Jesus Christ. In His Passion, at the height of His agony, when dying on the Cross and exclaiming, "My God, My God, why hast Thou forsaken Me?" the soul of Jesus was in perfect peace; for crying with a loud voice, He said, "Father, into Thy hands I commend My spirit." (*Luke* 23:46). And according to the testimony of the Evangelists He prayed for His enemies even on the Cross. In like manner the Holy Souls suffer the most excruciating torments, while at the same time they are filled with heavenly consolations; the flame of the love of God and man burns more strongly within them than does the flame of the fire that surrounds them; and this love it is that urges them to become our advocates with God.

St. Thomas also maintains that the souls in Purgatory are not aware of our thoughts, desires and prayers, because as yet they do not enjoy the Beatific Vision of God; hence we can not effectually address our prayers to them. True, the Church does not address official prayers to the Suffering Souls for the very reason adduced by the Angelic Doctor. Besides it would be against the general rule of divine order, if God were to grant special revelations to the Suffering Souls during their term of punishment. Granted moreover that they cannot, without God's special permission, have a full and clear knowledge of all particular circumstances and occurrences of our lives, at all events they know as much of us as we do of them. We know that they are in a state of suffering, that they are in need of our help, and that we can help them. This is sufficient to induce us to pray for them. *They* know of us, by their own experience, that we on earth are exposed to many trials, combats, temptations and dangers; they

know—better than we—the efficacy and necessity of
divine grace: hence they feel impelled to pray for all
wayfarers on earth, especially for their relations and
benefactors. The learned Suarez doubts not that the
Suffering Souls pray for us effectively, because they
are in the friendship and love of God, and united with
us in holy charity. They remember us, he says; they
know our needs at least in a general way, and are
probably informed of our special wants by the Angels
or by various other means. He even goes further and
adds, that they are continually informed concerning
us by such souls as come to them from this world, and
according to St. Augustine by special revelations of
God. At all events, whenever God permits them to
experience our aid, He can also reveal to them from
whom they have received it, and what return their
benefactors expect.

The following lucid explanation why the Church does
not address the Holy Souls officially in prayer is given
by the learned Scheeben: "The Church, at least in her
official prayers, views the Saints of Heaven as being
the persons who are specially and properly called and
empowered by God to be the true mediators for mankind
on earth. Enjoying the beatific vision of God and participating in His heavenly glory, they are themselves
not in need of intercession. The Church therefore practices invocation of the Saints reigning with Christ as
an act of veneration due to them. The souls in Purgatory on the other hand are themselves still in need
of the intercession of others, the same as are the faithful living on earth; and hence their intercession can
naturally be implored only in the manner in which we
implore the intercession of holy persons during their
earthly life. The invocation of the Poor Souls is therefore a private act of the faithful; and the Church has
no occasion, and in fact no commission, to approve or
authorize this act or practice of her children by officially addressing her own prayers to the Holy Souls.
To draw an adverse conclusion from this act of the

Church would be permissible only in case that she reproved or prohibited this invocation when publicly practiced. As a matter of fact however, this practice is tolerated not only in Bavaria, but also in Italy, under the very eyes of the Supreme Pontiff."

The Holy Souls are not invoked by the Church in her official prayers, they are not recognized officially by her as intercessors, because public invocation, as officially addressed to the Saints by the Church, is at the same time an act of veneration—an honor reserved solely for those who are in the state of glory, and not accorded to saints on earth nor to the souls in Purgatory. True, here on earth we may privately ask saintly servants of God, and even our relatives and friends, for their prayer; and we do so often, saying, "Pray for me," or, "Let us remember one another in prayer." This is not, nor can it be, offensive to anyone. But the Church cannot officially accord this honor to any mortal, since it is reserved by God to the sharers of His eternal bliss. Hence she does not officially invoke the intercession of living servants of God, nor of any living person whatsoever. Thus also the invocation of the Holy Souls must be left to private devotion; and the confidence in the power of their intercession will increase in the hearts of the faithful in the same measure as they multiply their suffrages for them.

This private invocation of the Holy Souls is not only permitted in the same way in which we invoke the prayers of saintly persons, good friends, or the poor to whom we give alms asking their prayers in return; it is moreover very commendable to invoke them with particular confidence, because the Holy Souls being most grateful will show their gratitude by their intercession, which easily finds favor with God on account of their sanctity. God will then grant our requests not simply in reward for our charity, but also to prove thereby that the intercession of the Holy Souls is very efficacious. When Onias and Jeremias prayed for Israel, were they not heard? St. Thomas teaches that the Holy

Souls, with God's permission, can leave their place of confinement and appear visibly in this world, both for the purpose of exhorting and warning the faithful, as also to obtain help for themselves. He adds that God also employs them sometimes as His messengers instead of the Angels. St. Gregory relates that God wrought miracles through St. Paschasius even while the Saint was still detained in Purgatory. The same is related by St. Peter Damian of St. Engelhart, Archbishop of Cologne.

Hence we conclude with Suarez and many other learned and holy theologians, that the devotion to the Holy Souls and the invocation of their intercession are both lawful and profitable.

The Gratitude of the Suffering Souls Toward Their Benefactors is Manifested Interiorly and Exteriorly

The gratitude of the souls in Purgatory toward their benefactors is marvellous indeed. True gratitude manifests itself both interiorly and exteriorly—interiorly, by evoking sentiments of grateful and lasting acknowledgment; exteriorly by giving expression to these sentiments in words, and by returning the favors received from others whenever there is an opportunity of doing so. The souls in Purgatory show their gratitude to us in all these ways. Above all they acknowledge the reception of benefits. In Holy Scripture we find the following examples of gratitude: Pharaoh was grateful to Joseph, Raguel to Moses, the Israelites to Rahab, David to Abiathar, Elias to the widow of Sarepta, Saul to the Cinites, Naaman to Elias the prophet, Tobias, father and son, to the archangel Raphael, the inhabitants of Jabes to Saul, Assuerus to Mardocheus, Nabuchodonosor and Darius to Daniel, St. Paul to Phoebe, etc. It has already been demonstrated that the souls in Purgatory can show themselves grateful toward their benefactors. Why should they not do so?

During the late Franco-Prussian war several wounded and captive Germans, officers and privates, were quartered in the chateau of a noble French lady. She, an aged widow, not only ordered her servants to look after the welfare of her guests, but also convinced herself by her own personal observation that they were well cared for. She ministered most kindly to the wants of all. Such as understood French she encouraged with comforting words, while on those who could not understand the language she bestowed special acts of kindness. Many a grateful prayer ascended to Heaven for this humane lady. A young officer, whose wounds she bandaged personally, was deeply touched by her devotedness; and accordingly he one day addressed to her the question, "My dear madam, why are you so anxious for the welfare of the enemies of your country?" Sorrowfully she replied, "My son is an officer in the French army. He was wounded and made a prisoner. A German mother took pity on him, received him into her house, and nursed him. He recovered, and it is to this good woman that I owe his preservation. I now imitate her example from gratitude to her and to our good God."

Tears glistened in the good lady's eyes. The officer was silent; his thoughts wandered to his far-away home, to his own dear mother, of whom this kind French lady reminded him so much. The lady had written several letters to her son's benefactress, but had as yet received no answer. While she was still standing at the couch of the wounded officer, a servant entered and handed her a letter. Glancing hastily at the address, she opened the envelope; and soon she exclaimed, "Thanks be to God! My benefactress, the benefactress of my son, has at last sent me her photograph." She showed the picture to the officer. Scarcely had he glanced at it, when he exclaimed, "My mother's picture!" "Your mother's?" tremblingly asked the lady; and on being assured that she had not misunderstood the officer's words, she fell on her knees and gave vent to her feelings in the following prayer: "O God, Thou hast entrusted to me the son of my benefactress. How I thank Thee from my inmost soul!" If the feeling of gratitude is so deeply rooted in the human heart here on earth, how strong must it be with a soul in the other world, a soul unalterably confirmed in the love of God?

Can there be even the smallest doubt that the Suffering Souls, these spouses of Christ, are inwardly grateful for benefits received? The souls in Purgatory become aware that their punishment has been mitigated and shortened; and immediately they ask themselves the question: "Who may the charitable person be to whom I am indebted for so great a favor?" And the greater and more intense the torments which the souls had to endure, the greater and stronger will be their inner sentiment of gratitude. It is probable, as was already observed, that the souls are informed by special divine revelation or through their Guardian Angels who the persons are that come to their relief. Their gratitude toward these persons will last throughout all eternity; for such is the will of their Divine Spouse, expressed in Holy Writ, "Forget not the kindness of thy surety; for he hath given his life for thee." (*Ecclus.* 29:19). And St. Paul says, "But above all these things have charity, which is the bond of perfection: And let the peace of Christ rejoice in your hearts, wherein also you are called in one body: and be ye thankful." (*Col.* 3:14, 15). "In all things give thanks; for this is the will of God in Christ Jesus concerning you all." (*1 Thess.* 5:18).

The sentiment of gratitude felt interiorly soon finds expression in words. If this is the case even in this life—if grateful men become eloquent when thanking their benefactors; how much the more so may we expect the same of the Holy Souls in Purgatory! This was experienced by Father Conrad, a zealous servant of God in the seraphic Order of Friars Minor. One night, while praying for the soul of a lately deceased brother, and having said only one "Our Father" with the versicle, "Eternal rest," etc., the brother appeared to him; and having reverently thanked him, he added, "O Father, if you could but know how greatly I was relieved in my torments by this short prayer, you would instantly repeat it. For the sake of God's mercy, continue in prayer!" The good priest continued his prayer, persevering in it till he saw the brother's soul gloriously ascend to Heaven. St. Bristan, a holy Bishop, was accustomed to pass the night in the cemetery. When closing his prayer with the words, "May they rest in peace!" he would often hear from the graves the response, "Amen! Amen!" Father Julius Mancinelli, of the Society of Jesus, had an almost continual intercourse with the souls in Purgatory. They visited him, thanked him, and assured him that he had lessened their pain by his prayer. Blessed Frances, a Carmelite nun, was also frequently visited by souls from Purgatory. They followed her wherever she went, some thanking her, others recommending themselves to her prayer. If she said the Rosary, they would devoutly touch and kiss the beads.

Anna Mary Taigi, a holy woman of Rome, was also privileged often to see released souls, who came to thank her. One day she intended to receive Holy Communion in the basilica of St. John Lateran, and to offer it for a certain deceased person. During the first Mass at which she assisted, and which was celebrated by her confessor, she was suddenly attacked with a great depression of spirit joined with severe bodily pains. Nevertheless she continued in prayer and offered up her illness in atonement to divine justice. Then Cardinal Pedicini began his Mass. At the *Gloria* the saintly woman was suddenly seized with great supernatural joy and consolation. Then a soul just released from Purgatory appeared to her and said, "I thank thee, my sister, for thy compassion. I will remember thee at the throne of God; for thanks to thy prayer I now go to enter Heaven, where I shall be in bliss forever."

Omitting a great number of other instances that might

be cited in confirmation of the fact that the departed souls may personally express their gratitude for the least help by which we assist them, we append one related by Pere Lacordaire in his "Conferences on the Immortality of the Soul." The Polish prince *N.*, an infidel, had just finished and was about to publish a book combating the immortality of the soul. One day, as he was walking in his park, a woman fell at his feet weeping. She addressed him sorrowfully, "Illustrious prince, my husband died a short time ago. Probably his soul is now in Purgatory, suffering greatly. I am so poor that I cannot even afford the customary alms to have a Mass celebrated for the repose of his soul. Please help me to come to the aid of my husband." Despite his own disbelief in the future existence, he was moved by her appeal and gave her a gold coin which he happened to have with him. The happy woman hastened to church and had a Mass said for her husband. Three days after, toward evening, the prince retired to his library, and there began to occupy himself with reading and correcting his book. Hearing a noise he looked around, and he saw before him a man dressed in the peasant's garb of the village. Astonished and angry at the disturbance, the prince arose and was about to address the intruder, when lo, he disappeared. The prince now called his servants and asked, "Why do you permit people to enter here without my leave?" "What people?" they asked in reply. "That man, that peasant, who just left this room." "Please be assured, sir, that no one has been admitted here," they all replied. "There was no stranger here, not even in the palace." The prince silently dismissed them, but was convinced that somebody had been in the room. Next day he had forgotten the incident, when the stranger again appeared in the same place and at the same hour, not saying a word. This time the prince's anger knew no bounds; and rising to chastise the intruder, he saw him again vanishing before his eyes. He aroused the whole house to capture the man, but he was nowhere to be found.

Nobody could explain the strange occurrence. The prince now anxiously awaited the next evening, resolved to have an explanation from his strange visitor. And he came. But before the prince could utter a word, the unknown man addressed him as follows: "Prince, I come to thank you. I am the husband of that poor woman to whom you gave an alms a few days ago to enable her to have a Mass said for the repose of my soul. This your charity pleased God, and He permitted me to come and thank you, and to assure you that there is a next life, that the soul is immortal. It must be your task to make good use of this favor for your own eternal welfare." After these words the Polish peasant disappeared. The prince's book against the immortality of the soul was not published.

The Holy Souls are not content to express their gratitude in words; they return the benefits conferred on them by manifold services rendered to their benefactors. It was already explained that the Holy Souls can pray for us, and that while they are unable to do anything for themselves, they can exert themselves in their fiery prison in favor of others. They continually practice various exercises of virtue; but they cannot thereby obtain for themselves a hastening or increase of their glory, or a lessening of their punishment. They are in a state of suffering until the payment of "the last farthing" is made; for they can no longer atone. Hence they are dependent on the atonement made for them by their brethren on earth. The more strictly divine justice insists on due satisfaction, the more liberally divine mercy grants the favors which the Suffering Souls implore for their benefactors. Thus God encourages us in our charity for them, and consoles them by granting their petitions. The possibility of the intercessory power of the Holy Souls being beyond doubt, their exercise of this power must not be questioned.

St. Bridget heard the souls in Purgatory call to Heaven, saying in a loud voice, "O merciful God, reward a hundredfold the charity of them that by their good works assist us to come from out of this darkness to the eternal light and to attain to Thy beatific vision." If the Holy Souls pray thus to God, whose beloved children they are: will He not hear them? And should we therefore not be inspired with great confidence in their help? Their aid will be for us a continual source of favors; for their prayer possesses all the qualities that render it efficient and pleasing to God: a living faith, great frequency, ardent charity, the purest of intentions. Unlike ourselves, they have not to repel the thousand distractions of a troubled imagination; their love for us is not impaired by selfish, interested motives. Even their tears, their torments and their loving resignation to the Will of God are prayers—sweet incense in golden censers borne by the Angels to the throne of the Lamb, there to find a gracious acceptance.

St. Catherine of Bologna testifies that whenever she asked a favor of God she always had recourse to the Holy Souls, and that she almost always obtained what she asked for. And she adds that many favors which she did not obtain through the Saints of Heaven were granted to her through the intercession of the Suffering Souls. The Venerable Frances of the Blessed Sacrament assures us that the Holy Souls assisted her in all dangers, and disclosed to her the snares of the devil. A soul appearing to her said, "However much the evil spirits may persecute you—fear not; we will always defend you." Another soul assured her, "We pray daily for you; and as often as anyone remembers us, we also remember him and intercede for him with God. Especially do we implore for him the grace to serve God well and to die a happy death." The same was declared by a holy soul appearing in 1870. The contemplation of the faults for which the Holy Souls are suffering induced the Venerable Lindmayer to avoid these same faults herself. The Holy Souls reminded her of her spiritual exercises and warned her when she was in danger of committing a fault. Hence she remarks, "By devotion to the Holy Souls our progress in virtue and perfection is greatly hastened." The Venerable Crescentia was accustomed to invoke the aid of the Holy Souls whenever she wished to obtain special favors from God; and she assures us that as a rule she was heard immediately.

The same is true today of thousands of devout Christians who present their petitions to God through the Holy Souls: as a rule they are successful in obtaining what they desire. If the Holy Souls can and do achieve such results while still in torment, it follows that they can and do obtain still more for us after their entrance into Heaven. There is every reason to believe that the very first favors they ask of God's mercy are for those to whom they owe their more speedy entrance into glory; and that they will continue their intercession as long as they see their benefactors in spiritual or temporal danger. St. Gregory says that there are thousands of instances from which may be learned how efficiently the Holy Souls can help in distress, illness, danger of war and death, etc., even while they are yet in torments. They obtain for us health in sickness, aid in poverty, relief in distress, counsel in doubt, and protection in danger; they assist us in temporal affairs and in the affairs of our salvation, coming to our aid especially at the hour of death and before the tribunal of judgment. Even after death their benefactors experience their gratitude, for they implore for them a speedy release from Purgatory. All this will be made apparent by the following theses and examples.

The Suffering Souls Aid Their Benefactors in Temporal Affairs

There are many examples from which we can learn to what extent the saints on earth exercised charity toward suffering humanity. St. Mary Magdalen was wont to say that she was happier serving her fellowmen than she could be by engaging in contemplation; and she gave the following reason: "If I am engaged in contemplation, God aids me; but when I aid my neighbor, I serve God. Our Divine Saviour Himself declares that we do unto Him all that we do for our neighbor." Even the common sentiment of humanity demands that we aid one another. Henry IV and a number of his courtiers one day engaged in hunting in the woods. A young nobleman of his train found a poor old man, who had gathered faggots and had fallen beneath the weight of his burden. Scarcely had the young man noticed this when he sprang from his horse, went to the poor man and raised him up. Noticing that he was hurt by the fall and bled profusely, he not only gave him all the money he had about him, but also ordered his servant to place him on his horse and to conduct him to a physician. Then he rejoined the king's train. One of the courtiers reprimanded the young man for his behavior, and asked him if he was not ashamed at having left the king for a beggar. "Why should I be ashamed?" rejoined the truly noble young man. "Should I uncharitably omit a humane action which does not interfere with the service I owe to the king? You should rather be ashamed for not being willing to do the same." The good king, who had secretly and from a distance observed the whole affair, and had also heard the young man's reply, was so well pleased that he thenceforth placed the greatest confidence in the young nobleman.

If a human ruler thus highly esteems a charitable action done by one of his subjects to another, what a reward may he not expect who performs charitable acts for the sake of Him who said, "Amen I say to you, as long as you did it to one of these my least brethren, you did it to Me!" (*Matt.* 25:40). God often rewards such charitable acts even here on earth. St. Elizabeth one day came down from the Wartburg castle bearing in her apron food for the poor, when suddenly her husband stood before her. "Let me see what you have there!" he said, drawing back her cloak. And to his astonishment he beheld the most beautiful white and red roses. To reassure his beloved wife he was about to address some words of encouragement to her, when behold, there appeared above her a shining crucifix. And greatly wondering, he took one of the miraculous roses, which he reverently preserved. In her childhood this charitable saint played at jumping-rope in the churchyard; and as often as she jumped she said, "May they rest in peace!" meaning the souls of those interred there. And her playmates had to repeat the same ejaculation. St. Zitta, a holy servant girl was one day accosted by a beggar. As she had nothing else to give, she went to the well and filled a pitcher with cool, sparkling water, which she presented to the beggar to refresh him. And he found the water turned into generous wine. At Amiens in France St. Martin met a beggar shivering in the cold from want of clothing. Taking his sword he cut in two the soldier's cloak he wore, and gave one-half to the beggar. His soldier comrades laughed at him; but during the following night Our Lord appeared to him wearing that very half of his cloak; and addressing the Angels that surrounded Him, He said, "Martin, still a catechumen, covered Me with this cloak." St. John of God one day found a poor boy shivering with cold and walking barefoot in the street. He took him up into his arms to bring him to an asylum. At first his burden was very light, but its weight continued to increase, so that he finally fell to the ground. And the boy appeared to him as Christ, Our Lord, who said to him showing him a pomegranate surmounted by a cross, "John, thou wilt find thy cross at Granada." And Jesus disappeared, leaving in the charitable man's heart that ardent desire of serving Him in His poor, by which he attained to such great sanctity. St. Paulinus sold himself into slavery to ransom a poor widow's son. God was so well pleased with this heroic act of charity, that he inspired the Vandal king to set the holy Bishop free, together with all the slaves belonging to his diocese, and he moreover presented him with several shiploads of provisions. St. Elizabeth, mentioned before, was moved by compassion for a poor leper to cleanse his wounds; then she anointed them with oil, and put the sufferer into her own bed. Her husband, the landgrave, when informed thereof, thought it an excess of charity, and went to see the man. On removing the coverlet, behold, before his eyes appeared the Crucified. And turning to his holy spouse he said, "Elizabeth, dear sister, such guests are ever welcome to my bed. Let no one prevent thy charitable practices."

If charity causes Omnipotence to perform such miracles even in this world; if we poor sinners can help one another by our prayers here below; is it probable that God will show less favor when the Suffering Souls desire to come to our aid, when they implore His mercy for us? The thought is repugnant to a religious mind, and God Himself signifies that the idea is proved untenable; for He graciously hears and grants in our favor the petition of the Holy Souls. Gregory Carfora, a canon regular, writes, "At Naples a poor man, the sole support of his family, was imprisoned for debt. His wife was in great distress not only because now the burden of providing for the family rested on her, but also because she was expected to cancel her husband's debt. In this strait she had recourse to a rich man, who was noted for his charity toward the poor. She presented a well-written petition, but received only a small coin. Still more depressed by this repulse she went to the next church to pour out her heart before God, the true Father of the poor. While praying fervently before the altar, a thought suddenly occurred to her mind, suggested perhaps by her Guardian Angel: she remembered the powerful help rendered by the Holy Souls to those who invoke their aid. Filled with great confidence she took the little money she had, and gave it to have a Mass said for them. On leaving the church she was met by a venerable old man, who addressed her most pleasantly and inquired for the cause of her sadness. Having told him her misfortunes, he gave her a letter which she was to deliver to a certain nobleman in the city; and then he left her. She immediately set out to fulfill the errand. The gentleman to whom the letter was addressed was greatly astonished, when on receiving it he recognized the handwriting of his deceased father; and accordingly he asked her who had given her the letter. She answered that an old venerable looking gentleman had given it to her. Glancing around the room her eyes rested on a portrait; and in great surprise she added that he looked exactly like the figure on that picture, only more cheerful. With trembling hand the man now opened the letter, which contained the following words, "My son: At this very moment thy father is leaving Purgatory to go to Heaven, released by means of a Mass which this poor woman caused to be celebrated. Therefore I commend her to thee. Be grateful, and reward her well; for she is greatly in need." The gentleman repeatedly read these words, tears meanwhile streaming from his eyes; and the oftener he read them, the more they consoled him. "Oh, my poor friend!" he exclaimed, "with your little alms you conferred so great a favor on my father. I will reward your charity most bountifully; henceforth neither you nor yours shall suffer from want."

By the command of Pope Gregory VIII Christopher Sandoval, Archbishop of Sevilla, proclaimed to the world what had occurred to him while a student at the university of Louvain. From early youth he had been accustomed to give all the money he could save in alms for the Suffering Souls. Once, when his usual allowance failed to arrive from Spain, he was in such distress that he even suffered for want of food. But what grieved him most was that he could no longer give alms. Not being able to help the Poor Souls in any other way, he one day denied himself his customary meal; he went to church hungry, there at least to pray for the Suffering Souls. He had scarcely knelt, when he saw at his side a beautiful youth in traveler's costume, who courteously invited him to dine with him and to receive news from Spain. Christopher accompanied him, somewhat awed by the unusual demeanor of the stranger. At the end of their meal the visitor gave him a purse filled with gold, telling him to use it to defray his expenses. As to himself, he would apply to the student's father for the refunding of the money. And with this he took his leave. Christopher searched everywhere for the mysterious stranger; but neither in Louvain, nor later in Spain, did he ever hear of him. His father also never was asked to make good the loan. Hence the young man took it for granted that a soul from Purgatory had come to his aid in gratitude for his charity. He was still more confirmed in this view because the sum of money he had received lasted just till his usual allowance arrived, which had been delayed by an accident.

Sister Macrina Mieczystawska, Superioress of a convent at Minck, a victim of the persecution under Czar Nicholas, came to Rome and had an audience with Pope Pius IX. He desired her to publish a description of the sufferings endured by her and her Sisters during a period of seven years. She relates as follows: "In 1843 the apostate Simearsko had us cast into prison and restricted us for six days to a fare of salt herrings. Daily every Sister received half a herring, without bread and water, thus to force us by thirst to abjure our Faith. During the first two days we were tortured fearfully by thirst, so that the skin was parched from our lips and palates. In this torment we contemplated the thirst of the Suffering Souls in Purgatory, and encouraged one another, saying, 'If our thirst is so painful, when it might be relieved by a glass of water, how great must the thirst be that consumes the Suffering Souls! They are surrounded by fire; and yet they do not yearn for earthly water, but for the fountain of living waters, God Himself, by whom alone their thirst can be quenched.' And we prostrated ourselves on the ground to pray for the Suffering Souls. God had mercy on us: thenceforth we suffered neither from hunger nor from thirst. When on the seventh day our prison was opened and we were driven to our usual hard labor, the guards imagined we would hasten to the well; but we voluntarily abstained from drink also on the seventh day in honor of the seven dolors of our Sorrowful Mother Mary. During those six days Wierowkin and two Russian popes often visited us, threatening us with new tortures if we did not apostatize. When the former saw us well and in good spirits, he angrily exclaimed, 'Forsooth, it seems I cannot kill them; they do not eat, and yet they are healthy and strong. It seems every one of them is possessed by a devil that suffers for her.'"

A poor servant girl, who had been well instructed in her religion in youth, had the pious custom of having a Mass said every month for the faithful departed. Even after she removed to the city with her employers, she never omitted it once. Moreover she had made it her duty to attend the Mass herself, and to unite her prayer with that of the priest, particularly for that soul whose purification was nearest to completion. This was her usual prayer. God tried this poor servant girl by a tedious illness, during which she not only had to suffer great pain, but also lost her place and had to expend her last savings. On her recovery, when she was able to go out for the first time, only one franc, (equivalent to nearly twenty-five cents), was left to her. After sending a devout appeal to Heaven she looked about for a new position. She had heard of an employment office at the other end of the town, and on her way there she entered the church of St. Eustace. Seeing the priest at the altar it occurred to her that she had not ordered her usual Mass that month; and moreover, that this was the very day on which it had been her custom to have the Mass said. What was she to do? If she parted with her last franc, she had not even wherewith to appease her hunger. She struggled between piety and human prudence, but the former triumphed. "At all events, God knows that I do it for His glory; and He will not abandon me." She resolutely entered the sacristy, made known her request, and then devoutly assisted at the Holy Sacrifice. Afterwards she proceeded on her way, not without apprehensions concerning her future. What will become of her, entirely destitute as she is, if she finds no position? While she went her way troubled with these thoughts, a pale young man of noble bearing addressed her, "You are looking for a place, are you not?" "Yes, sir!" "Well, go to ___ street, number ___, and ask for Madam ___. I think she will engage you, and you will have a good home with her." He disappeared among the crowd without taking notice of the girl's expressions of gratitude. She inquired for the street, found the number, and rang the doorbell. While she was waiting, a servant girl left the house with wrathful mutterings of discontent. Of her she inquired, "Is the lady of the house at home?" "Yes," was the reply. "She may answer the bell herself; I am done with her." And angrily she descended the steps and left. Immediately after a mild and noble-looking lady opened the door, and in a soft voice inquired about her wishes. The girl replied, "Madam, I was told this morning that you were in need of a chambermaid, and I have come to ask you for the place. I was assured that you would treat me kindly." In great astonishment the lady answered, "My dear child, this is indeed a great surprise. It is scarcely half an hour since I dismissed the rude servant you met at the door; and I thought, with the exception of us two, nobody could know anything about the affair. Who can have sent you?" The girl replied, "It was a young man, Madam. He met me on the street after I had left the church. And I thank God with all my heart for this providential meeting, for I must find a place today since I have not a cent left." The lady was greatly perplexed, and could find no explanation for the extraordinary occurrence. Meanwhile the girl glanced around the room, and her eyes rested on a portrait hanging against the wall. "Oh, Madam!" she now joyfully exclaimed, "see, there is the picture of the young man that sent me to you." At these words the lady showed great emotion and almost fainted. After recovering her composure, she bade the girl to tell her the whole story. Thus she became acquainted with the poor servant's devotion to the Holy Souls, heard of the Mass she had caused to be celebrated for them that morning, and received a detailed account of her meeting with the young man. When the simple recital was finished, the good lady embraced the girl and said, "Dear child, you shall not be my servant, but my daughter. It was my son who sent you to me. He died two years ago; and to you he owes his release from Purgatory. I do not doubt it in the least; and I am certain God permitted him to send you to me. I bid you welcome. Let us henceforth jointly pray for all souls still suffering in Purgatory, that they may be admitted to eternal bliss."

In the life of Eusebius, Duke of Sardinia, who lived in the thirteenth century, we read the following extraordinary occurrence. Not content with praying for the Suffering Souls, he had devoted the tenth part of his income to suffrages for their release. Compelled to engage in war with Ostorgius, king of Sicily, he was so hard pressed by the army of his foe, that he was about to leave the city. That very morning he saw a mighty army come to his assistance—an army numbering apparently about forty thousand warriors, horse and foot, all clad in white uniforms. Ostorgius, too, saw them and was seized with such consternation, that he sued for peace. Eusebius thanked God and his strange allies for the help he had received, when the leader of the unknown army addressed him as follows: "Know, Eusebius, that the soldiers you see here are souls who were, nearly all of them, released by you from Purgatory. The Lord of hosts has sent us to your aid. Continue in your devotion to the Holy Souls. The more souls you release from Purgatory, the more protectors you will have in Heaven, where they will continually implore God for your welfare." Father Louis Monaco, a canon regular, had a similar experience. Once while travelling alone, he recited the Rosary for the deceased, as was his custom to do on every such occasion. Two robbers, seeing him approach, intended to murder him. But the grateful souls came from Purgatory to protect and assist their benefactor. They surrounded him as a guard; and the robbers, seeing the priest suddenly encircled by soldiers, fled in precipitate haste.

The following incident also occurred in the middle ages—that eventful period, when Italy was convulsed with internal strife, when might triumphed over right, when blood was profusely spilt in private feuds. There was a soldier who amid all this tumult of war and personal hatred had persevered in piety, rectitude and purity of morals. He was a devout patron of the Holy Souls, and had even made a vow never to pass a cemetery without entering it if possible, and spending some time in prayer for the faithful departed. One day while taking a solitary walk he was met by a party of the enemy's soldiers. Being entirely without weapons to ward off an attack, he betook himself to flight. Scaling a wall in his way, he found himself in a cemetery. He remembers his vow; but if he tarries one moment he is lost, for his pursuers are at his heels. Nevertheless his faith and devotion assert their power. "For the love of God and the Holy Souls," he says; and then he kneels down to recite his customary prayer. But lo, his enemies have espied him; they too scale the wall and are astonished to see him kneeling devoutly in prayer. Still they push on, thinking it impossible for him to escape. But what is this? In a moment the cemetery is alive with soldiers. They form in line of battle, attack the enemy and put him to flight. All this happened in a few moments. The pious soldier had heard a disturbance going on behind him, but had not interrupted his prayer to look around. Having finished his devotion, he arose to continue his flight; but no enemy was to be seen. Soon afterwards peace was declared between the opposing factions, and then the soldier received an explanation of the sudden disappearance of his pursuers. They told him how bravely he had been defended. Considering all the circumstances, there was no doubt that the Holy Souls had come to defend their benefactor, who prayed for them even while his life was in the greatest peril.

A still more marvellous occurrence is related of another friend of the Holy Souls. This man had some enemies—as even the best of men sometimes may have. He was a devout client of the Blessed Virgin Mary, and had a great love for the Suffering Souls. It was his practice to say every evening the Litany of the Blessed Virgin for the relief of the Poor Souls. One night, after saying his accustomed prayer, he retired as usual to his bedroom; and soon after he was profoundly asleep. Meanwhile his enemies forced their entrance into the house, went to his room, saw his clothing on a chair, and looked for their man in the bed. But it is empty; he is nowhere to be seen. To save his life God had rendered him invisible to the miscreants. Perplexed and angry at having missed their opportunity, the intruders left the house. After some days they returned. In the evening the man retired to his room and began his usual prayer. But he was drowsy, sleep overcame him; and after saying one-half of the Litany he went to bed. Meanwhile his enemies were watching him. This time he is surely in bed and shall not escape them. They enter the room and advance to the bed. Yes, he is there;—but what is this? From head to foot his body is divided into halves, and one half is gone! Full of terror at the sight, yet thinking that some other enemy had done his work before them, they hastened away. God had renewed His miracle in favor of His servant; but as he had said only half of his prayer, He had rendered only one-half of his body invisible. The next morning his enemies met the man in the street alive and sound. They regarded him with great consternation, believing to see a ghost. Explanations were made, and a reconciliation was effected. Then they confessed their attempts on his life. Neither he nor they doubted in the least that he owed his life to the protection of the Blessed Virgin and the Holy Souls.

The Oratorian, Father Maganti, also experienced the gratitude of the Suffering Souls. They obtained many extraordinary favors and graces for him; for instance knowledge of the future, of secret faults, triumphs over the wiles of the devil, etc. He attributed all these supernatural gifts to the intercession of the souls in Purgatory. One day while travelling from Loretto he arrived in the town of Nocera; and immediately he went to a church of the Blessed Virgin to say Mass. Afterwards he continued his journey in company with some other travelers. The road led past a dangerous place where some days before several murders had been committed. Meanwhile a party of brigands lay in ambush for the pious pilgrims. They attacked them when they arrived, overwhelmed them and bound them fast to trees. All at once two children appeared on the hill overlooking the road and began to call so loudly and perseveringly for help, as if they intended to arouse the whole country. The brigands, who are about twelve in number, take no notice of this, except to point their muskets at the children. But the children continue to call for help; they even advance boldly toward the robbers. Seeing this the bandits become afraid and betake themselves to flight; for they are convinced that they have witnessed a supernatural apparition. The children go from tree to tree, loosen the bonds of the pilgrims, and then disappear. The companions of Father Maganti are quite bewildered; but he simply informs them, "We owe our deliverance to two Holy Souls from Purgatory. God permitted them to appear in the form of children, to remind us of the word of our Divine Master, 'Unless you be converted, and become as little children, you shall not enter into the kingdom of Heaven.'" (*Matt.* 18:3).

The life of a petty prince of the middle ages furnishes us another notable example of the gratitude of the Suffering Souls toward their benefactors. This nobleman had for a time led a rather dissolute life with his

courtiers. But the grace of God did not desert him—
he was converted quite unexpectedly. He settled his
affairs, and devoted a considerable portion of his income
to foundations for the relief of the Suffering Souls. The
sycophant courtiers, seeing themselves thus deprived
of their customary amusements and revels, were very
indignant, and conspired with a neighboring prince to
rob their converted master of his estates. When he
sought the aid of his former friends, they jeeringly
replied, "Go to your Mass-priests and prayer-reciters
among whom you have distributed your wealth. We
have neither the power nor the will to help you." Abandoned by almost everyone the good prince retired to
one of his castles, resolved to defend himself to the
best of his ability. But his troops were greatly inferior
in number to those of his adversary, who had meanwhile invaded his territory, and was now advancing
with his army to drive him forth from his citadel. One
morning, when his distress was at its height, he was
informed that a stranger desired his presence in the
courtyard. Arrived there, the prince was met by the
leader of a great army, who thus addressed him, "Fear
not! We are come to help you, and victory shall be ours.
We are the souls that were released by means of your
pious foundations. God sends us to your aid. Continue
in your prayers for the faithful departed in order that
on the day of battle our number may be still greater."
With these words the leader and his whole army disappeared. The prince returned to his apartments and
informed his servants of what had occurred, encouraging them like a second Machabee with the hope of
victory. A few days later the enemy's army appeared,
but to the great consternation of the troops the small
remnant of their adversary's adherents were reinforced
by a great host of unknown soldiers formed in battle
array. The enemy lost courage and sued for peace. After
the treaty was signed to the satisfaction of both parties, the prince was asked whence came the unexpected
assistance that had so opportunely appeared in his

defense. He told of his supernatural visitors and their promise. But when his opponent wished to see them they had vanished. When this miraculous occurrence became known, it served greatly to increase the devotion to the Holy Souls.

Another example: A merchant had laid in a full supply of goods, but they remained unsold for several years, so that bankruptcy seemed inevitable. In this strait he promised to have a number of Masses said for the Souls in Purgatory, and behold, in a short time he had sold out his entire stock. A patron of the Holy Souls recited the Office of the Dead every day for fifty years, and as a result he was successful in all his temporal affairs. He was assisted by the Holy Souls in many dangers, was comforted by them in his trials, and experienced their effective help in several lawsuits. A servant girl who was suffering much from rheumatism, and who had for a long time used all kinds of remedies without relief, at last had recourse to the intercession of the Holy Souls. She had three Masses said for them and was at once restored to health. A man affected in the same way promised to have a picture of the Suffering Souls erected near a much frequented place of pilgrimage, and immediately his illness disappeared.

Concerning personal services rendered by the Holy Souls, and their interest in our bodily comfort, St. Gregory the Great relates the following incident, which occurred during his time in the diocese of Civita Vecchia. A worthy priest, who had been advised by his physician to use steam baths, was served every time most attentively by an unknown man. To reward him the priest one day offered him two loaves of blessed bread, which at that time it was customary to distribute among the faithful at Mass. Sorrowfully the man refused them, saying, "O Father, why dost thou offer me this? This is holy bread, and I cannot partake of it. I was once proprietor of this place, and was sentenced after death to come back here. If you wish to release me, offer this bread for me to the Almighty, and thus you will aid me in atoning for my sins. In token that you were heard I will not appear to you again after I shall have been released." With these words he disappeared. The priest said Mass for him every day for a week; and when he returned on the morning of the eighth day, he found him no more.

Keller, in his book *Mirror for Earnest Christians,* relates the following: At the beginning of the sixties a devout young lady intended to found a religious community. A number of pious maidens had declared their intention of joining her, and an appropriate house had been selected, but the necessary sum for its purchase was wanting. Nevertheless, trusting in God and relying on the help of pious benefactors, the place was bought, the new community thereby incurring a heavy debt. While looking about for a loan, the Superioress was delayed on one of her journeys, so that it was already late in the night when she arrived at the railroad station nearest the town she was traveling to. As she had to be at the place early next morning, she resolved to proceed at once on foot. The road led through a dense forest, and she was very much afraid. Reassuring herself she began to say the Rosary for the Suffering Souls, when all at once she beheld at her side a young man with a lantern, who asked her to permit him to accompany her. After regarding his rather pale face for a moment she assented. On the way her guide asked her concerning the object that brought her there, and she confided to him all her doubts and anxieties. He replied with a few encouraging words. Arrived at the end of the forest he showed her a house at which she should not fail to call; and then he was suddenly gone. Next morning she related the occurrence to the priest, asking him whether he thought it advisable to apply at that house for the loan of the sum she needed. He replied, "You may try, but you will get nothing." Nevertheless she went there, but was received very coldly. Then she related how she had been directed to this house, and described the appearance of the young man. Immediately the behavior of the man and his wife changed. The wife began to weep, while the husband hastened from the room. But he soon returned with the desired sum, saying that he could not but show himself grateful to the benefactress of his deceased son; for it was he that conducted her through the forest and directed her to his house.

It is impossible to condense into one volume an account of all the instances in which the Holy Souls gratefully rendered assistance to their benefactors in the manifold relations of life—help in war and personal danger, in illness, and in distress of all kinds. But what was related above is sufficient to convince even the most skeptical of the efficiency of their intercession; and together with the examples adduced from Holy Scripture these instances of their gratitude ought not to fail in moving us to charity for them. Their intercessions for their benefactors on earth are graciously heard by Him who declares that he considers as done to Himself what we do to others. In making this declaration Our Lord confesses Himself our debtor, provided we exercise this charity in behalf of the Poor Souls. By our suffrages for them we secure for ourselves not only their own gratitude, but God Himself will be grateful to us for the help we have given to these Souls so pleasing to Him. He hears their prayers even when they pray to obtain temporal blessings for us.

The Holy Souls Assist Their Benefactors in the Affairs of Salvation

If the Holy Souls show themselves grateful even with regard to the temporal affairs of their benefactors, how much more solicitous will they be for the spiritual welfare of those who assisted them! They will do their utmost to preserve from the everlasting flames of Hell those by whose aid they were released from the purifying flames of Purgatory. The Venerable Colmar, Bishop of Mayence, writes: "A pious lady was greatly disturbed at the thought: 'What will become of me when I die and must appear before the tribunal of my Eternal Judge? There is a Hell—and I have so often offended my God! Woe unto me if I should be rejected by the Lord!' So great did this fear become with her, that she was quite disheartened. But recollecting herself, she regained confidence; for she said, 'I will pray for the souls in Purgatory; I will assist at Mass for them every day; I will offer for them the merit of all my good works. Perhaps I shall be so fortunate as to release some of them, and then I shall no longer have cause to entertain such great fear; for these souls will pray for me, and I shall not be lost.' She was immediately reassured, and thenceforth was a devout helper of the Holy Souls."

A Scotchman, whose brother was stricken with sudden death, was greatly affected by the sad loss. Though he was a Protestant, he knew that into Heaven "there shall not enter into it anything defiled." (*Apoc.* 21:27). As the religious denomination to which he belonged did not recognize a middle state, he was greatly concerned about his brother's condition in the next world, so much so, that he abandoned himself entirely to melancholy. God, who rewards the least solicitude for the eternal welfare of the deceased, led this loving brother to the true Faith. By the advice of his physician he traveled on the continent, where he met Abbe Paume. This saintly man took great interest in him, and explained to him the doctrine of the Church concerning prayer for the dead. On All Souls' Day the good man visited the priest and said to him, "I am resolved to ask admission into the Church from love of my brother. I shall find great relief in being able to pray for him, and your Faith not only permits, but directs me to do so, teaching that thereby I shall greatly benefit him. Your Faith thus deprives death of its terrors; your love does not cease with life, but extends beyond the grave. You know the frailties of human nature, frailties that are not grievously sinful; but yet they are obstacles to perfect purity. God has revealed that there is a middle state of purification between Heaven and Hell. Perhaps my brother is sentenced to it, and to release him I wish to become a Catholic. This Faith, which teaches me to pray for the dead, will console me and relieve my anxiety." And he was received into the Church.

Sister Margaret Ebner, of the Order of St. Dominic, was a great friend of the Suffering Souls, and released numbers of them by her prayers and austerities. And they were most grateful to their benefactress. As she had no greater desire than to serve God in the most perfect manner, and to arrive at the greatest degree of perfection, she recommended herself to the Holy Souls for this particular intention. And they assisted her most effectually, so that she often remarked, "Oh, that all persons striving after perfection would have recourse to the Suffering Souls, and would make them their intercessors and helpers! They would soon make great progress in virtue and would hasten their attainment of perfection."

Pope Benedict VIII relates the following: The saintly Jesuit, Father Alphonsus Lortesi, was troubled like St. Paul with great temptations. Having tried various means to rid himself of them, he had recourse to the Blessed Virgin Mary, the Mother of Purity, who thereupon appeared to him and requested him to pray fervently for the souls in Purgatory. He followed this advice and was freed from his temptations. A nobleman, a great benefactor of the Suffering Souls, was one night awakened from sleep and told that he should make his Confession immediately, because he was soon to die. He did so. He received Holy Communion, and died shortly afterwards. Such warnings by the Suffering Souls, such admonitions to penance and reformation of life, are frequent. Hence the well-known remark of Pope Adrian IV: "Whosoever prays for the Suffering Souls with the intention of helping them, imposes on them the obligation of gratitude and assistance."

Blessed Frances of the Five Wounds was notable for her intimate intercourse with the holy Angels and the Suffering Souls. In reference to the latter the history of her life recounts many well authenticated occurrences, one of the most remarkable of which is the following: Death bereaved her of a friend, a lady to whom she was indebted for various benefits. For a long time afterward Frances offered all her prayers, sufferings and good works for the soul of her deceased friend. One day her friend appeared to her while she was engaged in prayer and revealed to her many things regarding the future life. For instance Frances asked her whether her suffrages had benefitted her. The soul replied that their application was in the hands of the Blessed Virgin, and that by means of them she had received great consolation and a reduction of days and months of suffering. Frances then expressed a doubt concerning a certain offering she had made of a particular pain, and asked if it had been of benefit to her. "O, yes," the soul gratefully replied. "The very moment you began to feel the pain an Angel transferred me to a place so agreeable and pleasant that I seemed to be in paradise. When I asked the Angel if it were really so, he replied in the negative and said it was only an interruption of my sufferings. After your pain ceased I was returned to my torments." A short time afterward this soul was released and re-appeared to her benefactor, thanking her for her charity.

A priest relates the following: "Some years ago, when I was appointed pastor of my present charge, I found that the children of the Communion class had great difficulty in remembering the answers of the catechism. I did my best to assist them, advising various means from the use of which I hoped for an improvement of their memory. They did their best, but with little success. I was greatly perplexed, for they were good children, and anxious to receive their First Communion, which I was in conscience bound to refuse them as long as they did not know their catechism. All at once I remembered that I had read some examples showing how efficacious the prayer of the Holy Souls is for those who ask their aid. I now told the children to add thenceforth to their morning and evening devotions a prayer to and for the Suffering Souls, for the intention of obtaining a better memory. They followed my advice, and I was astonished at the result. The children, who had hitherto been unable to repeat any answers of the catechism that presented the least difficulty, now answered the most intricate questions very fluently; and they even comprehended and could repeat the explanations which I gave. I hope that by making this known the devotion to the Holy Souls will be increased, and that the belief in the efficacy of their prayers will be strengthened; and I am confident that my confreres will find in prayer for the Suffering Souls the same assistance in the performance of their duties as I did."

The following incident is related in the "*St. Benedict's Stimmen,*" 1881, number 1 and 2:

One hundred years ago the reign of terror in France was at its height. Louis XVI and Mary Antoinette had already fallen victims to the fury of the populace. France was deluged in blood. After the defeat of the Royalists near Quiberon Count Hyacinth of St. Florent, with over nine hundred of his comrades in arms, was imprisoned in Aubrey, where he expected his sentence of death. One day, while sitting near the window of his prison cell, the young Count was surprised at seeing a beautiful young lady looking in from the outside. He recognized in the lady his twin sister Hermania.

"Dear Hermania," he exclaimed, "how can you thus expose yourself to danger by coming to see me? You well know the penalty imposed by the republic on the intercourse with royalists. You promised to be careful."

"I know, dear brother," she replied in a low voice; "but today is our birthday, and I could not let it pass by without seeing you. Today we both attain the age of nineteen; and it is the first time in our life that we do not celebrate the feast together. And, Hyacinth, I felt so depressed; I could no longer resist the desire of seeing you, to reassure myself that you are alive and well."

"As you see, I am quite well," he replied, pressing her small white hand which she reached to him through the grating. "Do you remember," he continued, "that our dear deceased mother was wont to say that we both always had the same thoughts and sentiments? I also felt very melancholy all day, very likely because you did. But now you must regain your cheerfulness, or I also shall remain gloomy."

"Do they treat you well?" the girl anxiously asked.

"I have everything I wish for except liberty," replied the brother. "I almost feel ashamed at being so well cared for, while my royalist comrades are suffering . . . But I hear someone coming . . . Good-bye, sister dear; may our next birthday be a happier one!"

The girl left the window, walked across the grass-grown court and escaped through an opening in the wall. Hyacinth had scarcely seated himself, when the door was opened, and the republican commander entered. Politely saluting the prisoner, he addressed him as follows:

"The officers of my staff, particularly Oberon, seem to esteem you greatly."

"Oberon is always very kind to me," Hyacinth replied, without taking his eyes off a picture he had painted.

"He told me that you celebrate your birthday today. How old are you?"

"Nineteen, sir!"

"At your age a person expects to live for many years to come."

"Not always, sir!" the prisoner sadly rejoined. "In these times even youth may not hope for a long life. 'Tis said, 'In times of peace the son buries his father, in times of war the father buries his son.' My parents are dead, and strangers will have to bury me."

"You are melancholy today, St. Florent. You must

dine with us, and we will cheer you up by celebrating your birthday."

Hyacinth accepted the invitation with thanks. After dinner, when the desert had been brought and the servants had retired, the commander addressed himself to his guests:

"The republic promulgated a law today that concerns you, too, St. Florent. Hitherto the prisoners made at Quiberon—those of them that are not yet twenty-one years old—were not shot. Henceforth they, too, are to be executed; and therefore the sentence includes you also. That this is the case is proved by the fact that the soldiers detailed for this purpose are ready to execute the order at once."

Scarcely had he finished speaking when a detachment of troops entered the room. Several of the republican officers joined Oberon in pleading for the young royalist's life, but in vain. Hyacinth remained cool. Standing erect before the commander, he said, "I do not ask to be dealt with more leniently than my comrades. Since loyalty to our king has become a crime, I am as guilty as they are. But I request time to prepare myself before I go forth from the banquet hall to death."

His request was refused. Then the young nobleman turned courageously to his executioners, saying "I am ready." And he was led forth into the beautiful moonlit night.

The soldiers stood their prisoner up against the wall of the court and then retired a few paces. The commander observed the proceedings from the window of the hall. Suddenly a figure ran out from under the window of Hyacinth's cell, crossed the court and embraced the doomed man.

"Hermania, you're here!" thus Hyacinth softly addressed his sister, meanwhile trying to free himself from her embrace.

"Fire!" cried the distracted girl. "If my brother must die, let me die with him!"

One of the officers succeeded in loosening her hold on her brother, and led her away.

"Fire!" now cried the young royalist. It was the last time that his sister heard his voice as that of one living, for in the next moment the executioners leveled their muskets, and four bullets ended the mortal career of Hyacinth de St. Florent.

Fifteen years had passed since Count Hyacinth's death. Hermania de St. Florent was thirty-four years of age; and though her features were hard and cold, they still retained much of their former beauty. Her heart had been embittered and hardened by the cruel fate of her brother; it was, alas, inaccessible to the consolations of religion. In the first moments after her brother's execution she had cried in despair, "This trial exceeds my strength; I cannot bear it." She had to bear it; but she bore it without resignation. Her once so loving heart was closed to all human affection. Her life was blameless; she disdained the amusements and comforts of the world, and yet she did not seek peace where it was alone to be found—in resignation to the Will of God. "O how treacherous is life!" she exclaimed on the fifteenth anniversary of her brother's death. She stood at the window of her chateau, and was about to retire from it, when she observed the pastor of the village coming up the road. She hastened to meet him, for she held him in high esteem. After the usual exchange of greetings the conversation drifted to the occurrences of the day, when the priest had occasion to mention the date.

"Yes," sorrowfully replied the lady; "today is the third of August, a date I shall never forget. Today is the anniversary of my brother's cruel death."

The priest deemed this an auspicious moment to call her attention to the consolations of religion, and observed, "Blessed are they that mourn, for they shall be comforted."

"This is not the first time," she replied quietly but firmly, "that your reverence intimates that I should comply with the demands of religion. Your remarks indicate that you do not comprehend my character. The doctrines of the Gospel are known as well to me as they are to you, and I fully acknowledge their truth. You desire me to pray; but if I did so, I should also have to repeat the words of Our Blessed Lord, 'Forgive us our trespasses, as we forgive them that trespass against us.' But this I cannot do; for I have not forgiven the murderers of my brother, and I shall and will not forgive them. True, I can no longer do them harm, for the most of them were since called before the tribunal of God; but I still have the will and desire of revenge. The very thought of it fills me with delight; for then I feel that I still possess a heart. You tell me to seek consolation at the foot of the altar. If I did so, should I not be obliged to forgive my enemies? How can I, so full of hatred and desire of revenge, kneel at the altar? Now reverend sir, you know my exact position: can you continue to urge me to fulfill my religious duties when you know that doing so would on my part be mockery?"

"For the sake of your soul's salvation, my dear daughter, suppress such sentiments!" rejoined the priest in agitation. "Remember Our Saviour on the Cross. He prayed for His executioners."

"He was God, and I am only a frail mortal."

"But Christ is our example, and all the Saints strove to imitate Him."

"I am no saint!"

"True enough, alas! You are a poor, much-suffering woman. But you yourself have referred to a thought that should fill you with confidence and courage. Yes, He is our God; and because He is our God, He also has the power and the will to grant the grace and help necessary to observe His commandments. He demands that we forgive our enemies as He Himself did; and He will not refuse us His grace to do so if we place no obstacle."

"That is possible. I never thought of it."

Rising to take leave, the priest remarked, "I fear your case is a most difficult one. But I do not despair. I shall recommend you to the souls in Purgatory, by whose intercession I have often found help in cases that humanly speaking were hopeless. And if perchance your brother should be still among those souls, I will pray that he may be permitted to soften the heart of her who is so dear to him."

"My brother! You forget that he is dead fifteen years. It cannot be possible that he is still in Purgatory!"

"This is a question to which we cannot give a definite answer. But this we know for certain: God's mercy is great, especially to those who suffer from man's unmercifulness. Count Hyacinth was made to suffer death suddenly and unexpectedly, and we have no evidence that he had sufficient time during the few moments accorded to him between his sentence and its execution to prepare himself duly to appear before the tribunal of God. By no means do I question his Catholic Faith; but might he not have to atone for the youthful indiscretions so prevalent with young people of his class?"

Hermania was now alone; and as was her custom since her brother's death, she watched through the night following her birthday. She could not bring herself to seek repose during that night. The old servant, who was aware of this custom, had brought lights, and had securely fastened the doors and windows of her apartments. Now she was left to her musings. She sat in her easy chair, reviewing in her mind the sorrowful past. She thought of that night when she watched under her brother's window expecting his release, and saw him led to a cruel death; she saw the gleam of the muskets in the moonlight, and her brother, pale but firm, standing at the wall. But what is this? She rubbed her eyes. Yes, she is wide awake. She hears the slow ticking of the great clock in the hall. But there, before her—O God can it be true?—there stands her brother! Yes, it is he, not changed like her; he is still in the bloom and beauty of his nineteenth year. But oh, how sorrowful, how dejected! And yet his look betokens resignation! There was something in his appearance that restrained his sister from advancing to meet him; she felt that there was an impassable gulf between them. He was spiritualized; she still belonged to this material world. Placing her hands on her throbbing heart, she tremblingly addressed him:

"Hyacinth, my brother, what has brought thee back to the troubles of this world?"

"Sister," replied the spirit in a solemn tone of voice, "I am come to complain of the cruelty with which I have been treated."

"I know," she hastened to rejoin; "thy death is written as with characters of fire in my heart. Thy blood calls to me to be avenged. What can I do for thee?"

"I do not refer to my death. Viewed from eternity, life seems like a grain of sand on the seashore. Death is but a passing pain, the threshold of the King's palace. What saddens me is that thou hast forgotten—my dear sister, whom I so ardently loved."

"I forget thee? Did I leave a day pass without remembering thee? Were not my nights disturbed by painful dreams of thee? In the flower of my youth I rejected for thy sake every enjoyment and amusement of life, for my heart could not rejoice without thee."

"Thy tears and despair avail me nothing. I crave thy prayer, to help me to atone for my faults. I am suffering in Purgatory for the unatoned sins of my latter years. Above all, I suffer because in the haste of my execution I forgot to pardon my murderers. I did not remember the example of our Divine Saviour and of St. Stephen. I forgot that we are commanded to love our enemies. By this neglect I burdened my soul with a double guilt, because from it proceeded in part thy revengeful disposition. A long time was given thee to fulfill thy Christian duty of forgiving my murderers. Because thou would not, thou could not pray for me. For fifteen years I waited in vain; not a single prayer was said for me on earth. My body was interred without the blessings of the Church; no priest celebrated a Holy Mass for my soul. I saw innumerable souls ascend to heavenly bliss, released by the prayers and Holy Communions offered for them on earth. I had to remain behind. In my last moments, already at the threshold of eternity, I consoled myself with the thought, 'My sister's prayers will follow me beyond the grave.' This very night the first *De profundis* was said for me. It obtained permission for me to come here and implore thy help. Oh, take pity on thy brother, assist him to have his punishment abridged. Love thy enemies! Mortals on earth cannot comprehend the torments that harass a soul that has seen God for a short moment and is then again banished from His presence."

Hermania fell on her knees.

"O Hyacinth, pardon me! I was cruel toward thee, thinking to honor thy memory."

She covered her face with her hands and wept convulsively. Finally looking up again, the apparition had vanished; and the first dawn of morning appeared in the east. She remained on her knees, praying as she had not prayed for years. When the sound of the church bell, calling the people to five o'clock Mass, aroused her, she rose and hastened to church. The peasants were astonished at seeing their mistress kneeling in their midst, the first time in many years.

Her first prayer was for the murderers of her brother. She called to Our Saviour in His own words, "Forgive them, for they know not what they do!" The racking hatred that so long had tormented her and closed her heart to the soothing influence of grace vanished; and then, with scalding tears of contrition, she prayed for her brother.

After Mass she visited the good priest, and related to him her experience of the night, promising him to atone for her long neglect of duty by a truly Christian life.

"Thanks be to God" ejaculated the pious pastor.

"Whether your apparition of last night was a reality or a dream, it is certain that our Heavenly Father intended thereby to remind you of your duty."

"Most certainly it was no dream," she gravely replied. "Did you say a *De profundis* for my brother?"

"Yes, I did."

"Then it was Hyacinth himself whom I saw. He told me it had been the first prayer that was said for him."

A few days later Mlle. St. Florent knelt at the altar to receive her Divine Lord in Holy Communion, fully reconciled to Him by a contrite Confession. Thenceforth she devoted herself to works of charity; and though not very wealthy, the poor always found her their true friend, who gave them her service if she had no money to give. Soon she was known as "the good Lady of St. Florent." To those who thanked her for her aid she was wont to reply, "All I ask in return is a prayer for my brother, not for myself." Thus she lived for twenty-five years. Finally the third of August found her on her deathbed. She had already received the Last Sacraments, and calmly awaited the final summons. Suddenly her features were overspread with joy. "I see Hyacinth!" she exclaimed. "He is coming in heavenly splendor to receive me and conduct me to God. He is supremely happy, and I shall soon be united with him." She fell back: brother and sister were united in their God.

Not very long ago a pious Christian in Paris did his utmost to induce one of his friends, an old man who was near death, to return to God and religion by a sincere conversion. But all his efforts were in vain. Finally he had recourse to the intercession of the Holy Souls. He promised to have a certain number of Masses said for the release of the most forsaken soul, on condition that this soul would implore for his friend the grace of a true contrition. And behold, on that very day the aged sinner asked for a priest, made his peace with God and died soon after with all the signs of sincere penitence. In the neighborhood of the imperial castle of Ambras, near Innsbruck in the Tyrol, there is an open space in the midst of a vast forest, where the mortal remains of a great number of Tyrolese defenders of their country are buried, along with the bodies of the enemies against whom they fought. This place in the course of time became the destination of numerous pious pilgrims, who go there to pray for the Suffering Souls. So great is the number of extraordinary favors obtained there, that the trees for a great distance are covered with votive tablets testifying to the efficacy of the prayers of the Holy Souls. A new chapel recently built there also proves that the confidence of the peasants of the neighboring villages is as strong as ever.

To a saintly religious, Father Dominic of Jesus-Mary, there appeared the soul of a deceased artist, who asked him to warn a certain gentleman against retaining an immoral picture which the deceased had painted to his order, and to inform him that two of his sons would die in a short time. Moreover he should warn the gentleman that he himself would die soon if he did not do as requested. The good religious performed his errand, and the gentleman in great consternation gave him the picture to destroy it. Within a month his two sons really died. The gentleman repented; and he removed all his profane pictures, replacing them with religious ones.

To the Venerable Frances of the Blessed Sacrament there appeared repeatedly one of her relatives, deceased many years before, whose son was party to an unjust lawsuit. Despite all warnings he persisted for years in the unjust proceedings. Again his father appeared, declaring that his release depended on the termination of the lawsuit. Now at last the contending parties came to an agreement. They were not only reconciled, but fulfilled the other requests made by the departed soul to hasten its release. The son moreover was so affected by the occurrence that he thenceforth led a most exemplary life.

The gratitude of souls released and of souls still in torment, and the great relief given the latter by prayer, incited the Venerable Frances to the greatest fervor in suffrages for them; and not content to befriend the Holy Souls continually herself, she did her utmost to gain for the same devotion her Sisters in religion, priests, and all with whom she had occasion to converse in her position as portress of the convent. Thus she relieved and ransomed a countless number of Suffering Souls, whose gratitude she very frequently experienced.

The Suffering Souls Assist Their Benefactors in Death and at the Tribunal of Judgment

The renowned historian Cardinal Baronius relates: A man of great virtue was approaching his end and was violently assaulted by the evil spirits surrounding his deathbed. Suddenly he saw the heavens open and thousands of warriors in white garments coming to his aid. They told him that they were sent to defend him and to gain the victory for him. The dying man was greatly relieved and implored his heavenly defenders to tell him who they were. They replied, "We are the souls whom you released. We come to reward your charity, and to conduct your soul to Heaven." After receiving this assurance he died.

St. Margaret of Cortona died on the 22nd of February, 1297. At the very hour of her death a saintly religious in a distant city saw her soul ascend to Heaven in the company of a great number of souls whom Our Lord had released in consideration of the merits of His holy spouse.

The following remarkable occurrence was related a few years ago in the Italian newspaper *L'Unita Cattolica*: Two gentlemen, Parrini and De Witt, fought a duel in which the former was mortally wounded. Parrini was a freemason, as is evidenced from his will made two years before the duel, as follows:

FLORENCE, March 13, 1882.
To the Grand Master and the Masonic Brethren of the R∴ L∴ La Concordia.

Sound of mind and body, I hereby declare, on this the 13th day of March, 1882, my last will, and ordain by it as follows:

1) That no priest, of whatever rite or cult, shall enter my room in case I should be in danger of death by illness. 2) That after my death no religious fraternity, no priest, etc., but solely my brethren, friends and acquaintances shall attend my funeral. 3) That 500 francs be taken from my estate to be distributed at the pleasure of the Grand Master of the lodge Concordia amongst the poor widows and orphans of brethren of the said lodge. 4) That the execution of this my last will be entrusted to the Orient of said lodge, in whose secret archives a copy of it shall be preserved.

CESAR PARRINI.

On the morning of July 18th, 1884, the day of the duel, Parrini wrote another will which related solely to the settlement of his estate. In it he revoked nothing of the arrangements made in the former will relative to his death. After sixteen or more rounds had been fought, he fell mortally wounded. He was brought in a dying condition to the Villa Torrigiani. When informed of his approaching end, he said to one of his lady friends, "Call a priest as quickly as possible; I desire to have a priest! I promised it to you, and you know that I keep my word. Call a priest!" When the vicar of the parish, Don Louis Millinesi, entered the room, the dying man received him as a messenger from Heaven. After the vicar had been alone with him for a few moments, he went to the door and called for two witnesses. In presence of these the vicar read a revocation covering everything necessary to obtain absolution from the censures incurred by joining the freemasons, engaging in a duel, and calumniating the Church in newspaper articles and pamphlets. After the reading of this document, Parrini declared over the crucifix on his breast that he made solemn revocation; and then he added, "I pardon everybody the same as I implore pardon of God." The act of revocation is preserved in the archiepiscopal archives. After these preliminaries he made his Confession, and everything was prepared for the ministration of the holy *Viaticum*. Meanwhile the dying man, still pressing the crucifix to his lips, continued to pray and to commend himself to the mercy of God. He received the Last Sacraments with all signs of piety and faith, so that all present, a non-Catholic included, were moved to tears. While the vicar administered Extreme Unction, Parrini continued in adoration of the Lord whom he had just received, and audibly repeated the acts of faith, hope, charity and contrition, and implored the aid of the Blessed Virgin. Soon after receiving Extreme Unction he expired with the name of Jesus on his lips and the crucifix on his breast.

Whence this miraculous change of heart in this man Parrini? The answer to this question is found in the fact that in his heart he had never abandoned the Faith of his youth instilled into his mind by a pious mother. His apparent unbelief had proved no obstacle to his charity. The poor, as also the Suffering Souls, ever found in him their constant friend. He gave bountifully in aid of both. During all the years of his association with the masonic fraternity he had never neglected to say every day the *De profundis* for the faithful departed. Whenever one of his friends died, he was sure to say the *De profundis* for him. That this charity, although wanting in supernatural merit, was nevertheless pleasing to God, is proved by his happy death, which blessing was obtained for him by the intercession of the Holy Souls.

Brother Henry, a native of Louvain in Belgium, had finished his studies in Paris. After receiving Holy Orders he was sent to Germany as professor of theology and to be a preacher of the word of God. Wherever he went he proved himself to be a steadfast friend of the Suffering Souls; and he often experienced their gratitude. Once while in Cologne, after assisting at the funeral of a Franciscan, he continued in prayer for the soul of the religious and other departed souls, when the lately deceased Brother appeared to him, saying, "Thanks to thee, Father Henry, thanks to thee! It is due to thy fervent prayer that I was only half a day in Purgatory; and now I ascend to Heaven in the company of twenty-four other souls, whom thy prayer has released from Purgatory together with myself." When this same Father Henry was sent to Wimpfen as professor of theology, his brethren related to him the recent death of a nobleman, who had ordained in his last will that he should be interred in the Dominican church at Wimpfen. They also informed him that the deceased had been a great benefactor of the Order. Good Father Henry was so moved at this recital that he thenceforth remembered the pious nobleman's soul every day in prayer. On the anniversary of his death the deceased appeared to one of his relatives who was just praying for him, and said, "Fear not; I am your cousin. Know that by the prayer of Father Henry, professor at Wimpfen, I am released from Purgatory. Go and thank him in my name for his great charity." At last the good Father's time to die arrived. He was suffering from a very painful illness, but not unexpectedly; for it had been revealed to him long before that he would have to endure this trial. He peacefully expected the visit of his dear Mother Mary and of the Holy Souls; for he knew that they would not forsake him in death after appearing to him so often in life; and he was confident too that they would not permit him to remain long in Purgatory. And the fulfillment of his hope was revealed to a pious old lady at the moment of his death. She saw the soul of Father Henry ascend to Heaven in the company of three hundred and thirty-six other souls.

A pious Christian of Britany in France, who among other virtues that he practiced excelled also in charity for the Suffering Souls, was fast approaching the hour of his death. The pastor was notified to give him the Last Sacraments, but on account of great fatigue he sent his curate. The curate administered the last rites of religion to the dying man, and then set out to return home. On passing the cemetery which adjoined the priest's house, the curate to his great astonishment heard a voice loudly calling out, "Arise, ye dead! Arise from your graves and hasten to the church to pray for the soul of our great benefactor who has just expired. We owe this to him in gratitude for the prayers he so often said for us." And like the prophet Ezechiel the curate had a vision. The church door, which he had carefully closed before answering the sick-call, was wide open. In the sanctuary the lights were burning; and again he hears the voice, this time from the altar, calling the dead to prayer. At the same time he hears a great noise, the moving and rattling of bones in the graves. The dead come forth and go in procession to the church. In the sanctuary they sit down in the choir-stalls and recite in mournful accents the Office of the Dead. After it is finished, they silently return to their graves. The candles on the altar extinguish of themselves, and silence reigns as before in the deserted church. Pale with terror the curate hastens to inform the pastor of what he had seen. The latter would not believe him, but ascribed the vision to his assistant's vivid imagination. "First of all," he said, "you must find out whether your patient died, which is scarcely probable." He had not yet ceased speaking, when a messenger appeared giving due notice of the good parishioner's death. The curate was so impressed with this vision that he became a religious in the monastery of St. Martin of Tours. Later, when elected prior, he stated the occurrence in detail to his brethren.

Ackermann, in his book on the Poor Souls, relates that the Jesuit lay-brother Simon, and Father John

Fabricius, also a Jesuit, having been great benefactors of the Holy Souls in life, were assisted by them in death. A great number of souls whom they had released surrounded their deathbeds to console them in their last moments and to conduct their souls to Heaven.

But the Holy Souls are not content with assisting their friends in death; they also show their gratitude by releasing them from Purgatory. A saintly religious in Naples, Paula of St. Theresa, in a vision saw Our Lord descending into Purgatory and singling out souls here and there to release them from their punishment. When she asked Him why He selected these souls from among so many, Our Lord replied, "Because these souls during their mortal lives were noted for their charity to the Suffering Souls. I reward like with like; and therefore I release them earlier from their torments according to My promise, 'The merciful shall obtain mercy.'" Thus we see the prayer of the wise Noemi fulfilled in behalf of those who are true friends of the Holy Souls: "The Lord deal mercifully with you, as you have dealt with the dead." (*Ruth* 1:8).

From the foregoing we may conclude how profitable to us is our charity for the dead, and that we thereby suffer no loss, but are rewarded a hundredfold by the grateful souls themselves. If nevertheless there be Christians with hearts so indifferent and unfeeling as to be unmoved by all the motives hitherto adduced; and if these same Christians be so fortunate as to escape Hell and to be imprisoned in Purgatory in order that they may cancel their debts—be assured, they will have to pay their indebtedness "to the last farthing;" for thus the Word of God clearly states, "Judgment without mercy to him that hath not done mercy." (*James* 2:13).

The Venerable Archangela Panigarola, prioress of St. Martha's convent in Milan, on All Souls' Day had an apparition of her Guardian Angel who led her in spirit through Purgatory. Among other souls she saw that of her father. As soon as he recognized her he exclaimed,

"O Archangela, my daughter! How can you forget your unfortunate father, suffering so terribly here! I saw so many souls released by your prayers; but me, your father, to whom you owe so much, you have forgotten." Archangela was greatly agitated at hearing this plaintive reproach; but her Guardian Angel said to her, "God has permitted it thus, because thy father during his life neglected the care of his salvation and had no charity for the Suffering Souls."

Christian soul, be more charitable: it will be to your spiritual and temporal profit. Let us resolve to do everything in our power for the Suffering Souls. If at times we know of no soul for whom we are bound to pray in particular, let us follow the example of many pious Christians, and set apart every day of the week for a certain class of souls for whom we offer up our suffrages. For instance, today for the souls that were most devout to the Blessed Virgin; tomorrow for those who had a great veneration for their Guardian Angels; the next day for the clients of St. Joseph; again, for the most fervent adorers of the Blessed Sacrament, etc. Charity is inventive, as the saying is. If true charity inspires us, we will find many ways of helping and ransoming the Suffering Souls.

Chapter 6

Apparitions of a Suffering Soul in 1870

IN CONCLUSION of these treatises on Purgatory we append the following description of the apparitions of a soul from Purgatory, which occurred in the year 1870, and were published first in 1872 by the Rev. G. M. Curique, priest of the diocese of Metz, with the approbation of his Ordinary. The authenticity of these apparitions is established beyond doubt, and the account thereof may serve to confirm many of the theories advanced in this book.

Sister Mary Seraphine, member of a religious community in Malines, Belgium, was suddenly attacked, in 1870, by a great spiritual depression. She was at a loss to what cause to ascribe this melancholy, which with her was quite a new experience; and she did her utmost to overcome it. Formerly of a social, cheerful disposition, she had become silent and morose; and despite all her efforts she could not shake off the burden that oppressed her mind. It seemed to her that she was continually haunted by some invisible shadow which followed her everywhere, to the choir, refectory, etc., never permitting her to rest by day or night. She often felt this invisible power pulling at her scapular—a burden "like a leaden weight," she remarked, was pressing her right shoulder. She acquainted her Superioress and the mistress of novices with all these occurrences. Finally, on the 29th of July a letter arrived from France informing her that on the 17th her father had died. This explained all.

Thenceforth, while the Sister's depression continued, she often heard moanings and exclamations like those by which her father had been wont to relieve himself when suffering. She also continually heard a voice saying distinctly, "Dear daughter, have mercy on me, have mercy on me!" On the 4th of October her pains were increased; she now had to suffer also from an excruciating headache. On the evening of the 14th, when the Sister had retired to bed in the dormitory of the novitiate, and was just about to fall asleep, she suddenly saw her father between the wall and the bed. He looked very sorrowful and was enveloped in flames. She was so affected at the sight that she called loudly for help. It seemed to her that the flames were scorching her, too.

Next evening, on the 15th, and at the same hour, the Sister was kneeling at her bedside saying the *Salve Regina* before retiring, when she again saw her father in the same place and condition. From that time on till his deliverance she saw him every evening. On this second occasion she thought that perhaps her father was suffering for some act of injustice committed in business. But answering her unexpressed thought, he said, "No, I am not guilty of any injustice; I suffer for my continual impatience, and for other faults which I cannot mention."

She then inquired whether he had received no relief from the many Masses that his family had ordered to be celebrated for him. "O yes," he replied; "my soul is soothed every morning by a refreshing dew. But that is not sufficient. I am in need of the Stations of the Cross."

When the Sister was asked what she felt during the apparitions, she replied, "I feel as if I heard a certain rustling near me, and then I suddenly see my father. His aspect fascinates me, so that I forget where I am. I see and hear only him."

The mistress of novices often found her kneeling at her bedside, with hands folded and eyes open, and so oblivious of all around her, that nothing could engage her attention.

On the 16th of October the soul appeared again. The Sister had been instructed to say, "All good spirits praise the Lord!" As she received no reply she thought it was an evil spirit. But reading her thoughts, her father replied, "No, no. I am not a devil!" She answered, "Then say with me, 'Praise be to Jesus Christ and Mary!'" He repeated this ejaculation twice, and then added the words of the Gospel of St. John, "*Et Verbum caro factum est!* And the Word was made flesh." Then he continued, "Alas, alas, I am over six years in Purgatory, and you have no compassion for me!" "Poor father," the Sister replied, "how can you speak thus, when it is scarcely three months since you died?" "Oh, you do not know what eternity is! The soul, once having seen God, is consumed with an ardent desire of remaining in His presence. I am sentenced to Purgatory for six months; but if your community would pray perseveringly for me, my punishment would be reduced by one half. God has permitted me to implore you continually for my release. How senseless I was to have opposed your vocation. Now I am relieved only in your presence. The rest of my children think I am in Heaven, and scarcely one of them now and then says a *De profundis* for me. Poor Joanna (an old servant) alone continues to pray for me and thereby helps me."

This was really so. His children thought he was in Heaven, and expressed themselves thus in a letter to the Sister: "Father died like a saint, and is now in Heaven." How often we are in a like delusion concerning the fate of our dear ones!

"Poor father," the Sister replied, "I am entirely at your service. You may trouble me at will, if only the rest of the community are not disturbed. I will have many prayers said for you. Tell me what you particularly desire." He replied, "I wish that ten Masses be celebrated, and that the Stations of the Cross be visited for me often." The Sister asked him whether her mother was still in Purgatory. "No; on entering eternity I was informed that she went straight to Heaven after her death. You sacrificed your health by nursing her in her last illness, and now I come to trouble you for my deliverance."

On the 17th her father appeared to her in great sorrow, but without flames, and complained that he had been less refreshed on the previous day. "Dear father, do you not know that the Sisters cannot pray all day? According to our rule we must devote part of our time to our various tasks and labors." "I do not expect that they pray continually, but they might direct their intentions to my release. Every work, even the least, performed in the state of grace and offered to God, is meritorious and of atoning value, and serves to lessen our punishment. If the Sisters do not come to my aid, I shall continue to trouble you, for the Lord has given me permission. My dear daughter, remember the sacrifice you made on the day of your investment; now you must bear the consequences. Behold the fiery cistern in which I am confined. There are several hundreds of us in it. Oh, if people would but know what Purgatory is! They would then suffer everything in order to escape it and to release the Poor Souls confined in it. You must become a holy religious; you must faithfully observe all the rules, even those that may seem to be immaterial. The Purgatory of religious is terrible."

The Sister really saw a fiery cistern from which dense clouds of smoke arose. She said, "The impression it made on me is indelibly inscribed on my memory." Her father showed her his parched tongue, saying, "I thirst! I thirst!"

The next time he said, "It is long since I came to you." "Poor father," she replied, "You were here last evening." "If I shall have to remain in Purgatory three months more it will seem an eternity. At first I was sentenced to Purgatory for many years; and I owe it to the intercession of the Blessed Virgin that my time was reduced to a few months."

"This grace to come and ask me for aid," the Sister explained to the community, "was granted to my father in reward for his good works. Moreover he was a devout client of the Blessed Virgin Mary, in whose honor he received the Sacraments on all her feasts. He was also very charitable; he spared no trouble when there was question of assisting the unfortunate. He even begged from door to door to assist in establishing a home for the Little Sisters of the Poor.

Sometimes the Sister asked her father questions which he was not permitted to answer. One evening she gave him her hand and a book, the *Imitation of Christ,* saying, "You see me so perplexed, dear father, because I am always afraid of delusion, thinking these apparitions every evening might be productions of the imagination. Therefore leave the imprint of your hand on mine or on this book, so that I may know that it is really you whom I see." "No," he replied, "I will not do it. The pain you feel is according to the Will of God, and your uncertainty is to hasten my deliverance."

Later he nevertheless twice touched her, once on the right shoulder, and the next time over her heart, causing intense pain. But strange to say, though no indication appeared on her habit, her skin on both places had a black spot, as she modestly informed her confessor.

To her great consolation the Sister received full confirmation of the reality of these apparitions in the following manner: One evening a religious of the community suffered terribly from toothache, and Sister Seraphine suggested to her to pray for her father and in return to ask him to obtain relief for her. Scarcely had the Sister done so, when her pain vanished and she slept peacefully.

On the 30th of October, by command of her confessor, she asked her father what prayers would be most appropriate to be said on All Souls' Day. He replied, "Alas, the world does not believe that the fire of

Purgatory is similar to that of Hell. If a person could but once visit Purgatory, he would nevermore commit the least sin, so rigorously are the souls punished." Another time she asked him if he had been released from the cistern, as she had not seen him in it the last three days. "Oh, no," he answered; "see the proof!" And immediately she beheld the cistern, dense clouds of smoke and flames of fire ascending from it. And sorrowfully the poor man exclaimed., "Today we all were greatly relieved, and a great number of souls was admitted to Heaven."

About the same time he appeared to another Sister, who was greatly troubled because her father had died without the Sacraments after long neglecting his religious duties. He said to her, "Your father is saved; but he is sentenced to suffer in Purgatory for twenty years; for your consolation, however, I am permitted to inform you, that your Sister *N.* was released from the flames a short time ago, and is now in Heaven." The girl referred to had died sixteen years before, when she was only eight years old; and yet she had to suffer so long in Purgatory. Concerning the salvation of her father, the Sister ascribed it rightly to his great charity towards the poor to whom he had always been most liberal, and to the persevering prayer of his wife and children.

Sister Seraphine asked her father to appear again to this Sister, and to inform her concerning the state of her father; but he gave no answer. Nevertheless the Sister soon received full knowledge of it in some other way.

Sister Seraphine also questioned her father concerning other souls. For instance she asked him one day about the state of a Sister to whom she had been greatly attached. "She is in Heaven already for some time," he replied. Then she inquired whether any Sisters of her community were at present in Purgatory; but he confessed that he was not permitted to answer. "Do the souls in Purgatory know who prays for them, and are they permitted to pray for the faithful on earth?" He answered in the affirmative. "Do the souls also suffer for . . .?" and she mentioned some faults of daily occurrence. "Yes," he replied, "they are punished for them." He then related to her that on leaving this world he had seen the infinite majesty of God, the sacred humanity of Jesus Christ, the Blessed Virgin Mary, and that this vision had left in him a continually increasing and most ardent yearning to see them again. He also told her that St. Joseph was present at his judgment, and that he had since repeatedly visited Purgatory in company with the Blessed Virgin to console him; also, that he often saw his Guardian Angel who came to comfort him.

On the 23rd of November the Sister saw her father as usual; but this time he seemed closer to her, and her own suffering was thereby greatly increased. She felt as if she were all on fire. He informed her that if the community preserved in prayer as hitherto, he would be released during the Christmas holydays. We must here observe that he was aware of the most secret suffrages offered for the Suffering Souls, and immediately felt their beneficial effect. For example he saw all the pious exercises one of the Sisters had performed for him during her retreat; and he declared that she had aided him greatly by her zeal and heroic charity.

Always obeying the directions of her confessor and of her Superioress, Sister Seraphine asked her father whether it was true that the torments of Purgatory surpassed in their intensity the sufferings of the martyrs. "It is but too true," was his reply. Then she inquired whether all members of the Confraternity of Our Lady of Mount Carmel that wore the scapular are released from Purgatory on the first Saturday after their death. "Yes," he replied, "if they have faithfully fulfilled all the conditions." To the question, "Is it true that some souls must remain in Purgatory for fifty years?" he answered, "Yes; and there are souls that are sentenced to atone in it till the end of the world. These souls are the ones most tormented and the most forsaken."

On the 30th of November he said to his daughter, "It seems an eternity to me since I arrived in Purgatory. At present my greatest torment is the intense longing to behold God and to enjoy His possession. I feel continually elevated towards Him and am at the same time repulsed and cast into the abyss. Sometimes I am on the edge of the cistern seemingly about to be released from it, when I immediately feel divine justice detaining me because I have not sufficiently atoned."

For two weeks the Sister had not seen the cistern. She now implored her father again, as he had done repeatedly before, to obtain for her the grace of perseverance amid so many interior and external sufferings. "I have already prayed for you," he replied, "and I shall continue to pray for you, my dear daughter. But you will have to suffer still more before I am released."

On the 3rd of December she saw him again. Still sorrowful, he nevertheless appeared greatly relieved. He described to her the intense love of God that he felt and the increasing desire of beholding Him. Some time before she had asked him to repeat to her some of the acts of love which the souls in Purgatory made. He had not complied with her request then, but now he said, "I continually make these three acts of love: "O my God, grant me the love with which the Seraphim are enflamed! O my God, grant me still more: grant me the love which inflames the Immaculate Heart of the Blessed Virgin Mary! O my God, why can I not love Thee as Thou lovest Thyself?" Then he assured her that he implored for her the love of the Seraphim, adding, "Dear daughter, I am permitted to inform you, that though you are very weak—you will nevertheless have to suffer great pain between now and Christmas, on which day I shall be released." "And then, dear father, what then? Shall I regain my strength, so as to be able to serve God according to our holy rule?"

"That is a mystery not revealed by God," he replied.

Thenceforth, from the 3rd of December till the evening of the 12th, the apparitions ceased. On the 12th and the two following evenings he appeared again, brighter every time. From the 14th to the 25th he came no more. Meanwhile the good Sister suffered so intensely that she was scarcely able to visit the chapel. Nevertheless on Christmas night she succeeded in her effort to assist at the Midnight Mass, which she ascribed to the assistance obtained for her by her father, from whom she expected to receive the announcement of his deliverance on that blessed night. And so it happened. Between the first and second elevation of the Sacred Species, he appeared to her in supernal splendor and said, "My punishment is ended. I come to thank you and your community for all the prayers said for me. Henceforth I shall pray for you all."

On her return to her room he appeared to her again for the last time to convince her of his release; and again he thanked her. She implored him to obtain for her sufficient strength and health to observe the rule. "I will ask for you perfect resignation to the Will of God, and the grace of entering Heaven without having to suffer Purgatory." Then he vanished to appear no more. During this last apparition he was so resplendent that her eyes could scarcely bear the dazzling light. Her joy and happiness were now supreme. She felt an ineffable peace of soul, and she was glad to have the assurance that she had not been the victim of an illusion.

Thenceforth Sister Seraphine was affected with an illness scarcely known to our age—with homesickness for Heaven. Her father's yearning desire for the possession of God seemed to have been bequeathed to her. She became a victim of consumption; and after six months of intense suffering, borne with a martyr's fortitude, her pure soul was called to its eternal reward. She died on Friday, June 23rd, the octave of the feast of the Sacred Heart, at the early age of twenty-eight.

Appendix

Prayers for the Suffering Souls*

Seven Offerings of the Most Precious Blood

O HEAVENLY FATHER! Have mercy on all Suffering Souls in Purgatory, for whom Thine only begotten Son came down from Heaven and took human nature to Himself. For the sake of this Thy Divine Son, pardon their guilt and release them from punishment.

1. Eternal Father! I offer Thee the merit of the Precious Blood of Jesus, Thy well-beloved Son, my Saviour and my God, for my dear Mother, the Holy Church, that she may enlarge her borders and be magnified in all the nations of the earth; for the safety and well-being of her visible head, the Sovereign Roman Pontiff; for the cardinals, bishops and pastors of souls, and for all ministers of Thy sanctuary.

Glory be to the Father, etc.
Blessing and thanksgiving be to Jesus:
Who with His Blood has saved us!

2. Eternal Father! I offer Thee the merit of the Precious Blood of Jesus, Thy well-beloved Son, my Saviour and my God, for peace and union among all Catholic kings and princes, for the humiliation of the enemies of our holy Faith, and for the welfare of all Christian people.

Glory be to the Father, etc.
Blessing and thanksgiving, etc.

---

* The indulgences stated in this Appendix were valid when this book was first published in 1895. They are no longer in force since the Church issued the *Enchiridion of Indulgences* in 1968.—*Publisher,* 2008.

3. Eternal Father! I offer Thee the merit of the Precious Blood of Jesus, Thy well-beloved Son, my Saviour and my God, for the repentance of unbelievers, for the uprooting of heresy, and the conversion of sinners.

Glory be to the Father, etc.

Blessing and thanksgiving, etc.

4. Eternal Father! I offer Thee the merit of the Precious Blood of Jesus, Thy well-beloved Son, my Saviour and my God, for all my kindred, friends, and enemies, for the poor, the sick and wretched, and for all those for whom Thou, my God, knowest that I ought to pray, or wouldst have me pray.

Glory be to the Father, etc.

Blessing and thanksgiving, etc.

5. Eternal Father! I offer Thee the merit of the Precious Blood of Jesus, Thy well-beloved Son, my Saviour and my God, for all who, this day, are passing to the other life; that Thou wouldst save them from the pains of Hell, and admit them quickly to the possession of Thy glory.

Glory be to the Father, etc.

Blessing and thanksgiving, etc.

6. Eternal Father! I offer Thee the merit of the Precious Blood of Jesus, Thy well-beloved Son, my Saviour and my God, for all those who love this great treasure, for those who join with me in adoring it and honoring it, and who strive to spread devotion to it.

Glory be to the Father, etc.

Blessing and thanksgiving, etc.

7. Eternal Father! I offer Thee the merit of the Precious Blood of Jesus, Thy well-beloved Son, my Saviour and my God, for all my wants, spiritual and temporal, in aid of the Holy Souls in Purgatory, and chiefly for those who most loved this Blood, the price of our redemption, and who were most devout to the sorrows and pains of most holy Mary, our dear Mother.

Glory be to the Father, etc.

Blessing and thanksgiving, etc.

Ejaculation

Glory be to the Blood of Jesus: now and forever, and throughout all ages. Amen.

The Sovereign Pontiff, Pius VII, by a rescript, dated September 22, 1817, granted to all the faithful, every time they make these offerings devoutly and with contrite hearts, and say the *Glory Be to the Father*, etc. seven times, and the ejaculation seven times, as also the ejaculation, Glory be to the Blood," etc. once at the end, with the intention of thereby making reparation for all the outrages which are done to the Precious Blood of Jesus:

An indulgence of three hundred days.

A plenary indulgence once a month, to all who have said them every day for a month, on any day, when after Confession and Communion they pray for the intention of the Sovereign Pontiff.

Litany of the Most Precious Blood

Lord have mercy on us!
  Christ, have mercy on us!
Lord, have mercy on us! Christ, hear us!
  Christ, graciously hear us!
God, the Father of Heaven! *Have mercy on us!*
God, the Son, Redeemer of the world, *Have mercy on us!*

God, the Holy Ghost, *Have mercy on us!*

Holy Trinity, one God, *Have mercy on us!*

Most Precious Blood of my Redeemer, *Cleanse them, O Most Precious Blood!*

Blood of the new, eternal Testament, *Cleanse them, O Most Precious Blood!*

Price of our redemption, *Cleanse them, etc.*

Fountain of living waters, *Cleanse them, etc.*

Precious ransom of sinners, *Cleanse them, etc.*

Pledge of eternal salvation, *Cleanse them, etc.*

Sacrifice to eternal justice, *Cleanse them, etc.*

Key to the gates of Heaven, *Cleanse them, etc.*

Purification of our poor souls, *Cleanse them, etc.*

Salvation in our misery, *Cleanse them, etc.*

Remedy for our wounds, *Cleanse them, etc.*

Forgiveness of our sins, *Cleanse them, etc.*

Payment for our debts, *Cleanse them, etc.*

Remission of our punishment, *Cleanse them, etc.*

Source of salvation, *Cleanse them, etc.*

Hope of the Poor, *Cleanse them, etc.*

Nourishment of the weak, *Cleanse them, etc.*

Healing balm for the sick, *Cleanse them, etc.*

Reconciliation of sinners, *Cleanse them, etc.*

Joy of the just, *Cleanse them, etc.*

Refuge of all Christians, *Cleanse them, etc.*

Admiration of the Angels, *Cleanse them, etc.*

Consolation of the patriarchs, *Cleanse them, etc.*

Expectation of the prophets, *Cleanse them, etc.*

Strength of the Apostles, *Cleanse them, etc.*

Confidence of the martyrs, *Cleanse them, etc.*

Justification of confessors, *Cleanse them, etc.*

Sanctification of virgins, *Cleanse them, etc.*

Refreshment of the Suffering Souls, *Cleanse them, etc.*

Beatitude of all Saints, *Cleanse them, etc.*

Be merciful, *Spare them, O Jesus!*

Be merciful, *Hear them, O Jesus!*

From all evil, *Deliver them, O Jesus!*

From Thy wrath, *Deliver them, O Jesus!*

From the rigor of Thy justice, *Deliver them, O Jesus!*

From remorse of conscience, *Deliver them, O Jesus!*
From their great sorrow, *Deliver them, O Jesus!*
From the torment of fire, *Deliver them, O Jesus!*
From utter darkness, *Deliver them, O Jesus!*
From their moaning and lamentation, *Deliver them, O Jesus!*
Through this Thy Most Precious Blood, *Deliver them, O Jesus!*
Through this great price of our redemption, *Deliver them, O Jesus!*
Through the Sacred Blood shed in Thy circumcision, *Deliver them, O Jesus!*
Through the Sacred Blood shed on Mount Olivet, *Deliver them, O Jesus!*
Through the Sacred Blood shed in maltreatment by Thy enemies, *Deliver them, O Jesus!*
Through the Sacred Blood shed in Thy scourging, *Deliver them, O Jesus!*
Through the Sacred Blood shed in Thy crowning with thorns, *Deliver them, O Jesus!*
Through the Sacred Blood shed in Thy carrying of the Cross, *Deliver them, O Jesus!*
Through the Sacred Blood shed when despoiled of Thy garments, *Deliver them, O Jesus!*
Through the Sacred Blood shed in Thy crucifixion, *Deliver them, O Jesus!*
Through the Sacred Blood shed on the Cross, *Deliver them, O Jesus!*
Through the Sacred Blood shed when the spear pierced Thy holy side, *Deliver them, O Jesus!*
Through the Sacred Blood daily offered in Mass, *Deliver them, O Jesus!*
Poor Sinners, *We beseech Thee to hear us!*
Who didst absolve Mary and the Good Thief, *We beseech Thee to hear us!*
Who savest us through Thy grace, *We beseech Thee to hear us!*
Who hast power over death and Purgatory, *We beseech Thee to hear us!*

That Thou wouldst spare the Suffering Souls, *We beseech Thee to hear us!*

That Thou wouldst release from the torments of Purgatory the souls of our parents, relatives, friends and benefactors, *We beseech Thee to hear us!*

That Thou wouldst have mercy on the souls that are not remembered on earth, *We beseech Thee, etc.*

That Thou wouldst grant eternal rest to the souls of all the faithful departed, *We beseech Thee, etc.*

That Thou wouldst still their yearning *We beseech Thee, etc.*

That Thou wouldst cleanse them in Thy Sacred Blood, *We beseech Thee, etc.*

That Thou wouldst release them through it from their torments, *We beseech Thee, etc.*

That Thou wouldst grant them through it Thy beatific vision, *We beseech Thee, etc.*

Thou King of awful majesty, *We beseech Thee, etc.*

Thou Son of God, *We beseech Thee, etc.*

O Lamb of God, who takest away the sins of the world, *Eternal rest grant unto them!*

O Lamb of God, etc., *Eternal rest grant unto them!*

O Lamb of God, etc., *Eternal rest grant unto them!*

Christ, hear us! Christ, graciously hear us!

Our Father, etc. *Hail Mary,* etc.

V. From the gates of Hell:
R. Deliver them, O Lord!
V. Lord, hear my prayer:
R. And let my cry come unto Thee!

The Holy Rosary

We should make it a practice to say the Rosary every day, because this prayer is most pleasing to Mary; it is recommended urgently by the Church and is a source of blessings for us. Moreover, it is a most efficacious means of helping the Suffering Souls in Purgatory. If we cannot say the entire Rosary every day, let us say at least a part of it. We shall thereby merit the special protection of the Blessed Virgin Mary in life and death. For the prayer of the Rosary we ought to use beads blessed and indulgenced properly for the purpose. Then we can gain the following indulgences:*

1. *For the Rosary of St. Dominic*: 1) One hundred days for each *Our Father* and for each *Hail Mary*, if we say devoutly and without notable interruption at least five decades, meanwhile meditating on the mysteries. 2) A plenary indulgence once a year for all those who have said at least five decades every day for a year. Conditions: Confession, Communion and a contrite prayer for the usual intentions, the latter to be said on the day chosen for gaining the indulgence. (Benedict XIII, April 13, 1726). 3) An indulgence of ten years and ten quarantines, once a day; and a plenary indulgence on the last Sunday in every month—both these indulgences to be gained by those who say at least the third part of the Rosary, when it is recited *in common*. For the gaining of the plenary indulgence the third part of the Rosary must be said at least *three times every week*. Further conditions: Confession, Communion, visit of a church or public oratory, and prayer for the intentions of the Holy Father. To gain the indulgences of the Rosary when recited in common, it is necessary for only one to hold the beads; but the others must join in the prayer after having laid aside every other occupation.

2. *For the Confraternity of the Rosary*. The spiritual favors granted to the members of this most salutary Confraternity are very numerous. They are mentioned at length in the diploma of admission; here we give only a brief summary: a) An indulgence of five years and five quarantines for the devout mention of the name of Jesus in each *Hail Mary*; b) fifty years for the recitation of the Rosary of five decades in a church or before an altar of the Confraternity; c) a plenary

---

* See footnote on p. 297.—*Publisher*, 2008.

indulgence as often as they say the Rosary of fifteen decades without a notable interruption; d) a notable indulgence for devoutly bearing the beads about their persons. On the feast of the Holy Rosary, first Sunday in October, not only the members, but all the faithful can gain a plenary indulgence, provided they fulfill the conditions prescribed: Confession, Communion, visit to the chapel of the Rosary in a church wherein the Confraternity is canonically erected, and prayer during this visit for the intentions of the Pope. This indulgence may be gained *toties quoties*; that is, as often as the visits and prayers are repeated from Saturday afternoon about two o'clock until Sunday evening. These visits must be made separate one from the other by leaving the church every time. If a person cannot enter the chapel of the Rosary, it will be sufficient to see it from a distance. The prayers may be said kneeling, standing or sitting. Every member of the Confraternity who belongs to a religious community, to a college or association, can gain this indulgence by visiting the chapel of the community or association. (Pius IX, February 8, 1874). This precious indulgence, like every other indulgence of the Rosary, is applicable to the souls in Purgatory. (S. C. Ind., July 12, 1847).

3. *For the Rosary of the Crozier Canons*: An indulgence of five hundred days for every *Our Father* or *Hail Mary* said on such beads as are blessed by these Fathers, and as often as these prayers are said. A meditation on the mysteries is not required. (Leo X, August 20, 1516; Leo XIII, March 15, 1884.)

4. *For the Beads of St. Bridget*: One hundred days for each *Our Father* and *Hail Mary*. This Rosary consists of six divisions, each containing one *Our Father*, ten *Hail Marys* and a *Creed*. After these six divisions another *Our Father* is added to complete the number seven, in honor of Mary's joys and sorrows. Finally three *Hail Marys* are added. There are several more indulgences, plenary and partial; but like the one already mentioned they can only be gained

by saying the prayers on beads specially blessed for the purpose.*

5. *The Papal Indulgences,* among them a plenary indulgence for the hour of death, are often joined to the blessed beads.

One and the same rosary beads can be blessed for several kinds of indulgences; for instance, the cross on it can receive the Papal indulgences, the indulgence for the hour of death, and those of the Stations of the Cross. The beads can be blessed for the Papal, the Dominican and the Crosier Canons' indulgences; but by one recitation only one kind of indulgence can be gained, namely those indulgences for the gaining of which we make the intention.

A blessed object cannot be sold after being blessed and indulgenced; and after once being used it can also not be loaned or presented to anybody; if this is done, it loses the indulgences.

The rosaries with crucifixes attached, distributed *gratis* by the Spiritual Benevolent Fraternity, are all indulgenced as above explained. All these indulgences are applicable to the Suffering Souls.

Ejaculatory Prayers with Indulgences for The Suffering Souls

The friends of the Suffering Souls should accustom themselves to the frequent use of ejaculatory prayers. These aspirations, having their source in the Holy Spirit, are calculated to give us light, strength and consolation. We subjoin the following, for all of which indulgences applicable to the Holy Souls have been granted, which may be gained repeatedly during the day. The prayers are always to be said devoutly and with contrite heart.

---

* Indulgences are no longer attached to rosary beads or other objects since the *Enchiridion of Indulgences* was issued in 1968.—*Publisher, 2008.*

*I. Indulgence of Twenty-five Days**

1. For the invocation of the Most Holy Name of JESUS. Also a plenary indulgence at the hour of death for its repeated invocation during life. (Clement XIII, Sept. 5, 1759.)

2. For the invocation of the Holy Name of MARY. (Clement XIII, Sept. 5, 1759.)

II. Indulgence of Fifty Days

1. For the Sign of the Cross: In the name of the Father, and of the Son, and of the Holy Ghost. Amen. (Pius IX, July 28, 1863.)

2. Praise be to Jesus Christ: Forever, or, Amen. The indulgence is gained by both the one saying, and the one responding to this ejaculation. (Clement XIII, Sept. 5, 1759.)

3. Praise to Jesus and Mary: Today and evermore. (Pius IX, September 26, 1864.)

4. Jesus, my God, I love Thee above all things. (Pius IX, May 7, 1854.)

5. My sweetest Jesus, be not my Judge, but my Saviour! (Pius IX, August 11, 1851.)

Plenary indulgence for the daily recital of this ejaculation, on the feast of St. Jerome Aemiliani (July 20), or on any day during the octave. The usual conditions: Confession, Communion, visit to a church or public oratory, and prayer for the intentions of the Pope. (Pius IX, Nov. 29, 1853.)

III. Indulgence of One Hundred Days

1. For using Holy Water and at the same time making the Sign of the Cross. (Pius IX, March 23, 1866.)

2. Eternal Father! I offer Thee the Precious Blood of Jesus, in satisfaction for my sins, and for the wants

---

* Partial indulgences are no longer measured in terms of specific time periods but are designated simply by the words "partial indulgence."—*Publisher,* 2008.

of Holy Church (Pius VII, September 22, 1817.)

3. My Jesus, mercy! (Pius IX, September 24, 1846.)

This ejaculation was used frequently by St. Leonard of Port Maurice, especially when assisting the sick who could not join in long prayers.

4. Angel of God, my guardian dear,
   To whom His love commits me here,
   Ever this day be at my side,
   To light and guard, to rule and guide. Amen.

A plenary indulgence on the feast of the Holy Guardian Angels, October 2nd, and at the hour of death for those who have said it morning and evening throughout the year. A plenary indulgence once a month, if said every day. Conditions: Confession, Communion and prayer for the intentions of the Pope. (Pius VII, May 15, 1821.)

IV. Indulgence of Three Hundred Days

1. O sweetest Heart of Jesus I implore
   That I may love Thee ever more and more.

A plenary indulgence once a month, if said every day. Conditions as above. (Pius IX, Nov. 26, 1876.)

2. Sweet Heart of Mary, be my salvation!

A plenary indulgence once a month, if said every day. Conditions as above. (Pius IX, Sept. 30, 1852.)

3. Blessed be the holy and Immaculate Conception of the Most Blessed Virgin Mary! (Leo XIII, September 10, 1878.)

4. Jesus, Mary and Joseph! I give you my heart and my soul!

Jesus, Mary and Joseph! Assist me in my last agony!

Jesus, Mary and Joseph! Grant that I may die in peace in your company!

Also, one hundred days for each of these ejaculations, separately. (Pius VII, April 28, 1827.)

The invocations mentioned last may also be said in the form of a Rosary, thus: Instead of the *Our Father* say the acts of faith, hope and charity, for which there is granted an indulgence of seven years and seven quarantines, and a plenary indulgence once a month on the usual conditions. (Benedict XIV, January 28, 1756.) Instead of the ten *Hail Marys* say each time one of the invocations; at the end of each decade, *Glory be to the Father*, etc., or, Eternal rest, etc. Thus you may continue through five decades.

MAY THE SOULS OF ALL THE
FAITHFUL DEPARTED, THROUGH THE MERCY
OF GOD, REST IN PEACE! AMEN.

A Week of Prayers
For the Holy Souls

"A Week of Prayers for the Holy Souls"

Prayer for Sunday

O LORD God Almighty, I pray Thee, by the Precious Blood which Thy Divine Son Jesus shed in the garden, deliver the souls in Purgatory and *especially that soul amongst them all which is most destitute of spiritual aid*; and vouchsafe to bring it to Thy glory, there to praise and bless Thee forever. Amen.

Our Father. Hail Mary.

Eternal rest grant unto them, O Lord, and let perpetual light shine upon them.

Prayer for Monday

O LORD God Almighty, I pray Thee, by the Precious Blood which Thy Divine Son Jesus shed in His cruel scourging, deliver the souls in Purgatory and *especially that soul amongst them all which is nearest to its entrance into Thy glory;* that so it may forthwith begin to praise and bless Thee forever. Amen.

Our Father. Hail Mary.

Eternal rest grant unto them, O Lord, and let perpetual light shine upon them.

Prayer for Tuesday

O LORD God Almighty, I pray Thee, by the Precious Blood which Thy Divine Son Jesus shed in His bitter crowning with thorns, deliver the souls in Purgatory, and *in particular that one amongst them all which would be the last to depart out of those pains,* that it may not tarry so long a time before it come to praise Thee in Thy glory and bless Thee forever. Amen.

Our Father. Hail Mary.

Eternal rest grant unto them, O Lord, and let perpetual light shine upon them.

Prayer for Wednesday

O LORD God Almighty, I pray Thee, by the Precious Blood which Thy Divine Son Jesus shed in the streets of Jerusalem, when He carried the Cross upon His sacred shoulders, deliver the souls in Purgatory and *especially that soul which is richest in merits before Thee;* that so, in that throne of glory which awaits it, it may magnify Thee and bless Thee forever. Amen.

Our Father. Hail Mary.

Eternal rest grant unto them, O Lord, and let perpetual light shine upon them.

Prayer for Thursday

O LORD God Almighty, I pray Thee, by the Precious Body and Blood of Thy Divine Son Jesus, which He gave with His own hands upon the eve of His Passion to His beloved Apostles to be their meat and drink, and which He left to His whole Church to be a perpetual Sacrifice and the life-giving food of His own faithful people, deliver the souls in Purgatory, and *especially that one which was most devoted to this mystery of infinite love,* that it may with Thy Divine Son, and with the Holy Spirit, ever praise Thee for Thy love therein in eternal glory. Amen.

Our Father. Hail Mary.

Eternal rest grant unto them, O Lord, and let perpetual light shine upon them.

Prayer for Friday

O LORD God Almighty, I pray Thee, by the Precious Blood which Thy Divine Son shed on this day upon the wood of the Cross, especially from His most sacred hands and feet, deliver the souls in Purgatory and *in particular that soul for which I am most bound to pray;* that no neglect of mine may hinder it from praising Thee in Thy glory and blessing Thee forever. Amen.

Our Father. Hail Mary.

Eternal rest grant unto them, O Lord, and let perpetual light shine upon them.

Prayer for Saturday

O LORD God Almighty, I beseech Thee by the Precious Blood which gushed forth from the side of Thy Divine Son Jesus, in the sight and to the extreme pain of His most holy Mother, deliver the souls in Purgatory, and *especially that one amongst them all which was the most devout to her;* that it may soon attain unto Thy glory, there to praise Thee in her, and her in Thee, world without end. Amen.

Our Father. Hail Mary.

Eternal rest grant unto them, O Lord, and let perpetual light shine upon them.

————

All those who recite the foregoing prayers may gain 500 days' Indulgence, once a day. This Indulgence is applicable to the souls in Purgatory. *(Raccolta No. 594)*

Masses for Souls, Living and Deceased

THE HOLY SACRIFICE OF THE MASS is a continuation of Our Lord's sacrifice on the Cross. His sacrifice on the Cross merited our redemption. And the Sacrifice of the Mass applies the fruits of Calvary to souls on earth and in Purgatory. "The dead are aided by alms, by the prayers of the Church, and by the Sacrifice of the Mass." *(St. Augustine)*

HOLY WATER—
A Means of
SPIRITUAL WEALTH.
USED IN THE OLD TESTAMENT ALSO

The Holy Souls Long For It

Only in Purgatory can one understand how ardently a poor soul longs for holy water. If we desire to make a host of intercessors for ourselves, let us try to realize now some of their yearnings, and never forget them at the holy water font. The holy souls nearest to Heaven may need the sprinkling of only one drop to relieve their pining souls.

Holy Water

"They shall pour living waters . . . into a vessel. And a man that is clean shall dip hyssop in them, and shall sprinkle therewith all the tent, and all the furniture, and the men that are defiled with touching (the corpse of a man, or his bone, or his grave) any such thing." (*Num.* 19:17, 18, 16).

"Let them be sprinkled with the water of purification." (*Num.* 8:7).

"Wash me yet more from my iniquity, and cleanse me from my sin." (*Ps.* 50:4).

"Thou shalt sprinkle me with hyssop, and I shall be cleansed." (*Ps.* 50:9).

Numbers Chapter 5: 17

"And he shall take holy water in an earthen vessel, and he shall cast a little earth of the pavement of the tabernacle into it."

LaVergne, TN USA
17 November 2009
164403LV00003B/1/P